Praise for *Total Eclipse of the Mind*

"I read *Total Eclipse of the Mind* with the particular curiosity and attentiveness of one who has also entered into darkness as a spiritual practice and creative adventure. Andrew Holecek writes brilliantly not only about his own experience with the sacred tool of darkness, but also about the history and mythology of the practice. I love that he treats the absence of light not as an enemy but as a collaborator—one that strips distraction, sharpens perception, and invites wonder. This book will be a beautiful companion to anyone who, like me, is curious about how entering the darkness can bring us closer to the light."

Elizabeth Gilbert
New York Times bestselling author of *Eat, Pray, Love* and *All the Way to the River*

"There is immense value to spending time in darkness, and this book provides a pathway into this revolutionary practice—and helps you access more of what I call your Self. An original contribution that will reorient your relationship with darkness."

Richard Schwartz, PhD
author of *No Bad Parts* and founder of Internal Family Systems

"Physical and metaphysical light pollution is pulling us away from ourselves, distracting us from who we truly are. The result is a world that has lost its way in the light. Andrew's writing is like walking with a dear friend who is expertly and lovingly guiding us through the deepest passages of our mind. This book will help you find your way back—and reconnect to what really matters."

Judson Brewer, MD, PhD
New York Times bestselling author of *Unwinding Anxiety*

"Andrew Holecek's masterful introduction to the ancient Tibetan practice of dark retreat centers on a life-affirming but paradoxical contrast: the illusion of seeing in the light versus the profound wisdom found in prolonged darkness. This book offers a visceral path to experiencing the no-thing that is the self."

Christof Koch, PhD
neuroscientist and author of *Then I Am Myself the World*

"Andrew Holecek has written a masterpiece through his years of direct experience with the dark. Let this book guide you to inner change for the better."

Stephan Rechtschaffen, MD
founder of Blue Spirit (Costa Rica) and
Omega Institute (Rhinebeck, New York)

TOTAL ECLIPSE OF THE MIND

Also by Andrew Holecek

The Power and the Pain: Transforming Spiritual Hardship into Joy

Preparing to Die: Practical Advice and Spiritual Wisdom from the Tibetan Buddhist Tradition

Meditation in the iGeneration: How to Meditate in a World of Speed and Stress

Dream Yoga: Illuminating Your Life Through Lucid Dreaming and the Tibetan Yogas of Sleep

Dreams of Light: The Profound Daytime Practice of Lucid Dreaming

The Lucid Dreaming Workbook: A Step-by-Step Guide to Mastering Your Dream Life

Reverse Meditation: How to Use Your Pain and Most Difficult Emotions as the Doorway to Inner Freedom

I'm Mindful, Now What?: Moving Beyond Mindfulness to Meet the Modern World

TOTAL ECLIPSE OF THE MIND

UNLEASHING THE POWER OF DARKNESS FOR CREATIVITY, HEALING, AND TRANSFORMATION

ANDREW HOLECEK

ST. MARTIN'S ESSENTIALS
NEW YORK

First published in the United States by St. Martin's Essentials,
an imprint of St. Martin's Publishing Group

EU Representative: Macmillan Publishers Ireland Ltd, 1st Floor, The Liffey Trust Centre, 117-126 Sheriff Street Upper, Dublin 1, D01 YC43

This book is not intended as a substitute for the medical recommendations of physicians, mental health professionals, or other health-care providers. Rather, it is intended to offer information to help the reader cooperate with physicians, mental health professionals, and health-care providers in a mutual quest for optimal well-being. We advise readers to carefully review and understand the ideas presented and to seek the advice of a qualified professional before attempting to use them.

Book design by Rachael Murray
Jacket photograph by Rafal Suskievic (Other Peter)

www.stmartins.com

The Library of Congress has cataloged the hardcover edition as follows:

Library of Congress Cataloging-in-Publication Data

Names: Holecek, Andrew, 1955- author
Title: Total eclipse of the mind : unleashing the power of darkness for creativity, healing, and transformation / Andrew Holecek.
Description: Boulder, CO : Sounds True, 2026. | Includes appendix. | Includes bibliographical references and index.
Identifiers: LCCN 2025041807 (print) | LCCN 2025041808 (ebook) | ISBN 9781649634856 hardcover | ISBN 9781649634863 ebook
Subjects: LCSH: Meditation--Bon (Tibetan religion) | Rdzogs-chen--Bon (Tibetan religion) | Bon (Tibetan religion)--Doctrines
Classification: LCC BQ7982.2 .H65 2026 (print) | LCC BQ7982.2 (ebook)
LC record available at https://lccn.loc.gov/2025041807
LC ebook record available at https://lccn.loc.gov/2025041808

First Edition: 2026

10 9 8 7 6 5 4 3 2 1

To Prajñāpāramitā for holding the space,
and to Hermes-Mercurius for moving the pen.

Every man is two men; one is awake in the darkness, the other asleep in the light.

—Khalil Gibran

CONTENTS

Part 3: Navigating the Challenges of Darkness

FOREWORD

As the practice of dark retreat gains increasing popularity, I am delighted to introduce this work by my friend Andrew Holecek. Dark retreat is a profound and sacred practice in the Yungdrung Bön tradition of Tibet—where I was fortunate to undertake my own forty-nine-day dark retreat under the guidance of my beloved teacher, Yongdzin Tenzin Namdak Rinpoche, and with the loving support of my mother, who provided all my meals. This was a profound and unforgettable experience, and since then I have had the privilege of guiding many students through dark retreats—from short weekends to full forty-nine-day immersions—and seen the healing power of this practice to transform hearts and minds.

A dark retreat is not something to enter lightly. Andrew has put immense care and dedication into this book. His wisdom and compassion will undoubtedly guide many readers on a journey of understanding and healing.

In our daily lives, we often fear the unknown depths within us and fill our time with activities and distractions. The dark retreat invites us to step away from these distractions and meet ourselves in a space of silence. In that silence, we may find both profound peace and the clarity to face our hidden wounds. With the right preparation and guidance, this journey can bring profound clarity, meaning, resilience, and joy to our lives, gently guiding us toward the realization of our own luminous and authentic self—the inner light that has never been apart from us.

With my blessings,

Tenzin Wangyal Rinpoche

INTRODUCTION

The seeing commit a strange error. They believe
that we know the world only through our eyes.
—Jacques Lusseyran

I have engaged in deep inner work for most of my adult life, centered around fifty years of meditation. My journey has been a quest to discover who I am and to find answers to the big questions: Why are we here? What's the meaning of life? What happens after we die? Part of this journey has included the traditional Tibetan Buddhist three-year retreat, where I had the luxury of engaging in dozens of meditations in the most supportive environment. To enhance my understanding of the mind, over the past few years I have systematically explored some of the most potent psychedelics on the planet.[1] Eastern or Western, ancient or modern, natural or technological, if there is a legitimate method for psychological and spiritual development, I have probably tried it. As rewarding as many of these approaches have been, nothing compares to my experience with dark retreat. It is easily the most transformative practice I have ever done.

For nearly thirty years, this unusual practice has delivered life-changing insights. It has illuminated dimensions of being beyond my imagination. It has birthed creativity at breathtaking new heights. It has shown me, repeatedly, what really matters. It has healed fractures in my mind and heart I didn't even know existed, and it has connected me to others and to the planet at the most profound levels. As I age and contemplate the ultimate dark retreat, it has become my main preparation for this final journey, one that has removed all fear of death. And the return on investment is profound. Just a few days in the dark pays dividends for months or even years.

Dark retreat is also the most challenging practice I have ever done. Nothing has asked more of me. Nothing has stretched me to such an extent. Nothing has commanded such levels of honesty. And absolutely nothing has demanded so much surrender. Every requirement and demand has been rewarded tenfold. It's almost like cheating. How can such brief durations in darkness deliver so many life-altering experiences (chapter 4)? Where do the transformations come from, and why do they last (chapter 5)? Why is dark retreat the most experiential and revelatory practice for so many people (chapter 6)?

But this practice is not for everybody. Dark retreat is big medicine. This book is just as much about keeping people *out* as it is about inviting them *in*. If you approach dark retreat as you would an ancient temple, you will be blessed. If you approach it as the next peak to conquer or the latest exotic experience to check off your list, you will be reproached. When darkness isn't engaged with the respect it deserves, it spanks you. With the proper guidance and respect, this medicine can save you. In his book *Beauty: The Invincible Embrace*, John O'Donohue writes, "What you encounter, recognize, or discover depends to a large degree on the quality of your approach . . . When we approach with reverence, great things decide to approach us."[2]

Before we go any further, pause for a moment. Take a deep breath. Now, reflect on the deepest and most meaningful experience of your life. What do you do with your eyes? Where do you go? Almost everybody closes their eyes or lowers their head and goes within. In moments of silence or commemoration before a big public event—in moments of depth—virtually everyone turns inside. To reflect is to literally "bend it back." Dark retreat is possibly the most mind-bending thing you can do. Deep reflection, provided by the metaphysical mirror of darkness, turns the mind and heart back upon itself, allowing you to see what really matters. In Antoine de Saint-Exupéry's *The Little Prince*, a magical fox shares with the prince what he calls "my secret, a very simple secret," which is, "It is only with the heart that one can see rightly; what is essential is invisible to the eye." Close your eyes to open your heart. Then you will see.

Origin of This Book

I have written nine previous books. Each one was a labor of love, requiring endless research, writing, and rewriting. The book you hold in your hands came almost fully written to me at the end of a recent dark retreat. On one hand, it's the easiest book I've ever penned, with pages flowing out of me as quickly as I could put words to paper.[3] On the other hand, it's turned out to be the most difficult book. The difficulty is fourfold. First, how do you illuminate darkness without destroying it with light? It's not easy to speak of the unspeakable. As Zen writer Alan Watts said, the task "is to say what cannot be said, to eff the ineffable." How do you shrink-wrap a practice of infinite depth into finite letters without eff-ing it up? At the deepest levels, dark retreat takes you all the way to nonduality because darkness is the color of nonduality.[4] When you try to speak about nonduality using dualistic language, you'll always eff it up. Irony, paradox, and contradiction abound. But irony, paradox, and contradiction are just the ways nonduality looks through a dualistic lens. Reality itself is not paradoxical; it's just not effable.

Second, dark retreat is a topsy-turvy journey probably unlike anything you've ever done. It's one reason the practice is drawing so much attention. It's just so unconventional and bizarre. Everything is turned inside out and upside down in dark retreat. Your daytime compass is worthless in the dark. Every traditional navigation system is left behind. Standard notions of directionality, accomplishment, and success no longer apply. So how do I orient you in a journey where disorientation is core to the journey? How do I help you keep your bearings when getting lost is how you find what you're truly looking for?

Third, darkness invites intimacy and exposure. Dark retreat strips you down to levels of nakedness you didn't even know were possible. To share experiences that are so exposed, so personal, and so vulnerable renders violence to the experience itself and can keep the experience from maturing into realization.[5] Why should I take that risk? And fourth, although there are a few esoteric books on tantric-level dark retreat, there is nothing of note that I can find for the general reader.[6] I, therefore, feel an obligation to represent this ancient practice as accurately as possible.

After my first formal dark retreat many years ago, I went to my teacher to share the experience and seek his counsel. This esteemed Rinpoche (an honorific term meaning "Precious One") offered his advice and then cautioned me, "You can talk about many things, but keep this practice to yourself."[7] For many years, I have heeded his instruction. But this book burst into my mind with the clear message to write it. What to do? I believe it's time to share for the following reasons.

It's Out There

Dark retreat is rapidly emerging onto the self-improvement and spiritual scene. The toothpaste is out of the tube, and it's not going back in. NFL superstar Aaron Rodgers went into a dark retreat a few years ago, and the press went ballistic about his strange adventure (which included an interview with former Fox News star Tucker Carlson). NBA icons Dwight Howard and Rudy Gobert, along with a host of other elite athletes, have posted social media clips about their experiences in dark retreat, inspiring a rush to see what the fuss is about. Movie stars, famous authors, artists, entrepreneurs, billionaires, and other celebrities have also gone into the dark and started to talk. Dark retreat centers are popping up around the world. My friends who run some of these centers tell me they're booked years in advance, with a waiting list of hundreds. A host of scientists in Europe and America are now studying dark retreat and darkness therapy.[8] The word is getting out, and it is fantastic. Or is it?

Dark retreat is remarkably similar to psychedelics in its promise and peril. Numerous studies proclaim the benefits of psychedelics, along with the proportional hazards. Without the proper set and setting, psychedelics can do more harm than good. Bad trips are not uncommon. *Set* refers to mindset, your motivation in taking the substance and your aspirations for the journey; *setting* refers to the holding environment, whether it's caring professionals in a psychedelic-assisted therapy session or your drinking buddies wanting a new high. When psychedelics surged onto the scene sixty years ago, the excitement stampeded over safety, and the medicines were banned. Decades of important research and beneficial use were lost due to impatience, misunderstanding, and lack of care.

Nearly every opportunity and obstacle in the world of psychedelics applies to dark retreat. With the proper set and setting, one good trip can electrify your life. Without the proper setup, one bad trip can electrocute.[9] It's critical to understand that darkness itself never hurts anybody. It's completely harmless. How you relate to the dark and what it reflects create the (self-inflicted) damage. Darkness is a truth teller, a mirror. But dark retreat is a magnifying mirror that shows you who you truly are and exactly what you're made of at atomic levels. Darkness is exacting. The questions to reflect upon are: How willing are you to be so exposed? How up close and personal do you want to get to yourself? How big a dose of *yourself* can you handle? Truth heals. But how much truth can you take?

Despite the burgeoning hype with psychedelics and dark retreat, nothing is a panacea. I'm going to tout the outrageous benefits of this practice, but as with any method, don't put all your eggs in one basket. We so quickly project all our hopes onto new techniques, only to have them dashed as our projections fade and we fall out of love and back into reality. Don't turn to dark retreat to cure all your ails, and don't view it as the latest self-help method in the New Age supermarket or the trendiest form of Goth meditation. There's a reason the formal practice (versus informal home use) is historically guarded. It's not because dark retreat admits you into a secret club, but because such an exotic practice tends to magnetize spiritual thrill seekers, reckless psychonauts, and poorly motivated explorers, who then suffer the consequences of such a flippant attitude.

When my teacher told me not to speak about dark retreat decades ago, times were different. Perhaps he felt that people weren't ready. In 2002, only 7.5 percent of Americans meditated; in 2022, that number jumped to 18.3 percent.[10] Today it is estimated that about 35 million people in America and anywhere from 200 to 500 million people worldwide meditate.[11] Some 55 million people in the US practice yoga, and around 20 million people in the US alone have tried psychedelics. Since the pandemic, meditation has spread dramatically. The Global Wellness Institute found that since March of 2020, time spent meditating increased by 2,900 percent worldwide.[12] Is it possible that authentic meditators, yogis, and plant-medicine seekers are looking for the next step on their journey?

My aspiration in writing this book is to help you determine if this practice is right for you and if dark retreat could be your next step. With some honest checklists and a directory of indications and contraindications (chapter 11), you can evaluate if this practice has something to offer. If it does, this book provides everything you need to know to have a safe and fruitful journey. How do you prepare for dark retreat (chapter 9)? How do you integrate the insights (chapter 10)? What do you do when challenges arise (chapter 14)? How long should you stay in, when do you come out, and should you go back for more (chapters 8, 14, 10)? And what exactly do you do in there (chapter 7)? Starting with easy home practice, I will guide you step-by-step and show you how applicable this ancient practice is for our modern age.

A Return to Source

The world is deeply mired in what the Hindu tradition calls the Kali Yuga, the "age of vice and misery," and what Japanese Buddhism refers to as mappo, the Degenerate Age.[13] Fifty years ago, meditation master Trungpa Rinpoche wrote, "This is the darkest hour of the dark ages. Disease, famine, and warfare are raging like the fierce north wind."[14] Political upheaval, ecological devastation, social injustice, cultural divides, gender inequality, poverty, homelessness, and endless conflict are just a few of the many crises that comprise our present metacrisis. Many reasons are given for this metacrisis (also called the polycrisis, systemic crisis, or permacrisis), with an equal number of suggested solutions. A broad-spectrum approach is needed to address broad-spectrum problems.

I will argue that the multitudinous display of problems can be reduced to fundamental principles and addressed by a return to our origins.[15] Dark retreat delivers us to the reduction base of innate wholeness and helps us understand what's really going on, not merely within ourselves but within the world at large (chapter 2). It may seem initially facile and dismissive of the complexity of the metacrisis, but societies are comprised of individuals, and every individual shares the same fundamental principles of being. It's not a tired cliché but a ceaseless proclamation of the truth:

Despite our superficial differences, at the ground of being, we're essentially the same. But in this light-polluted and highly distracted age, we lose our shared essence in the complex display of modernity. We forget.

The multiplicity effectively obscures the underlying unity. And multiplicity arises in broad daylight, when our most superficial and dualistic sense of sight splinters the world, dominates our perception, then seduces us out and away from ourselves. If left unchecked, outside light turns into a thermonuclear weapon of mass distraction. With the advent of artificial light, the damage is only getting worse. We've ironically lost our way with too much light. By taking us underground, dark retreat returns us to our common base, removes the divisive splinters, and initiates healing. It heals because it helps us remember.

Satellite data has revealed that artificial light is spreading and growing brighter, producing more light pollution and a "widespread loss of the night."[16] Because of electric light, outdoor illumination has grown 3 to 6 percent annually in the second half of the twentieth century. "While this has benefited productivity and safety, it has come with a dark side. The night is no longer dark enough."[17] We're suffering from a massive darkness deficit disorder. Franz Hölker, coauthor of a *Science Advances* study, warns, "From an evolutionary perspective, now, artificial light is a very new stressor. The problem is that light has been introduced in places, times, and intensities at which it does not naturally occur, and many organisms have had no chance to adapt to this new stressor."[18] It has devastating implications for the environment, for human health, and most importantly for our psychological and spiritual (psychospiritual) evolution. Darkness deficit disorder leads to an introspective deficit disorder. It's a disorder because we think what we're looking for is outside in the light when it's actually to be found in the darkness within.

Because light in general and artificial light in particular tend to pull us away from ourselves, we've lost contact with who we really are. We're living on the surface of ourselves, then wondering why something is missing. We're equally out of touch with this sacred earth and can no longer truly feel each other. As earth is losing its darkness, we are losing our way. Darkness deficit disorder is a disorder of depth. So much of the psychospiritual path is associated with light and height. We clamor for peak experiences and strive for the light. But if we're not careful, this can lead to high-altitude sickness and serious sunburn. I'm not dismissing the value of light nor the importance of lofty achievement, but merely pointing out the imbalance of the Kali Yuga and the need for darkness and depth. For every step we take up and out, we need to take another step down and in. Otherwise, we get dizzy and disoriented with the height and blinded by the light.

When I spend time in the dark, it is to recover the night and restore my sight. In dark retreat, with absolutely nothing to seduce me out, with no trace of light pollution, I'm drawn deeply within and see things never seen before. I find what I'm truly looking for and what really matters. These retreats reestablish the natural curfew of the night and cure the darkness deficit disorder. They keep me from getting into discursive trouble, the inevitable turmoil that accompanies an insatiably outward-bound mind. Barbara Brown Taylor, author of the bestselling book *Learning to Walk in the Dark*, writes, "I have learned things in the dark that I could never have learned in the light, things that have saved my life over and over again, so that there is really only one logical conclusion. I need darkness as much as I need light."[19] Perhaps there's a symbolic reason we have two eyes. Keep one eye on the dark, and you'll never lose sight of your depth.

Lunar Spirituality

In this Degenerate Age, humanity has been seduced away from the center of itself and as far away as possible from the divine. This divinity lies at the core of our being, which is pitch-black.[20] Poet Christopher Dewdney writes, "It is always night inside the body." Sunlight only penetrates a few millimeters past the skin, beyond that is absolute darkness. "The perpetual night of the body is where each of us began, so we are truly children of the physical night."[21] In that deep silence and stillness, in the darkness at the center of ourselves, we will find the exalted. But silence and stillness, held under the cover of darkness, scare us. So we jump out of the bed of darkness and search outside for our version of the divine, misplacing ourselves in the light. In countless ways, we are solar-powered beings, light eaters, and ours is a solar spirituality.

Mine is a lunar spirituality. I worship the night and am consumed by it. "The night is our window on the Infinite," writes naturalist Chet Raymo. I have spent my life exploring the infinity within, the origins of life, the beginning of consciousness, the basis of all. And this always leads me back to the dark. In Greek mythology and the Book of Genesis, darkness precedes light. In Hinduism, the darkness of dreamless sleep is called "causal consciousness," which means that both dreaming and waking consciousness arise from it. The flash of the Big Bang arose from a womb of primordial darkness. Seeds germinate in the dark. I was probably conceived in the dark, spent nine months bathed in it, and was then born from it.

You and I are children of darkness. Literally and allegorically. Every morning we arise from darkness, and every night we return to it. Every flash of insight or flicker of thought arises from the background darkness of the mind and returns to it, like a campfire spark melting into the nighttime sky. One day our bodies will melt back into the dark. Whether we like it or not, darkness is our primal home. It behooves us to become familiar with it.

Origins of Dark Retreat

Even though dark retreat is making a splash as a new method of transformation, forms of this practice have been around for millennia. It's difficult to say when the practice began, but one can easily imagine our ancient ancestors doing natural forms of dark retreat in the recesses of their caves. Practicing in sensory deprivation has been part of religious, shamanistic, and Indigenous cultures for ages. "Temple sleep" rituals were part of ancient Egypt, going back some 4600 years, where initiates spent time in darkness to seek spiritual guidance and commune with the divine.[22] In ancient India, dating back to around 1500 BCE, yogic practitioners went into the dark to nurture evolved states of consciousness and deepen spiritual practice.

Ancient Greek and Roman mystics performed practices in caves and other sequestered settings to invoke religious experiences. The Greeks specifically engaged in incubation rites for healing or to receive prophetic dreams from the gods.[23] The ritual use of darkness to evoke altered states of consciousness in the Neoplatonic tradition is also well documented.[24] Dark retreats have long been part of

Taoism and are actively practiced with modern masters like Mantak Chia.[25] The Indigenous Kogi population of Colombia has engaged in dark practice for at least six hundred years. Children destined to become spiritual leaders, called Mamás, are sometimes placed in darkness (or near darkness) right after birth and can stay there for up to nine years as they nurture their relationship with the spirit world, Aluna. The ancient Japanese Shinto tradition works with the practice of komori ("child of the night"), their version of dark retreat.[26] Tibetan and Bön Buddhism, where most of my training comes from, have engaged in dark practice for over a thousand years.

Sūtra vs. Tantra Dark Retreat

Dark retreat comes in two forms, sūtra and tantra.[27] The Sanskrit word *sūtra* means "discourse, sermon, or scripture," and refers to exoteric teachings delivered in a public setting. Sūtra-level dark retreat is for anyone. This is an accessible practice you can do at home or in formal retreat settings, and it is our main focus in this book.

Tantra-level dark retreat, explored in a future volume, is a different matter. This is prescription-strength medicine that must be prescribed by an authentic teacher, then used as directed by a genuine student. When my teacher admonished me not to speak about dark retreat, he was referring to this form of practice. *Tantra* means "weave, continuum" but is notoriously difficult to define, which is one reason it can be readily distorted into domains like "tantric sex" or "tantric speed dating" (no kidding). For our purposes, tantra refers to esoteric teachings delivered in a private setting for a select group of prepared individuals. The tantras themselves are intentionally opaque, or self-secret. Without a commentary, a knowledgeable guide, and previous experience in the sūtras, the tantras are impenetrable.[28] It's like trying to understand advanced calculus without having studied basic math.

Tantra dark retreat transcends but includes sūtra dark practice. It involves retreats of up to forty-nine days, engages methods designed to elicit a particular set of experiences, and, according to Tibetan Buddhism, is the ultimate preparation for death. This does not mean that sūtra-level practice isn't as transformative as its tantric counterpart. As we'll see, sūtra-level practice has tremendous benefits—without the risks of tantra (chapter 5). To give you a sense of how far dark retreat can go, I'm going to use the classification of tantra dark retreat to discuss the deeper aspects of this practice. These interjections are a form of "trickle-down spirituality," where a lofty teaching is briefly engaged to show you what is possible and elevate subordinate levels of material.

For purposes of contradistinction, sūtra dark retreat is more psychological in nature and deals with self-improvement, while tantra dark retreat is more spiritual in nature and deals with self-transcendence. While these distinctions are helpful, in the end it's all fuzzy. You can have full-blown tantric-level experiences in a sūtra retreat and, conversely, harvest mostly sūtra-level insights in a tantric retreat. Like everything in the dark, the boundaries break down and these levels blend into each other.[29] As we go further into this book, we'll drop deeper into tantric levels of dark retreat, mirroring the experience of dedicated dark trekkers. Many of these deeper insights came to me after a number of dark retreats. They are inserted to give you a sense of just how much is possible if you stick with this practice.

Dark retreat is not about darkness. It's about you. It's about depth. It's about getting to know yourself, without distraction, at the deepest possible levels. If you don't know who you are, how can you possibly know what you really want? Dark retreat reveals the extents you go to in order to avoid yourself and how that avoidance strategy causes all your suffering. Go into the dark to find yourself, to find what you truly want, and to end suffering. It's a marvelous practice of "lost and found." What is lost in the light can be found in the dark.

How to Read This Book

This book will progress, like your time in darkness itself, from relatively accessible introductory material to progressively deeper topics. If you don't want to go this deep, just skim or skip the deeper sections. As with darkness altogether, do what feels right for you. You may find that coming back to the deeper dives in a later reading makes more sense, especially if you have the chance to explore dark practice and get a feel for it. Keep in mind that dark retreat is not amenable to skimming. It's a disservice to the practice to keep things lite. Dropping into the depths should be done slowly. Just like in scuba diving, you don't want to go down too fast. Take your time, get used to the gravity of the material and the density of these waters, and you'll enjoy the plunge. Otherwise, you're likely to dart back up to the surface, not unlike the desire to head for the door when things get heavy in the dark.

The first seven chapters create the view that supports dark retreat. For those who are anxious to get going, the nuts and bolts of dark practice are introduced in chapter 8. Copious endnotes accompany the text and can be read after completing the book or upon a second reading. My favorite books are the ones that give me pause or stop my mind altogether. Books where I need to take a breath and feel into what's being said. When I enter darkness, I have to slow down or come to a full stop to get my bearings. Take your steps in this journey mindfully, respectfully, even reverentially, and darkness will gradually reveal its secrets.

Part 1

Introduction to Dark Retreat

1

The Two Faces of Darkness

> If we decide to keep going beyond the point where our eyes or minds are any help to us, we may finally arrive at the pinnacle of the spiritual journey toward God, which exists in complete and dazzling darkness.
>
> **—Barbara Brown Taylor**

"You're going to do what?!" is the most common response I hear from people when they learn I'm going into dark retreat. And that I've been doing so for decades. For most people, the idea of voluntarily going into solitary confinement in a pitch-black cave or cabin is just crazy. Why on earth would anyone engage in such an insane venture? Even a psychologist friend, someone who works with the mind, said upon hearing of my dark exploits, "That sounds like absolute torture!" It can indeed be torturous to your ego, but for those who really want to grow in this brief and precious life, it could be the most sensible thing you ever do. One retreatant, after just three days in dark retreat, said, "It's the best gift I've ever given myself. My life will never be the same."[1] Contrary to unexamined assumptions, dark retreat is actually a sane asylum. What's truly insane is being swept away by the madness of the modern world, trapped in the sphere of superficial appearance, blinded by light pollution, and essentially distracting yourself unto death. Where's the real darkness today?

Dark retreat is the perfect "Rorschach meditation." The Rorschach test is a psychological assessment that analyzes the way a person projects onto the image of a neutral inkblot, allowing the psychologist to examine emotional functioning and personality. What's more perfect than the inkblot of total darkness to reflect one's projections? Darkness itself is neutral, but as we'll see, when we explore shadow work at the deepest possible levels (chapter 12), it provides an ideal metaphysical mirror that reflects our projections. It's totally unfair to darkness, but the dark is okay with that. You can use it or abuse it any way you like, turning it into a refuse heap or a treasure trove. We're going to use it to learn as much about ourselves as we can, in the shortest possible time, under the most intense but transformative of conditions. And that treasured education begins before we ever set foot in the dark.

If you think solitary confinement in sensory deprivation is crazy, why do you think so? If dark retreat sounds like torture, why is that? If the thought of going into the dark makes your knees tremble, or you're freaked out by the thought of being so alone with yourself, what spooks you? If you feel that darkness is ominous, dangerous, or even evil, where is that feeling coming from? If you insist that this ancient practice should be shelved in the dustbins of history and kept secret, why the insistence? Dark retreat begins to teach you the minute you start thinking about it. It's a unique form of "night school" that can inform every aspect of your diurnal and nocturnal life.

I've used the following psychological principle to great effect in my life, a maxim that comes front and center in the dark: If something *affects* you more than it *informs* you, if you *react* more than you *respond*, you're probably dealing with a projection. Why are we so adversely affected by the dark? Why are so many people afraid of darkness? It's because we project the crap out of it! Or more accurately, we project all our crap *onto* it. The level of our reactivity is directly proportional to the level of our "projectivity." We project all our inner refuse, the metaphysical darkness we don't want to face, onto outer physical darkness and end up fearing something out there that's actually the dread of what's in here. The intensity of dark retreat is not due to darkness. It's due to everything we've plastered onto it. And these projections come home to roost when we spend time in the dark.

Perhaps the only thing we project onto more than darkness is death itself, which is why we're even more adversely affected by death. They're kissing cousins. Death is absolutely smothered with our projections, a convenient refuse heap for all our refused, rejected, and projected experience. We'll return to the relationship of darkness and death in chapter 16, when we explore some of the further ends of dark practice.[2] Voluntary dark retreat in life helps us prepare for the involuntary dark retreat waiting for us at the end of life. If we own up to our projections now, which is but one gift of dark practice, we can remove the darkness and fear that surround all things shadowy, including death itself. Psychologist Carl Jung said, "Projections change the world into a replica of one's unknown face."[3] In the dark, you're forced to come face-to-face with all your projections, which allows you to strip off all the makeup and become familiar with your real face. As the perfect metaphysical mirror, dark retreat flips external projection into internal reflection, showing you all the godly and ungodly aspects of your unmasked face.

Janus

Not only do we come face-to-face with all our projections in the dark, but once we own up and integrate those projections, darkness then delivers us head-on to the deepest dimensions of our being. This is where we meet the deified nature of ourselves and come face-to-face with who we really are. We're going to greet many gods and deities in the dark and in this book, for they represent the archetypes, or first forms, of personal and collective reality. As we work our way down to the source, we're going to bump into all sorts of dirty and divine things. We're essentially going to remove the dirt to reveal the divine.

While I was raised on Buddhist and Hindu deities on my path, I have developed a deep respect for their Western counterparts in Greek and Roman mythology. At these foundational levels, they're all cross-dressers. Formless wisdom is poured into countless forms to skillfully communicate with different cultures. Mythology is an ancient rendering of depth psychology, and depth psychology can be viewed as modern mythology.[4] By learning about Western gods and Eastern deities, you're learning about the depths of your unconscious mind, precisely what you're going to plunge into when you dive into the dark.

Janus is the Roman god of gates, doorways, and thresholds, and, by implication, the god of beginnings, endings, and transitions. He is known as "the god of good beginnings," which help ensure good endings, so it seems appropriate to have him head the way. Janus is depicted with two faces, one young and one old, with the young face looking forward and the old face looking back. We're going to emphasize the youthful face at the outset of our journey and return to the elderly face at the end.

The temple of Janus extended east and west, where the day begins and ends, and had two gates facing in both directions. Janus presides over the first hour of the day, the first day of the month, and the first month of the year. His name is enveloped in the month of January (I'm actually writing these words on the first day of January 2024), and his symbols are a set of keys and a doorkeeper's staff. We'll be using his keys to unlock the doorway to creativity, healing, and happiness for authentic seekers, and his staff to keep the mere shoppers out.

Something that is Janus-faced has two sharply contrasting characteristics, like darkness itself. In other words, we need to distinguish higher-phase darkness, which symbolizes origins, birth, creativity, and source, from lower-phase darkness, which represents ignorance, fear, loathing, and death. African shaman Malidoma Patrice Somé writes, "Indeed, it is in the redefinition of darkness that we discover an entryway into a potent transformational experience that can assist us in rethinking the nature of both reality and healing. What might we learn about ourselves and the powers of the 'other world' by surrendering to the beauty and opportunity for greater vision afforded to us in darkness?"[5] What if the darkness we've been avoiding holds the light we've been seeking?

The backward-facing aspect of Janus represents diabolical darkness. This frightening face helps to keep the dilettantes out, but it can also scare genuine seekers from exploring the divine qualities of the dark. In the following quote, scholar Peter Kingsley writes about death, but his comments apply equally to darkness. As such, I've taken the liberty to replace "death" with "darkness" when he writes:

> It's such a perfect arrangement for wisdom to hide away in [darkness]. Everyone runs from [darkness] so everyone runs away from wisdom, except for those who are willing to pay the price and go against the stream . . . night and darkness are the equivalent of ignorance. This can seem amazing: that [one] should go to the depths of ignorance in search of wisdom instead of straight to the light . . . It's ignorance simply because it's ignored, ignored by people who run from [darkness]. And what everyone ignores—that's where wisdom lies.[6]

Diabolical darkness is associated with evil and all things "dark" in the negative sense. We talk about the darkness of death, the darkness of ignorance, and the dark ages. People dress in black when they're mourning, suffer when they're in a dark mood, and feel depressed when everything looks black. *Darkness* comes from a root that means "to hide," as well as "the place where dirt collects."[7] Just look at all the dirt that has collected around the word *dark*, where synonyms include *dismal, dreary, bleak, grim, funereal, somber, grave, heavy, gloomy, melancholy, blue, depressed, dejected, cheerless, joyless, sad, sorrowful, disconsolate, sullen, dour, morose, crestfallen, brooding, frowning, scowling, glowering, evil, wicked, villainous, infamous, base, vile, ominous, threatening, menacing, sinister, ignorant*, and *unenlightened*. When Dylan Thomas exhorted us to rail against the dying of the light, it was good poetry but bad advice. He didn't seem to realize that the night is good and raging against darkness is counterproductive. Kingsley shares that "the underworld isn't just a place of darkness and death. It only seems that from a distance. In reality it's the supreme place of paradox where all the opposites meet."[8] And all dualities are healed.

Christianity, with all its nobility, doesn't help when it comes to dark matters. Christians often use *darkness* as a synonym for *sin, ignorance, spiritual blindness*, and *death*. "Deliver us, O Lord, from the powers of darkness. Shine into our hearts the brightness of your Holy Spirit, and protect us from all the perils and dangers of the night."[9] Or "God is light and in him there is no darkness at all" (John 1:5). Or "I am the light of the world. Whoever follows me will not walk in darkness, but will have the light of life" (John 8:12). In the Book of Genesis, we find, "And God saw that the light was good. And God separated the light from the darkness." This is the ugly face of darkness that keeps people looking away. If we see through these fearful eyes, there's no way we're going to go into the dark. Diabolical darkness represents the death space, and who in their right mind wants to head into a grave? If we don't understand what the forward face is looking at, even people who could genuinely benefit from dark retreat are scared off. Darkness is often associated with the devil, whose very name includes evil. But even Christianity points out that the devil can transform into Lucifer, "the bringer of light." Here is the face of divine darkness and the glittering gift of dark retreat. Sanskrit scholar Christopher Wallis writes, "There is no darkness within, only light unseen."

If you realize that tucked within the darkness is the most dazzling light of wisdom, you're more likely to step into the dark. In her classic book *Mysticism: A Study in the Nature and Development of Man's Spiritual Consciousness*, Evelyn Underhill writes, "The Dark Night (of the Soul) brings the Self to the threshold of that completed life which is to be lived in intimate union with Reality. It is the Entombment which precedes the Resurrection, say the Christian mystics."[10] Many people come out of dark retreat feeling reborn. Dark retreat democratizes resurrection, which is now available to anyone willing to go into the dark and "die." Darkness mandates this dying or letting go of the distractions of life, of habitual ways of relating to everything, and of much of what you've been taught about the nature of mind and reality.

I casually mentioned to a new friend recently that I was going into dark retreat for a month this year, and his response was, "That sounds awful!" Little did he know the hidden truth of his words. *Awful* literally means "full of awe." The word took on awful connotations, as did darkness itself, when people lost sight of its true meaning. Whether darkness is awful in the positive or negative sense depends on how we face it. If we contract around darkness, we make it awful; if we open to it, darkness reveals itself as full of awe.

As Janus leads us across the threshold of the anxiety and fear we harbor around darkness, and we transition from diabolical darkness into divine darkness, we end our old relationship to the dark and begin a new one, transforming obstacle into opportunity. We avail ourselves of opportunities for growth we couldn't have imagined in the light of day. Malidoma Somé said that the village elders of his tribe once told him, "Let's turn the lights *off* so that we can see." When Malidoma asked for more light, the elders told him, "No, if we light the lamps, we won't be able to see." The elders explained:

> You can't see anything real in the daylight. The only thing you see in the daylight is what you want to see. When you turn the lights off in the night, you see what wants to be seen, which is a whole different story . . . We need to turn off the light of what we think, of our diurnal consciousness. We need to descend into the night.[11]

Descend into the night and meet it on *its* terms. Don't bring your diurnal strategies into the dark. Don't try to illuminate it with your waking consciousness, which is so floodlighted, ego-centric, and heady that it stomps on the nuances of the nocturnal. Open to what darkness has to teach you. Let it enter your life and help balance the equation.

We suffer when appearance is not in harmony with reality, when what seems to be happening is not aligned with what's really happening. Darkness allows us to drop below superficial appearances, the gloss of diurnal consciousness, and into deeper underlying realities. When we face outward and get lost in the surface display, we get seduced into mere appearances and suffer. When we turn off the distracting lights and face inward, we dis-cover reality and put an end to our suffering.

Finally, Janus has played a delightful role in my life over the past few years as I've shifted my gaze from the ancient wisdom of the East, namely Buddhism and Hinduism, to include the remarkable wisdom from the West. I've spent time with pre-Socratic philosophers, sages like Pythagoras, Heraclitus, and especially Parmenides. Plato remains the shining star, but the influence of Aristotle is close behind. Twentieth-century philosopher Alfred North Whitehead wasn't exaggerating when he said that all of Western philosophy is but a series of footnotes to Plato. The Neoplatonic giants Plotinus, Iamblichus, and Proclus have opened new eyes to the mystery traditions of the West. I was delighted to learn that dark retreat was part of many of these ancient schools. While my training has been largely from the Tibetan Buddhist and Bön traditions, I have learned much by looking in my own backyard. I consider Carl Jung to be a modern heir of these Greek titans, so his influence will also be felt in the pages ahead.

My Bias

By going temporarily blind in the dark, my dark retreats have ironically revealed countless blind spots. Pointing out these blind spots is a central theme of our journey. One such revelation that needs to be illuminated at the outset is that we're all suffering from an insidious form of discrimination, an unconscious prejudice that borders on bigotry (defined as "an obstinate or unreasonable attachment to a belief, opinion, or faction"). It's a segregation of consciousness and perception that severely restricts every aspect of our lives. The most damaging forms of discrimination are those we don't even know we're afflicted by. These are the true blind spots, and they do real damage. As Mark Twain allegedly said, "It ain't what you don't know that gets you in trouble. It's what you do know that just ain't so."[12]

Hidden biases and blind spots are nasty and hard to detect.[13] The Buddha understood this, which is why he was more interested in questioning answers than answering questions. His bumper sticker was "Question Authority." Socrates had a similar gadfly orientation, one that resulted in his execution by Greek authorities. His focus on critical thinking privileged proper questions over definitive answers. Both rebel thinkers challenged the status quo and strove to overthrow the tyranny of appearance.

What's the status quo being challenged? What's the authority in question? That the best way to perceive and understand things is in the full light of day; that the appearances revealed by your eyes reveal the truth. Barbara Brown Taylor writes:

> [I]t makes me wonder how seeing has made me blind—by giving me cheap confidence that one quick glance at things

> can tell me what they are, by distracting me from learning how the light inside me works, by fooling me into thinking I have a clear view of how things really are, of where the road leads, of who can see rightly and who cannot. I am not asking to become blind, but I have become a believer. There is a light that shines in the darkness, which is only visible there.[14]

And what's the sinister discrimination? Our extreme bias for daytime consciousness, our favoritism toward light, and the limited reality they disclose. We're all afflicted with an acute light-centric and sight-centric prejudice. And like all blind spots and prejudices, these centricities are highly limiting, creating a near-total eclipse of the mind. They reduce what we can know about mind and reality to what we perceive in the light of day. Going blind in dark retreat corrects this poor vision. Jacques Lusseyran, a French author and political activist blinded at age seven, writes:

> I believe that blindness has its own function. It has the task of reminding us that the despotism of one sense, sight, is unjust, and of cautioning us against the form of perception prevalent today . . . That a blind person should speak up and warn the seeing to be cautious about the use of their own eyes, as I am doing, may appear unseemly and even comical. Yet it is not the process of seeing that I attack. I accuse only a certain idol worship. The idol is the conviction that seeing is the principal activity of the spirit, and sufficient for it.[15]

Why do we have this prejudice? Why do we idolize light and sight at the expense of our other senses and the night? We'll explore many reasons in this book. The first is shared by Arab trickster Mullah Nasruddin in a parable I've taken the liberty to update.

A neighbor is walking home one evening when he sees Nasruddin underneath a streetlight in front of his house, searching intently for a lost key. The neighbor offers to help, unsuccessfully, and eventually asks, "Where exactly did you lose this key?"

Nasruddin replies, "Back in my house."

Incredulous, the neighbor exclaims, "Then why on earth are we looking out here!?"

Without missing a beat, Nasruddin says, "Because there's more light out here."

Dream researcher Stephen LaBerge lends a hand: "The outside world may have more light, but it isn't where the key was lost and hence might be found: that is, inside, in the darkness within, our innermost home, beyond the self, in the beginning of all."[16]

We tend to look where the looking is easy, even if it's in the totally wrong place. We're blinded by external light, which seduces us out and away from that which we truly seek. The Greek word for sin is *hamartia*, an archery term that means "to miss the mark." Many of us feel that something is missing, like the key to happiness, so we look for it outside. But if our aim is 180 degrees off, it's no wonder we continue to miss the mark and feel empty inside. What we're looking for is indoors, in the darkness and depths within. One retreatant shared, "How much of our experience is completely painted by our imperception of it. It's like there's an entire world that you have when there's no [outer] form at all, and there's no world that's there. Like an entire [inner] world of emotions and fears and pain and enjoyment and pleasure."

We already have what we're looking for. We just need to set our sights in the right direction. By erasing externality, darkness aims us in the right direction. As psychotherapist and meditation teacher Sylvia Boorstein put it, "Happiness is an inside job."

2

Installing the GPS

Turn out the lights—and leave them off—and we will experience a consciousness our minds have never known but our bodies still remember . . . We can't find our souls in the daylight, since we lost them in the night . . . Turn out the lights and leave them off and, in short, you remember who you are.

—**Clark Strand**

The journey into darkness is so unfamiliar. Having some light, in the form of orienting generalizations, will help us find our way. This chapter installs several global positioning systems that we'll continually update throughout this book. Fictional sage Dumbledore said of death what equally applies to darkness: "To the well-organized mind, [darkness] is but the next great adventure." Organizing your mind before entering a bewildering environment helps you turn the trip into a fruitful adventure.

At first glance, dark retreat may seem to be a wildly esoteric practice, beyond the reach of most people. While the container of darkness may be novel, the spirit of this practice is logical and practical. Dark retreat is just a concentrated way to work with your mind and heart. Anybody who has one of those may be interested in how darkness helps them explore these dimensions of being. On one level, dark retreat is simply meditation on steroids. Anyone interested in meditation will find it to be a treasure, and anyone already practicing meditation will realize how darkness ramps things up. As NBA superstar Rudy Gobert put it after three days of retreat, "Dark retreat is meditation times a thousand."

The Soul of Darkness

Dark retreat is a journey of the soul. While spirit is often expressed in metaphors of ascent, height, and light (and is more masculine in nature), scholar Patrick Harpur reminds us that "[s]oul is expressed in metaphors of descent, depth, and darkness," and is more feminine in nature. "She favors the Underworld and the circuitous route. She is not transcendent but immanent, lying hidden within the world. Slowly, meanderingly, she follows the downward spiral of Imagination towards its dark wisdom. She prefers the twilight to the light, where things mingle and worlds intersect."[1] Author Thomas Moore lends his voice: "*Soul* is not a thing, but a quality or a dimension of experiencing life and ourselves. It has to do with depth, value, relatedness, heart, and personal substance."[2]

Physicists work with particle accelerators to study the substance of the physical world. Dark retreat is like an inner-work accelerator that allows you to study the substance of the psychospiritual world. But they work in opposite ways. Particle accelerators work by drastically speeding things up; dark retreat works by radically slowing things down. With the former, particles slam into each other at blinding speeds; with the latter, you collide with infinity by coming to a full stop.

Dark retreat is akin to what happens when you step outside of a brightly lit room and into the night. At first, you can't see a thing. Your pupils are so contracted from the light that you're temporarily blind. But if you remain patient and keep your eyes open, your pupils will relax, and you will start to see things previously hidden in the dark. Darkness represents the unconscious mind, so in a similar way, when you step out of your brightly lit and speedy world into a dark cabin or cave, at first you can't see a thing. Your mind's eye is so contracted that everything inside is black. But if you remain patient and keep your mind's eye open, your mind relaxes, and you start to see things within that you've never seen before. You're opening the aperture of your awareness and perceiving a wondrous new world inside.

The more time you spend in the dark, the more open and sensitive you get, the more you dilate your consciousness, and the more you see. When I first step into my dark room, I can't see a thing with my physical eyes. But if I stay in there long enough, I'll often see a pinpoint of light leaking in. I'll fumble around to block it out with duct tape and return to complete darkness. But after a few more days, when my eyes dilate even more, I'll see tinier light leaks coming through the tape, which I cover up with more tape. (Scientists say it's possible to see a single photon.) It's not just my physical eyes that dilate, but my mind's eye, and eventually my entire body. I'm opening my mind, heart, and body and seeing deeper into the previously dark recesses of my being. Unconscious processes then slowly emerge into the light of consciousness.

Phenomenology is the study of experience, and microphenomenology is the study of microscopic experience. Because you're slowing down and opening up to such an extent in the dark, you're putting yourself under the most powerful microscope and revealing dimensions of being that were previously lost in the glare of day. You eventually get down to the atomic nature of experience, nurturing a super refined perception with your "innerscope," dare I say extra-sensory perception (ESP). But this form of ESP is not about anything extra. It's about removing all the extras. It's about heightened *intra*-sensory perception, cultivating the exquisite sensitivity of *feeling*. Dark retreat then becomes a recovery and restoration project. At physical levels, you're going to rest and recover as never before, restoring your health. At psychospiritual levels, you're going to restore your relationship to fractured dimensions of your being and recover from a splintered mind and broken heart. But mostly, you go into the dark to restore your sight and recover a lost way of seeing.

The Three Circles

Imagine three concentric circles. The smallest inner circle represents your comfort zone. Think of it as your bubble bath or happy place, the space where most of us want to be. There's nothing wrong with soaking in comfort and fulfilling your comfort plan, but the bubble bath turns into a toxic tub if comfort becomes your primary objective. Have you noticed that the more time you spend in your comfort zone the smaller it gets? People who strive for luxury and ease get fussier, more irritable, and increasingly small-minded. Look at the lives of the rich and famous, with their inability to tolerate any level of inconvenience or discomfort. The comfort zone readily flips into a contracted zone riddled with defensive or offensive strategies. Comfort is an important aspect of life, but is this where growth takes place?

Outside of the comfort zone is the challenge zone. In order to evolve, you have to stretch out of your bubble bath. It may not always feel good, but stretching is good for growth. Whether it's physical exercise, emotional discipline, or spiritual training, accepting some discomfort is necessary for evolution. As cliché as it is, truth abides in the adage "No pain, no gain." Whether it's working out at your local gym or "working in" with deep inner work, countering your comfort-ridden habits is where growth occurs.

Anybody who works their way into the challenge zone knows that the more time you spend here, the *bigger* your comfort zone gets. Instead of getting fussier and more close-minded, you become more tolerant and open-minded. Small mind is replaced with big mind, and mountains return to molehills. In the world of yoga, which is largely about the benefits of stretching, the most important pose is Savāsana, the "Corpse Pose." At the end of a rigorous session, the practitioner "drops dead" into Savāsana and lies still on the ground, fully relaxed. Dark retreat is in the family of Savāsana, which is simultaneously the easiest and most difficult pose in yoga. The big stretch into the challenge zone comes from the difficulty of doing absolutely nothing! The challenge is to let go or "die" to all activity, and simply be.

In Tibetan Buddhism, dark retreat comes from the tantric tradition, or the Vajrayāna. *Yāna* means "vehicle," and *vajra* means "adamantine, indestructible," so Vajrayāna is often translated as the "Diamond Vehicle." Diamonds are made deep within the darkness of the earth, under intense pressure. Diamond-like qualities of the mind and heart are cultivated in dark retreat, but with workable levels of pressure. You don't have to endure crushing forces to harvest the benefits of darkness; you just have to do nothing. The trick is doing it well. Indian sage Ramana Maharshi taught, "Don't meditate. Just be." And after three days in the dark, one retreatant shared, "I did not have to be guarded at all. I could just take a deep breath and be. I don't have to act a certain way. I don't have to do anything. I could just let it take me—and totally be freed." Dark retreat only puts the squeeze on you if you're a "human doing" more than a human being. Darkness puts all my relentless activity under house arrest and forces me into simple human being. It has shown me that who I *think* I am is defined by what I do; who I *really* am is revealed when I finally stop doing.

Because you literally can't do anything in the dark, it squeezes all the doing out of you, forcing you into the diamond-like nature of your being. That's the painful point. When you're feeling the squeeze, remember this: no pressure, no diamond. As you'll see in the pages ahead, the healthy pressure of the challenge zone shows you what you're really made of: indestructible (diamond-like) awareness.

Outside of the challenge zone is the danger zone. This is when you've gone too far. A healthy stretch transforms into a hurtful snap. If you bend the mind too far, it can break. In dark retreat, this means grinding it out like an ultramarathoner. If you're toughing it out and enduring the retreat, you're trying too hard. Dark retreat is not an extreme sport with a summit to reach or a finish line to cross. Darkness tends to smack down type A personalities. Like death itself, dark retreat is something you can't actually do. You have to let it do you. It's so simple, which is precisely what makes it so hard. The invitation, and eventual command, of entering the challenge zone of darkness is to surrender. Replace white knuckling with a white flag, or the ensuing battle with yourself will hurl you into the danger zone.

Studies suggest that voluntarily shocking your system with things like fasting, cold plunges, sweat lodges, interval training, or even psychedelics can be good for you. You can cautiously view dark retreat as a voluntary shocking of your system, but only if you keep in mind that the shock comes from doing absolutely nothing. Flipping from a crazy-busy "human doing" sprinting around in the light to a dead-still human being sitting motionless in the dark can be shocking. There's nothing inherent in the dark that's going to shock you. You're going to jolt yourself with the truth. Dark retreat tases your established habits, any form of deception, and all manner of distraction. It's designed to disrupt or stun your karma. Intentional shock is a risky analogy, however, because dark retreat already lends itself to thrill seekers. This practice is not about walking on burning coals and bragging about it. It's not about seeing how many days you can endure in darkness. Learning about the danger zone is not meant to seduce extreme meditative "athletes" into dark retreat, to challenge anybody to see how close to the edge they can go, or to test the limits of someone's stamina, but to keep the sincere practitioner from putting too much pressure on themselves in the dark. Even diamonds can crack.

These three zones will come into play throughout our journey to help us find the balance between comfort and risk, and work with the meditative dictum "not too tight, not too loose" (we'll return to this balancing act in chapter 14). If you're too loose in life, or in dark retreat, you're going to sleep your way through both. If you're too tight, you can hurt yourself. Janus can help us relate to the three circles. Keep one face looking forward in the direction of growth, but keep the other face looking back and in touch with comfort. This way you'll come face-to-face with the middle way and find your balance in darkness.

To Erase

The power of dark retreat comes from its ability to erase. This practice is about subtraction, not addition, a theme you'll encounter many times in the pages ahead. Darkness itself is the result of negation (of light), not addition. It's defined by absence, not substance. *You can make light, but you cannot make darkness.* You can make lies, but you can't make the truth. You can fabricate deception, but you can't fabricate reality. You can only reveal it. The very "structure" of darkness suggests its benefits as the primordial eraser. Only elemental truth is allowed in the dark, which is precisely where dark retreat takes you.

When brought to fruition, dark retreat erases you altogether and points out the un-erasable. With everything that is happening these days—our crazy schedules, ridiculously busy lives, and endless obligations—do we really need to add anything else to our lives? I take the greatest delight when I can remove things from my packed day, and recently I had a dream where an authoritative voice boomed out repeatedly, "Less is more!" Relate to dark practice as the addition of a tool designed for deletion, like a snow shovel, sponge, or dust mop.

In this regard, dark retreat is the most "retro" thing you can possibly do. Darkness will restore your identity, return you to the nature of your being, and eventually revert you to the reduction base of reality itself. And it does all this through the process of removal and cessation. Just stop all the diversion, and reversion naturally ensues. Stop rerouting reality, and you'll find your way back to it. Stop all the detours, and the path to what you truly seek is revealed. We'll unpack this critical topic throughout our journey.

As we've seen, darkness is about returning to origins, and the exploration of word origins, or etymology, is resonant with this return. A word about words is therefore in order. We can learn a great deal about ourselves by exploring the depths of our language. Language structures our perception and thinking in the most insidious way, so by deconstructing words back to their origins, we can invite a correlative deconstruction in our traditional ways of thinking and perceiving. The trick is to find the balance between etymological insight and silly wordplay. I hope my sense of balance works for you in the following pages because etymology is like an archaeology of consciousness, which coincides with our narrative of digging deep and bringing unconscious processes into the light of consciousness. If you find the etymology distracting, just skim or skip the brief interjections.

Two irreducible prefixes, *di-* and *re-*, frame our journey in this book. Keep these in mind as we progress into more nuanced topics. These two prefixes (described shortly) unpack a central theme that's been suggested several times already: The source of all our suffering arises when we lose the essence in the *di*splay, when appearance is no longer in harmony with reality. In other words, when we're *dis*-tracted, literally "pulled apart," from the truth. As theologian Paul Tillich said, "[T]he state of our whole life is estrangement from others and ourselves, because we are estranged from the Ground of our being . . . Man is split within himself . . . To be in the state of sin is to be in the state of separation."[3] Dark retreat *re*duces the display so we can *re*capture the essence and *re*turn to the ground. It's the most grounding practice I've ever done.

Dark retreat cuts through appearance to put us in contact with reality. If distraction is the disease, *re*traction is the remedy. This narrative is captured in perhaps the most famous parable in Western philosophy, Plato's Allegory of the Cave. In it, Plato describes a group of prisoners shackled inside a cave and forced to face a wall. Projected onto this wall are shadows from objects passing in front of a fire that is behind them. The shadows comprise the prisoners' reality, capturing their attention and becoming the entirety of their lives. Professor of religion Gregory Shaw summarizes the key points:

> The prisoners bound by chains and looking at the shadows on the wall is his image of the state of human beings *possessed by conventional reality,* caught up in the *consensual trance* [the display] that keeps us isolated and cut off from the Universal Mind [the essence] . . . [inner work] loosens our chains so that the individual is no longer identified with the conventional . . . what is relevant . . . is a radical shift in one's habitual orientation.[4]

We are prisoners bound by the chains of our infatuation with mere appearance, the outward-bound mind, the shadowy display. What an elegant irony: Go into a dark retreat cave and lose the display to find the essence. Get out of Plato's cave by going into a real one.

To Align

The metacrisis is the result of individual and collective misalignment. We're meta-misaligned, seriously out of sync. Erasing these misalignments with practices like dark retreat leads to alignment. *Align* is embedded in nasty misaligned words like *malign* and *malignant*. So many things today are skewed, out of tune, out of kilter, or otherwise wonky. There's little sense of resonance, harmony, flow, or ease in a world riddled with discord, divisiveness, and disease. The Sanskrit word for this is *duhkha*, usually translated as "suffering" or "dissatisfaction." The image is that of a wheel with its axle off-center. Whether we feel that something is not quite right with the world today or we clearly see that things are definitely not right depends on the extent of misalignment.

Imagine a cart with both axles off-center. Such a bumpy vehicle would quickly stray off course and never get to its destination. Cyclists talk about "truing a wheel," which refers to bringing it back into alignment. To overcome duhkha, we need to align ourselves with our true center. Only then can we see straight. Only then can we be straight with ourselves and with others. By going into the dark, you tune into your true self by turning so deeply into yourself. All sorts of things naturally come into alignment when the sources of misalignment are removed. This is why so many people come out of darkness feeling true to themselves, aligned with their mission in life or otherwise in tune with reality.

The sages who lived in accord with reality were called rishis. The Buddha was sometimes referred to as the Maharishi, or "Great Rishi." *Rishi* can be translated as "the straight ones, the aligned ones." Trungpa Rinpoche wrote that rishi refers to the person "who constantly leads a straightforward life. The Tibetan word for rishi is *trangsong. Trang* means 'direct,' *song* means 'upright.' The term refers to one who leads a direct and upright life."[5] The principle of alignment applies across a spectrum, from physical to psychological to spiritual, with the metacrisis resulting from one misalignment upon the other. The metacrisis makes sense from the perspective of hamartia ("missing the mark"), which we can now interpret as missing the center. If you set off in the wrong direction, in a vehicle with axles that are off-center, it's no wonder everything feels off and you keep missing the mark!

Realignment ranges from aligning ourselves to the present moment with practices like mindfulness; tuning into others with empathy, understanding, and compassion (with practices like metta, or "loving-kindness," described in chapter 7); resonating with the gods and deities, or any greater power (with Western practices like theurgy, or Eastern methods like deity yoga); and getting in harmony with reality altogether with practices like dark retreat.[6] Therapy is about getting into alignment with emotional and psychological dimensions of our being; physical health is about getting into alignment with our body. Alignment is behind Carl Jung's work on synchronicity; it's at the heart of Plato's visionary work of aligning the microcosm with the macrocosm. You'll find it in experiences of coincidence and in flow states of optimal performance. Alignment is how you enter the "zone" where good fortune abounds. It's virtually synonymous with happiness. Once you align yourself to the principle of alignment, you'll start to see expressions of it everywhere.

Because dark retreat is so deep, it acts as the great aligner. The challenges in darkness are directly proportional to how far out of alignment you've become. If you're already straight with yourself, with others, and with reality, dark retreat is a breeze. But if you're not, darkness will straighten you out. It will force you to line up with yourself, with others, with truth itself. Darkness stretches and bends you back into alignment with reality. It sets things straight.

Here's one example of how dark retreat has helped me back into alignment. I spent many years trying to figure out the question: "What should I do with my life?" I looked outside for the answers, for what other people were doing, and listened to what other people thought I should be doing. With so much time to reflect ("bend back") in dark retreat, I realized that my question was out of alignment because I wasn't following my inner voice. I couldn't hear it in the bluster of daily life. In darkness, I could finally listen and hear the true, aligned question: *What does life want to do with me?* I then discovered the purpose of my life by aligning, surrendering, to life itself. My life is not about me. What a relief! It's about opening to, and becoming employed by, reality itself. It's about getting out of my own way and going to work for others. Dark retreat erased the wrong question, aligned me with the right one, and changed everything. Instead of being bossed around by my ego, which is so out of line with reality, my new superior is reality itself.

When I'm feeling off-center during the day, I drop into my dark room to realign. When I'm about to lose my cool in a difficult situation, I close my eyes to realign. My annual dark retreats are where I go for regular and more extensive tune-ups. Depending on how far off-axle I've become, it can take several hours, or even days, to get back into alignment. I go offline in the dark to get back in line with my body, my heart, and the stars. The initial dissonance, the difficulty up front, is always revelatory of how far I've strayed. Realignment is at the heart of dark retreat. As we'll see, it's where creativity, healing, and happiness all line up.

The Big Two

Here's how the Janus principle ties into the two central vectors of our journey, as represented in two core prefixes. The first prefix, *di-*, points to the source of all our discord, the essence of every form of dissonance and the heart of the disintegration comprising the metacrisis ripping the world apart. This dismal prefix describes how we get diverted from the essence and find ourselves so far out of alignment. It's the outward face of Janus. *Di-* is a diabolical prefix that means "two, twice, double, or apart." My thesaurus lists thirty pages of disrupting words beginning with this most divisive prefix, starting eerily after the word *demonic*. *Di-* is the essence of duality, the heart of the conventional world of disorder and dis-ease, known in Sanskrit as samsāra. (Samsāra itself comes from a root that means "to wander or distract.") *Di-* or *dis-* is that which distances us from reality, dismembers us from what is true, and divorces us from ourselves and each other. All this dissing is condensed into one wicked word that's at the heart of our journey into and out of the cave: *distraction*. Lakhar Rinpoche says, "To end distraction is to end samsāra." Conversely, to amp distraction is to amp samsāra. Distraction is the central player of the Degenerate Age.

Dys- is a closely allied prefix, which means "bad, ill; abnormal, imperfect; hard, difficult" and culminates in the collective dysfunction that is the dystopia of our world today. A dystopia is literally a utopia gone astray, a lost paradise born of the countless forms of dissing ourselves, each other, and reality itself. We only have to remove all this distraction to find our way back, retrace our steps, and revert to our natural state. It's a reparative journey that takes place as we recover and restore our natural condition in darkness. Thomas Moore writes, "When I see those three letters 'dys-' in 'dysfunctional,' I think of 'Dis,' the old Roman name for the mythological underworld. Soul enters life from below, through the cracks, finding an opening into life at the points where smooth functioning breaks down."[7] Moore is hinting at the alchemical principle of transforming obstacle (lead) into opportunity (gold), an alchemy that takes place in the crucible of darkness. Let's use all our dysfunction to allow soul to reemerge. If we relate to it properly, rupture transforms into rapture.

The second prefix, *re-*, describes how to retreat from the dysfunctional display to find the restorative essence, how to get realigned. It's the inward face of Janus. The "radical shift in one's habitual orientation" that Shaw referred to in the previous quote is the shift from *di-* to *re-*, from outside to inside, from the display back to the essence. *Re-* means "again" (indicating repetition), as well as "back" or "backward" (indicating withdrawal or retreat). It's almost a religious prefix (to "link back") in its import. I have over fifty pages of words in my thesaurus beginning with this regenerative prefix. *Re-* (going back again and again) is the essence of the return to nonduality, the heart of the world of reordering and ease known in Sanskrit as nirvāna. The Vajra Regent, a meditation teacher, said that the essence of spiritual practice is remembrance. We can reduce this even further to say that the essence of spiritual practice is *re-*, coming back again and again to the present moment, to our true nature, to what *is* before we dis ourselves from it. *Re-* is that which reverts us to reality, reinstates what is true, and reestablishes our connection with ourselves and each other. *Nirvāna* itself means "to extinguish" and is related to the word *nirodha*, which means "cessation." The many words for liberation in Sanskrit are mostly terms implying cessation, negation, or reversal—of all the dissing. Negation is at the heart of traditional religious and spiritual approaches represented by apophatic theology ("to say no"), the via negativa ("by way of denial"), or kenosis ("the way of emptying").

Cessation is at the core of dark retreat. Everything is put on hold. Your life, your habits, your movements, and your distractions all come to a hard stop. That, indeed, is what makes it so hard. But it's the ceasing that initiates the erasing. Dark retreat erases all the adventitious defilements—all the dust, all the activities, all the doing—that obscure who you really are. Starting with outer levels of cessation, darkness eventually erases all the dualities that obscure nonduality, leaving a wake of healing, creativity, and unconditional happiness.

Reductionism is a loaded term, often viewed in a negative sense when we attempt to reduce everything into matter (as in scientific reductionism and materialism). But when harnessed properly, reductionism is a powerful way to reduce complexity into simplicity.

Healthy reductionism cuts to the quick, gets down to what really matters, and leads a more simplified and meaningful life. Henry David Thoreau wrote,

> I went to the woods because I wished to live deliberately, to front only the essential facts of life, and see if I could not learn what it had to teach, and not, when I came to die, discover that I had not lived . . . I wanted to live deep and suck out all the marrow of life, to live so sturdily and Spartan-like as to put to rout all that was not life, to cut a broad swath and shave close, to drive life into a corner, and reduce it to its lowest terms.[8]

In other words, Thoreau went to the woods to contemplate and meditate, and dark retreat is going into the woods as deeply as possible. After three days in the dark a retreatant shared:

> That's crazy. It's beautiful. I never was as close to myself as I was in there. It's just a layer that isn't often peeled back out here. There is no way you can experience that and not come out the other side with a different take on yourself or a different approach to life. It reprioritized me by trimming the fat. You realize how much you *don't* need by being in there. Now I can move accordingly because I know what matters. Now I can really home in on what's important.

Can the essence of all our suffering, of samsāra itself, of the metacrisis, be reduced to the nearly infinite iterations of *di-*, represented archetypally in distraction? Can the essence of happiness, of nirvāna itself, be similarly reduced to the essence of *re-*, represented most directly in retraction?[9] Could it really be this irreducibly simple? Don't take my word for it. Test these prefixes, which represent the core vectors of going out or going in, against your own experience. And remember that simple doesn't always mean easy. Retreat to the dark woods, where you withdraw from the display in the most impactful way, and see for yourself.

3

Dark Retreat as an Observatory

To go in the dark with a light is to know the light. To know the dark, go dark. Go without sight, and find that the dark, too, blooms and sings, and is traveled by dark feet and dark wings.
—**Wendell Berry**

I first received instruction on dark retreat in 1996 within the context of a twelve-year cycle of teachings offered by meditation master Khenpo Tsültrim Gyamsto Rinpoche. One hundred or so seasoned students gathered annually for several weeks to study the loftiest teachings in Tibetan Buddhism. Dark retreat was presented as part of the Dzogchen, or "Great Perfection," teachings.[1] The notion of sensory deprivation as a form of meditation was interesting, but it didn't grab me at a visceral level. There was also no place to do the formal practice three decades ago. Rinpoche suggested we start by going into a dark closet for a few hours at a time, just to get a feel for it. Being a good student, I followed his instructions and became a true "closet meditator."

Things took off when I was asked to start teaching on death and dying a few years later. In the Tibetan tradition, bardo yoga (*bardo* means "gap, transitional process, in between") is a set of teachings and practices designed to help you prepare for the end of life. Bardo yoga is specifically directed toward the gap between lives but also applies to the gap between any two states of consciousness. It's not hard to see the connection between the gap of bardo and the gap that dark retreat inserts into your life. I started reading everything I could find and kept coming across references to the forty-nine-day bardo retreat, one of the most advanced practices in Buddhism, during which a rigorously prepared practitioner goes into a pitch-black cabin or cave for seven weeks to simulate the alleged forty-nine days one spends in the bardo after death. The practice fell out of favor because instead of attaining enlightenment, ill-prepared practitioners attained madness.[2]

After several years of home practice, I went to my main teacher, Dzogchen Ponlop Rinpoche, and asked for his permission and guidance to start doing formal dark retreat. He recommended I start with three days, then gradually build up. I'm not sure he knew about this, but Christ allegedly spent three days in a cave, a literal tomb, before his resurrection. Three days seems to be the average time at a number of dark retreat centers. Being apprehensive, I started with one day, which you can easily do at home. I then found a small dark retreat center and went in for three days, then five, then a week, then a month, etc. (You do *not* need to go in for so long to have deep transformation.) Every retreat got easier, more enjoyable, and eventually blissful. For the past dozen years, I've done annual dark retreats (sometimes as many as three retreats a year) and sustained a sturdy daily practice in the dark. What I originally approached with trepidation, I now venture into with anticipation. Every time feels like I'm coming home.

In the following pages, I'll share insights and experiences from my time in darkness. Keep in mind that these are just my experiences, and yours may be entirely different. When I was in the traditional Tibetan three-year meditation retreat over twenty years ago (that did not include dark practice), we alternated solitary practice with group practice. The ten of us (five men, five women) would periodically gather under the guidance of a retreat master to talk about a practice we had been doing for months. It never ceased to amaze me how different the shared experiences were. One person talked about ecstatic experiences, while the next person talked about hell, with both of them doing the exact same meditation. Psychospiritual practice works in idiosyncratic ways. Don't let my experiences color yours. Don't expect to have the same experience as anybody else.

I continue my daily practice at home with my Manta™ or Mindfold™ or MyHalos™ eye mask, lightproof masks designed so you can open your eyes underneath them. Several years ago, I walled off a corner in my basement to create a pitch-black holding cell. I step into delicious darkness for at least an hour a day and periodically do one or two days of dark retreat at home. The word for meditation in Tibetan is *gom*, which means "to become familiar with." Over the past twenty-nine years, I've become more and more familiar with physical and metaphysical darkness, to the point that I now savor every moment I spend in the dark. Because I've followed the guidance of my teachers, and listened to the darkness, I've never had any unworkable problems in the dark. I've definitely been stretched, but I've never pushed. I've had mind-blowing experiences, but I've never looked for them. I just go in to see what darkness has to teach me. As cliché as it may appear, I've discovered that I may not always get what I want, but I always get what I need. So I've stopped wanting. I go into retreat, get out of the way, and let the darkness do its magic.

Beginner's Mind

Zen master Suzuki Roshi said, "In the beginner's mind there are many possibilities; in the expert's mind there are few."[3] One risk in reading a book about dark retreat is becoming an expert. Too much information (TMI) is a real issue because it's so easy to confuse information with experience and because the map is never the territory. Even the best map can lead you astray. TMI can create expectations or color your approach, and that's a killing jar of genuine experience in the dark. Make no appointments, have no disappointments. TMI can shrink-wrap direct experience, bending it out of shape as we try to fit our fresh experience into premeditated boxes. When I was in my three-year retreat and about to begin three months of subtle māhamudrā meditation, we were instructed not to prepare and not to read anything.[4] The retreat master was enforcing a traditional protection of not allowing conceptual understanding to stain direct experience.

A big part of the magic of dark retreat is the process of emergent design, which means having no designs on what might happen. Welcoming whatever arises and being receptive to surprise are keys to successful retreat. A beginner's mind is an open mind. Even deeper is the notion of emergence as a meditative principle, referring to conditions that allow for the emergence of deep psychic material from the unconscious mind, specifically the emergent unconscious mind.[5] Jeffrey Kripal, summarizing the work of French philosopher and theologian Henry Corbin, writes:

> [H]e understood the imaginal to name a noetic organ or intellectual-spiritual capacity that was meditating an actual dimension of reality, whose appearances were nevertheless shaped by what he called the *imagination créatrice*, or "creative imagination," an astonishing imaging or mythmaking dimension of consciousness that acts well outside any conscious control or apparent human agency—hence the phenomenology of revelation [emergence] as something given or shown.[6]

Dark retreat works with emergence on all these levels. You will be shown dimensions of consciousness you had no idea even existed. Be open to anything, trust yourself, and follow the thread of your experience. This is how you find your way back: follow the leader of embodied experience. Go in with the attitude, "What's it going to be like this time?" Submerge into the dark and allow things to naturally emerge.

But not having enough information is also an issue. It's easy to get lost when the terrain is this foreign, and a good map is helpful when things get dark. While I had barebones instruction from my teachers and bits of advice from a few dark retreatants, my guides left most of it up to me. In retrospect, I wish I'd had more handholding. A few bumps and bruises could have been avoided as I fumbled around in the dark. For example, no one told me that if I was feeling smothered by the darkness I could briefly flick on the lights. I also didn't know how critical it was to stay fully embodied with yoga or exercise. No one informed me about the importance of humor or loving-kindness toward myself. When I was in retreat, except for the delivery of food, I was completely on my own, hermetically sealed in a lightproof and soundproof cabin. Hermes, the Greek god of boundaries, paths, travel, commerce, and messaging, acts as an intermediary between mere mortals and the gods. He's associated with the hermetic seal because he was able to close a container so effectively that it could not be breached. There were times on retreat when an assuring voice, a welcome breach, would have helped. Perhaps this book will lend such a helpful voice and be there for you when things get dark.[7]

Using the maxim "not too tight, not too loose," if you're too prepared (or expecting too much), you're too tight and not open to the spontaneous emergence that can arise. If you're too laissez-faire, you're too loose, and the dark can slap you for your flippant attitude. One of the reasons dark retreat is considered advanced is that you become your own guide and meditation instructor.[8] No one can follow you into the dark. No one knows your quirks and idiosyncrasies better than you. Dark retreat is empowering in this regard. You learn to trust yourself, the goodness of your heart, and the strength of your own mind.

We're going to have lots of traffic with the conscious and unconscious mind in the coming pages, so it's important to remember that in both Pali and Sanskirt the same word, *citta* or *chitta* respectively, is used for both "mind" and "heart." Every time I use the word *mind*, it's more accurately "heart-mind." The deep explorations of the mind afforded in dark retreat are equally explorations of the heart, and the heart is always embodied. Dark retreat is, therefore, a journey of the body-heart-mind. It's not merely cerebral insights that emerge in darkness but rich emotional experiences and profound somatic feelings. One retreatant shared, "The fragile pieces that I try to bypass are there, and they're asking to be nurtured. I don't think I've ever been more in my body than inside that cave. It's like a homecoming."

Restoration Project

My first few retreats were not easy. Everything was so unfamiliar, way out of my comfort zone. It was a stretch. After a challenging four-year wandering retreat on the streets of India, meditation master Mingyur Rinpoche wrote, "I wanted to put myself in situations where I was unfamiliar to myself . . . to explore the deepest depths of who I really was . . . to test my own capacities in new and challenging situations. If I can truly disrupt my established routines, find my own edge and then keep going . . . let's see what happens to the virtues of patience and discipline when no one is watching, when no one even knows who I am; when perhaps I don't even know who I am."[9] There were times when the darkness felt heavy, claustrophobic, even crushing. The worst moments were the feelings of being buried alive, when the retreat cabin turned into a tomb. But the challenges were precisely where the blessings and opportunities emerged. Poet John Keats spoke of the gift of Negative Capability: "that is when man is capable of being in uncertainties, mysteries, doubts, without any irritable reaching after fact and reason."[10] Dark retreat can get very unreasonable. So don't try to reason your way out. It's not a comfortable place to be, but the growth zone rarely is.

When things got rough, I remembered traditional meditative advice, echoed by Mingyur Rinpoche: "Do not run away from these unpleasant feelings. Do not manipulate them into pleasant feelings. Stay with what is, with whatever arises. I was trying . . . but the newness of everything all at once, and especially the shock of being alone, kept knocking me back."[11] Because of my analytic disposition, I started to examine what was going on. Reason can be engaged in this inquiring way, which is a way to stay *in*. Why am I feeling so much pressure and moments of anxiety or fear? Why the desperate need to run away? What is really burying me here? I'm just sitting alone in the dark doing nothing; why is this so hard!?

The darkness responded, and insights emerged in the form of dreams, visions, and unexpected thoughts. I discovered that the darkness isn't heavy and hard. I am. *Dark retreat is only as hard as you are.* As the darkness gradually worked me over, I started to soften, and the retreat softened. When *I* began to ease up, it got correspondingly easier. That's when I realized I was buried alive in my own habits and projections, or in Sanskrit language, my karma. The weight of those habits was crushing me because they could no longer be expressed out and, therefore, diluted. Everything gets concentrated in the dark because experience is no longer watered down with distraction. Psychologist John Welwood writes, "Unless we bring our larger intelligence to bear on our defensive postures, they will harden further, freezing us into a living rigor mortis. This cannot be emphasized too strongly: If we do nothing, our karma *will bury us*."[12]

What John didn't say is that in dark retreat (as opposed to normal life) doing nothing is actually the way to purify karma. In other words, by being fully with whatever is happening, not repressing or indulging your experience, you purify whatever emerges by not reacting adversely to it. If you don't contract against your experience, but let it emerge into open welcoming arms, it will naturally move through those arms and go its merry way (a process referred to as self-liberation).[13] The next time an experience emerges and is "held" in this open way, it has less power. Eventually the habit/karma will exhaust itself, and you, along with the darkness, will feel lighter and freer. Darkness accelerates this form of enlighten-ment, or the shedding of all weighty habits.

In my dark retreat experience, when my habits can no longer move out and express themselves, they exert their formidable pressures within. When I'm unable to ex-press my normal habits in the dark, they im-press, creating a sense of pressure that seems to come from the darkness, from outside. But the straitjacket is entirely self-imposed. Other external pressures were also revealed to be the result of internal projections. For example, my fear of the dark was the fear of the unknown and what darkness might reveal. It was also the fear of dying, or having to let go of everything comfortable and familiar. My desire to run away was a manifestation of my need to get away from *myself*. As these habits were revealed and released, the pressure was released. The tomb gradually transformed into a womb. My struggles were labor pains, and one thing that was birthed is the baby you're holding in your hands.

We come from darkness and return to darkness. It's not so much "ashes to ashes, dust to dust" as it is "darkness to darkness." Like the two faces of Janus, darkness is both beginning and end, origin and termination. The entire play of life and death—the arising and ceasing of every kind of experience—takes place in a highly concentrated manner in dark retreat, which is what makes it so challenging and so rewarding. You're basically doing nothing in there, yet absolutely everything is revealed. In one early dark retreat, I had a dream about stepping into a supercharged race car, a hybrid supersonic white vehicle that looked like a blend of a Corvette and a Ferrari. I took it for a spin, in awe of the massive horsepower at my disposal, and at one point, I hit the gas to see just how fast this beast could really go. To my utter surprise, instead of entering warp speed and having my hair blown off, the race car came to a screeching halt! The message was clear: I'm going to arrive at my destination in the fastest possible way by coming to a full stop. In other words, I'm already there. I'm already where I want to end up. The other crazy thing that happened is that as the car came to a dead stop, it changed color from white to black. The white color represented waking consciousness and daylight, and black symbolized the unconscious mind and stepping into the dark. The dream was a perfect summation of the spirit of dark retreat.

Dark retreat can be viewed as the archaeology of consciousness, an excavation project that gets down to the essence of things. Just by sitting alone in the dark, you're digging deep into the nature of your mind and heart, recovering and then repairing the entire spectrum of your being. You're accessing and reconditioning a beautiful soul that's been buried in the sedimentation of the unconscious mind and the deposition of your habits. Dark retreat then transforms into a magnificent restoration project, bringing to light all that has been buried within, chiseling off the debris and restoring yourself to life. It's not just a lost arrowhead or trinket that's discovered in there, but the entire architecture of your life. The lost temple of your innermost being is finally recovered, brought to light, and restored.

My Personal Hubble

When astronomers want to peer into the depths of the universe, they go to the tops of distant mountains. Observatories are built as far away as possible from any source of light pollution. The scientists then polish telescopic mirrors to such a degree that even a speck of dust interferes with the incoming light. Finally, they point their telescopes to the darkest spots in space, keep the lens of their instruments open, and wait. The openness of their instruments and the patience of the scientists are keys to the process of discovery. For example, when astronomers wanted to estimate how many stars there are in the known universe, they took the lens of the Hubble telescope, which was orbiting the earth in dark outer space, and pointed it to a pitch-black point in space the size of a drinking straw. They kept the lens of the Hubble fixed on that black point, and tiny dots of light began to appear. Over the course of ten days, some ten thousand points of light appeared in that dot of darkness. Each point of light wasn't merely a star but an entire galaxy, containing one hundred to two hundred billion stars! They estimated that there are more stars in the known universe than there are grains of sand on every beach on this planet.

The similarities between exploring inner and outer space, as well as the correspondence of external light and the internal light of the mind, are striking.[14] Dark retreat is an observatory that explores the inner light and space of the mind, revealing insights as wondrous as any that the Hubble can deliver. The darker it is, the more finely polished the mirror, and the longer you look, the more you can see. It's why the new Webb telescope, a million miles from earth, with a new generation of refined mirrors, is peering farther back in time and getting closer to the origin of the universe than any instrument in history. Webb is revealing things never seen before and revolutionizing our understanding of the cosmos.

Similarly, dark retreat removes you from any form of light pollution that could pull you away from yourself. It then focuses the lens of your mind into the darkness of inner space, revolutionizing your understanding of the cosmos within. With absolutely nothing to distract you, you can peer *back* to the origins of your being, bringing to light the deepest recesses of your unconscious mind. Once you see into and through the beginning and intermediate bandwidths of your unconscious mind (akin to interstellar dust), then the supernovas, quasars, and pillars of creation from the depths of your existence come into the light of consciousness. Creativity and insights erupt, healing surges forth, and wondrous visions unfold. Eventually all the contents of the unconscious mind, the "dark matter" and "dark energy" within, are brought into liberating light.[15] This illuminating process is yet another rendering of en-lighten-ment. The remarkable discoveries of the Webb telescope pale in comparison to the revelations that unfold in the observatory of dark retreat because these inner discoveries can illuminate your entire life.

Wisdom of No Escape

Over the years, I've noticed more and more homes with miniature observatories poking out of rooftops. I imagine how nice it must be to peer into the cosmos in the luxury of your own home. My dark holding cell, or inner observatory, is in my basement, as far underground as I can get. I can tell you how nice it is to peer into deep inner space in the luxury of my own home. This holding cell has a meditation cushion in a four-foot-by-six-foot corner of my basement, perfect for several minutes to several hours of retreat. Super simple. If I'm doing a day or two in the dark, I seal off my study, which is near a bathroom I can easily find with my eye mask on. Throw a mattress on the floor, have my wife bring me some food, and I'm good to go. For longer retreats, as I'll share in chapter 8, I head to a retreat center.

I savor stepping into my observatory every day and soaking in the darkness. It feels like my entire body is gulping it in, as if I'm steeping in a "drink-tank," absorbing the delicious darkness through every pore. There's something elemental about it. My initial contraction and resistance have been replaced with an almost sensual surrender. It's the ineffable sensation of every cell in my body opening to receive this mysterious medicine. Darkness feels embryonic, nurturing, and deeply restorative. There's something indescribably perfect about pitch-black.

One economic feature with dark rooms is that you don't have to invest a lot in décor. The moment you turn off the lights, it just doesn't matter how things look. Right here is one of the liberating gifts of darkness. It doesn't matter what expensive or shiny objects you have in there. You could be in a mansion in Beverly Hills or a shack in the woods, and it all looks the same when the lights go out. Darkness equalizes external appearances by erasing them. Everything flatlines in the dark. Darkness doesn't care if you look like a movie star, have the wealth of a billionaire, or wield the power of a dictator. You could be disfigured or a beggar on the street, and it all looks the same in the dark. It doesn't matter if you wear your finest clothes or put on your best makeup. Fashion doesn't matter. Fame and fortune don't matter. Cosmetics don't matter. *Appearances don't matter.*[16] You can't have a "bad hair day" in the dark. The only thing that matters is the only thing you ever really have, and it's not your hair. It's your beautiful mind and good heart.

We suffer when we get sucked into superficial appearances, lose contact with what's real, and fall out of alignment with reality. At the deepest levels, we suffer because of our infatuation with duality, our addiction to frozen light, and our loss of contact with nonduality, all synonymous with Plato's shadows. By getting rid of dualistic appearances, darkness invites the restorative descent into nonduality. The longer you spend in the dark, the more real things get because more and more obscuring appearances are erased. But, as poet T. S. Eliot said, "Humankind cannot bear very much reality."[17] This is precisely why darkness can become unbearable. The challenge of dark retreat comes down to how much reality you can stand. If you can't stand what's happening—in darkness or in life—you'll try to find another place to stand, then another, all in an effort to dilute your concentrated experience. But a small dark space doesn't allow that exit strategy. Darkness frustrates any level of escape, and things get increasingly concentrated.

Because you can't move about in a small dark space, you'll transfer your escapist tendencies onto your mind, which manifests in the form of increased discursive thinking. It's a last-ditch effort to move away from the concentrated intensity of what's happening, or *not* happening. Most of the time, nothing is happening in the dark, and from the ego's point of view, which feeds on movement (distraction), the level of inactivity and boredom is deadly.[18] Ego is fasting in the dark and eventually starves to death. Hunger pangs set in with survival-level force, in the form of runaway mental browsing, excessive rumination, and catastrophizing. The monkey mind jumps into action as you swing from one mental place to the next in an endless attempt to distract yourself from what's (not) happening. That strategy only works for so long. Sooner or later, darkness forces you to stop swinging, and that's when the ego starts hanging. That's when you start to see that all the moving and shaking—all the distracting—is precisely what the ego is. By frustrating the ego's modus operandi, you flush it out of hiding and start to transcend it. But we're getting ahead of ourselves. We'll have much more to say about distraction, boredom, and self-transcendence in chapter 12.

Let's get back to the world of mere appearance and how darkness works with that. Anecdotal data suggests that women tend to do better than men in the dark. Many women come out and say, "I've never felt so safe and secure as in the dark. I've never felt so held." One woman said, "I no longer had to edit myself in the dark." When asked why they feel safe in the dark, one woman said, "In life, I always feel looked at. I feel that people, often men, are sizing me up, judging me on how I appear. In the dark, no one can see me! I can finally relax and just be myself!" They open and relax, the most important ingredients for a successful journey in darkness. Darkness invites you to let your guard down, take the cosmetics off, and be yourself. You can finally align with your true nature. With no one able to see you, you feel less contracted and self-conscious. Who cares what you look like? And most importantly, why should you care? Imagine what dark retreat could do for women (and men) as they age and their self-esteem diminishes because superficial appearances diminish. It's not just a form of women's lib, but liberation from superficiality altogether and the tyranny of mere appearance.

A central narrative of this book is that all our personal and collective suffering, all the ailments of the metacrisis devouring this world, arise from the principle that appearance is not in harmony (alignment) with reality. The display masks the essence. Looks can be deceiving. You can't judge a book by its cover. This principle applies across multiple levels of reality, from the superficial appearances of fashion, reputation, and social façade, all the way down to appearances manifesting as form altogether—the world as we perceive it, matter as we know it. The two faces of Janus come back into play, with one face being seduced *out* into relative truths and mere appearances, and the other face looking *in* toward absolute truth and reality. The face that looks out gets lost in the display; the face that looks within recovers the essence. Meditation master Tulku Urgyen Rinpoche said, "Samsāra is mind turned outwardly, lost in its projections. Nirvāna is mind turned inwardly, recognizing its true nature." And Carl Jung put it this way, "He who looks outside dreams. He who looks within awakens."

A big part of the psychospiritual path is bringing appearance back into harmony with reality, reducing misinformation back into real information, transforming fake news into real news, or otherwise looking below mere appearance to find out what's really happening. Cutting through the display to find the essence. Putting the axle back into alignment. Whether it's detective work and forensics looking below what seems to be true at the scene of a crime, or scientists penetrating below matter to see what it's made of, or medicine looking beneath clinical presentation into the underlying basis of disease, discovering the reality behind mere appearance is at the root of investigations across the full spectrum of existence. Meditation, therapy, and countless self-help strategies are all about this journey of revelation. By going into the dark, distracting appearances are removed in one fell swoop, and darkness forces you into underlying realities and, therefore, back into harmony.

4

Why Do Dark Retreat?

Blindness is a state of perception which—when taken in all seriousness, accepted, and used—is capable of increasing many faculties sorely needed in every intellectual and organizational activity.
—Jacques Lusseyran

[B]lackness is the preeminent site of the non-normal, the out-of-bounds, the "beyond" . . . the place where discourses and experiences of the super emerge.
—Biko Gray

There are almost as many reasons for going into the dark as there are people doing dark retreat. Many people are simply curious: "I wonder what it's like to spend so much time alone with myself?" "I'm curious how I'll react to total darkness." "What does darkness have to teach me?" Childlike curiosity lends itself to successful explorations in the dark. With this attitude, you're making yourself available to darkness, and the receptivity pays dividends. It also implies a healthy respect for what darkness has to offer. Relating to darkness with humility and reverence transforms it into a temple of insights.

Dark retreat is a very curious practice, as in "odd, peculiar, bizarre," so meeting it with your own curiosity invites a playful dance. Let darkness lead this dance. Allow it to take you wherever it wants. By going with the underground flow, you're surrendering to the darkness, and that's where magic happens. *Curiosity* is connected to the word *cure*, and we'll explore the curative aspects of dark retreat in chapter 6. Both the noun and the verb *cure* denote "looking after." With an open and curious attitude, sprinkled with respect, darkness will look after you and take good care of you. It may not be the care that your comfort-riddled ego is looking for, but it will be the care that your soul seeks.

Sleep

Most people don't go into dark retreat just to catch up on sleep, but relieving sleep deficits is a healthy by-product of spending time in darkness. I always spend the first few days catching up on lost sleep and allow myself to luxuriate in bed for the duration of the retreat. It's not like I have to leap out of bed to do something! Sleeping in is a delicious indulgence that allows you to explore liminal states of mind as you drift in and out of sleep for inordinate periods of time. The extra time in bed is an opportunity to practice liminal dreaming, the first of the five nocturnal meditations, which we'll explore in chapter 9.[1] Having the opportunity to rest and recover at this level also contributes to the restorative and healing properties of darkness.

Dark retreat allows you to play with the maxim "not too tight, not too loose" at a whole new level because dark practice invites "too loose." Most of us are way too tight in this stressed-out world, so time in the dark balances the equation. You can take naps whenever you want and for however long you want. I know dedicated spelunkers of the mind who stay in bed most of the time. Is sleeping so much just an escape? Maybe. But maybe not. It could be precisely what they need, and what Dr. Dark is prescribing. I've had some of the most interesting experiences in the boundary between awake and asleep, as this border becomes porous and eventually dissolves in darkness. There have been times when dreams continued upon waking, and other times when waking thoughts morphed into dreams. These normally disparate states of consciousness are no longer so disparate in the dark, and a marvelous form of "interstate commerce" opens as insights traffic back and forth from one state to another. From waking consciousness, down to the subconscious, then further down to the unconscious, and then back up, this unique trade route brings profits from every level of the mind.

As a determined micro-phenomenologist (and with the nocturnal meditations at my side), I could sometimes maintain consciousness, like a lucidity yo-yo, and witness this descent and ascent. One profound insight of this lucidity (awareness) was realizing that the accepted notion "*I* fell asleep, *I* had a dream, *I* woke up" is an illusion. There is no such person—no solid, lasting, and independent "I," that makes this nightly trip. To think there is a self, a real traveler that saunters along this trade route, is a costly mistake. It's another instance of appearance not being in harmony with reality. I discovered that there is *only* formless awareness, and that progressive degrees of contraction of this awareness are what create the illusion that there is someone sleeping, dreaming, and waking up. In other words, when awareness is fully open, *that* is the deep dreamless (formless) state. When awareness partially contracts away from that openness, *that* is the semi-formed dream state. When awareness fully contracts, *that* is the fully formed waking state. There is no "I" that contracts or expands and, therefore, no solid entity that falls asleep, dreams, and awakens. There is only the pulsation of formless awareness. Night after night, "I" would relax and fall partially apart into dreams, then fully apart into dreamless sleep. Then "I" would pop back up and witness the birth of the dreaming and waking self out of nothing but the contractions of formless awareness itself. After just three days in the dark, one retreatant shared a similar insight: "Everything is created from nothing!"

After a few days in the dark, there are times when I can't tell if I am dreaming or awake. In addition to the deconstruction of the contracted self-sense, coemergent with that sense of self arise space and time. Dark retreat eventually erases all three because they're all constructs. It's one of the most revelatory discoveries of dark retreat, and for the ego (self-sense), it's one of the most unsettling. The very things you took as axiomatic, as givens, are discovered to be made up. This is why so many miraculous things can take place in your dreams, because space and time are not fully constructed in that partially contracted state. The laws of physics don't apply here, so you can fly, walk through walls, and experience all sorts of otherworldly things. So it's not just the sense of self that falls apart in the dark, but its retinue of space-time. For many people, myself included, not knowing if it's day or night, or if you're awake or dreaming, is one of the most disorienting aspects of dark retreat. But it's precisely when you (the small, contracted, false self) get lost at these deepest levels that the real you (the big, open, true Self) can be found. Before an ayahuasca ceremony, one shaman advised, "May you lose great things to find great things." Before you can remodel, you have to demolish.

On rare occasion, when jolted awake in the dead of night, I couldn't even tell if I was dead or alive. I had to touch my body to assess that I was in fact still embodied and alive. It's akin to the feeling you get when you wake up with jet lag in the middle of the night in a foreign country, with no idea where you are or even *who* you are. At first, this porosity was unsettling as I struggled to find my footing in reality. But as I surrendered to this plasma of mind—not knowing what's real or not real and being totally okay with that—I found the experience spellbinding. What, after all, is reality? Curiosity replaced anxiety as I learned to watch my mind transition between previously separate states of consciousness. As we'll continue to see in our journey, dark retreat is a duality decimator. One example of this demolition derby is the dissolution of the boundaries between waking, dreaming, and deep dreamless sleep. When you finally realize there is only the flow of formless awareness, it takes the notion of "going with the flow" to a whole new level. What happens to your idea of flowing between things when the land of things dissolves and there is only the between?

By spending more time investing in sleep, you may find yourself withdrawing your accounts from waking consciousness. This "transfer of funds" serves the dual purpose of dereifying or liquifying the waking state as you disinvest time in that state, while simultaneously reifying or solidifying the other two states as you invest more time in sleeping and dreaming. As philosopher and psychologist William James said, "Reality is what you attend to."

Spend less time attending to the waking state, and it becomes less real; spend more time attending to the dream and sleep states, and they become more real. You're diversifying your portfolio of consciousness, which allows you to gain deeper respect for the dividends of the other two states. In the dark, all three states have equal footing. Author Jeff Warren writes, "In order to understand day consciousness properly, night is the best place to start. The forces that shape dreaming consciousness do not suddenly vanish when the sun arises; rather, they go underground and wield their mysterious influence from below."[2] Go underground in dark retreat to meet those forces, bring them to light, and their mysterious influence is no longer so mysterious.

Having the opportunity to sleep so much allows you to dream more and opens your "accounts" of reality to include all three states. This not only restores you physically, it also restores the way you perceive reality. Friedrich Kekulé, who discovered the molecular structure of benzene in a dream, said, "Let us learn to dream, gentlemen, and then perhaps we shall learn the truth."[3] Dark retreat doesn't merely show you what darkness has to offer; it also reveals what the previously dismissed states of dreaming and sleeping consciousness have to offer. Author Michael Pollan writes, "While the ego sleeps, the mind plays, proposing unexpected patterns of thoughts and new ways of relation. The gulf between self and world, that no-man's-land which in ordinary hours the ego so vigilantly patrols, closes down, allowing us to feel less separate and more connected, 'part and particle' of some larger entity. Whether we call that entity Nature, the Mind at Large, or God hardly matters."[4]

Mixing metaphors, dark retreat invites the democratization of consciousness. Darkness overthrows the imperialism of wake-centricity and empowers the usually oppressed states of dreaming and sleeping consciousness into the governance of our lives. We become more aware of these subtle states in daily life, and the insights they provide inform and transform how we live. The unconscious is only unconscious from the perspective of waking consciousness. Patrick Harpur lends a hand: "When [waking consciousness] sleeps or is placed in abeyance, the 'unconscious' reveals a striking consciousness of its own, which often sees and knows more than we do. Sleeping and waking need not be treated as opposites. The one can invade the other."[5]

A brief excursion into this deeper perceptual and cognitive restoration is in order so we can give ourselves permission to sleep away in the dark. The following is another dip into the depths of tantric-level dark retreat. With the right view, sleeping so much is not a waste of time at all. It's a healthy reallocation of resources to balance the books, to equilibrate our view of reality, to get all three states back into alignment. Falling asleep at these extended levels can truly wake us up. Here's how it works.

Western Eurocentric traditions derive their views of mind and reality almost exclusively from the waking state, a dominance referred to as "wake-centricity." The wake-centric stance dismisses other states of consciousness that waking consciousness can't fully experience. It's a form of epistemological empire-building (epistemology is the branch of philosophy concerned with knowledge and how we know), driven by egoic agendas, that then colonizes and dominates other states of consciousness. It's egoic because ego is only fully operational and online in the contracted waking state. Ego then dismisses other states it can't fully experience as either being less real (the dreaming state) or totally unreal (dreamless sleep). The nocturnal meditations of lucid dreaming, dream yoga, and sleep yoga are designed to remedy this imperialism by bringing awareness, or the light of lucidity, into these previously "dark" states of consciousness, states that magically come to light in dark retreat. The marvel of dark retreat is how it facilitates this infusion of light (awareness) by "stealing" it away from waking consciousness and, like Robin Hood, who steals from the rich and gives to the poor, distributing the funds to the impoverished other two states. By overthrowing the tyranny of waking consciousness, dark retreat ignites the revolution that leads to a new republic of mind, a real united states of consciousness.

In other words, the myopic and close-minded view of wake-centricity essentially throws out two-thirds of reality, the other two-thirds being the reality of the dream state and the deep dreamless state. Dark retreat restores our sight because it invites a much bigger view, an open-minded view that is nurtured in polycentric cultures associated with the East. These philosophies derive their views of mind and reality from all three states. You now have three lenses or perspectives upon which to view reality, a truly three-dimensional view, which is more complete than the one-dimensional, flatland, or wake-centric view. Dark retreat is like going to a psychospiritual optometrist where you're fitted with corrective lenses that give you a much clearer view of reality. You can wake up in the dark to see the world in a more integral and complete way. Isaac Lidsky chronicles his descent into blindness in the book *Eyes Wide Open* and shares, "Remarkably, as sight lost its previously unchallenged centrality in my world, other pathways of perception emerged, I was developing a new, nonvisual processing system for interacting with the world . . . I came to understand the true nature of my sight by losing it."[6]

The West offers a clunky and limited view of consciousness. It's a binary yes/no, on/off, awake/asleep, dead/alive model represented by a light switch. Dark retreat alone, or in concert with the nocturnal meditations, replaces this light switch with an Eastern dimmer. Instead of awake/asleep, you're now transitioning in a more refined way from gross to subtle to very subtle states of consciousness, leaving a few "photons" of awareness on. "Very subtle" is sometimes rendered as "divine," which implies that its opposite, the demonic, is associated with exclusive identification with the gross. The devil is not in darkness but in our exclusive identification with light. Spending so much time in bed allows you to play with this dimmer, turning on a nightlight usually overshadowed in the full light of day. You discover a granularity of consciousness usually blotted out by excessive light and our capitulation to wake-centricity.

In New Age language, by closing our two wake-centric eyes, dark retreat gives us the opportunity to open the "third eye," which is a portal to the inner realms and spaces of higher consciousness. This extremely sensitive eye is associated with insight and intuition, so it's no surprise that a much higher level of insight occurs when all "outsight" is curtailed. The third eye has the ability to see beyond normal perception, to literally perceive things in a new multiperspectival or multidimensional light. You can triple your perspective of reality in the dark and, therefore, markedly accelerate your evolution. It seems that everything electronic these days is about HD, or high definition. HD is redefined, and massively heightened, in dark retreat. Henry David Thoreau summarized it beautifully, "Only that day dawns to which we are awake. There is more day to dawn." Step into darkness to experience this dawn.

Creativity

More and more people are entering the dark to unleash the powers of creativity. I didn't initially go into dark retreat for this purpose, but after the volcanic eruption of creative forces in a recent retreat, I now have an even deeper appreciation for what darkness has to offer. My approach is to enter every retreat with a beginner's mind: "What does the darkness have to teach me this time?" An open attitude allows for whatever is right at that time to emerge. But there is no reason you can't go into the dark with the overt aspiration to receive creative insights. Setting this intention is akin to dream incubation. If you want to incubate a dream, you create the intention to have a specific dream, and dreaming consciousness responds. Darkness can respond in a similar way. As any fundraiser knows, it's amazing what you can get if you just ask for it.

Let's say you want to incubate insights for a musical composition or a book. Set the deep intention before going into retreat, then reiterate it while in retreat, that you *really* want some ideas to emerge. Add some emotional octane, which can be facilitated by visualizing the song being performed or the book being published. All this acts like a depth charge that goes off in your unconscious mind and serves to stir things up at these creative levels. Then open, relax, and wait.

Thomas Edison and Salvador Dali devised similar ways to trigger creativity in their respective fields. They would sit on a comfortable couch holding a spoon or some other implement above a plate on the floor, then allow themselves to doze off. As they were about to fall asleep, their grip would relax and the spoon would fall, clanging onto the plate and waking them up. They would repeat this maneuver as a way to troll the liminal and creative spaces between waking and sleeping, called hypnogogia, defined as "leading (agogos) to the god of sleep (hypnos)." Along the way to Hypnos, you might bump into Apollo, the god of the arts and creative inspiration, or Athena, the goddess of arts and crafts. If you're open to it, all manner of nonhuman intelligence (NHI) can come to visit, and some of the most rewarding visitations are when the gods come calling, as we'll see in the pages ahead.

How you interpret these visitations is up to you. You can view them as archetypal expressions of your unconscious mind emerging into consciousness, or as external agencies descending upon you.

Some people could misinterpret them as psychotic breaks, while others interpret them more accurately as mystical breakthroughs. When people ask me how I can handle so much time alone in the dark, I often say there comes a magical point when you realize you're not alone, and it's not really dark. It's hard to put into words, but the darkness changes. I'm sure that if a scientist were measuring the frequencies of darkness, nothing would change physically. But metaphysically, the color definitely changes. It just gets lighter, even though it's still pitch-black.

Releasing our grip on the spoon is more about releasing our grip on the constraints of waking consciousness, which is the most shallow, restrictive, and least creative of all states. When we relax and open, creative insights can finally emerge. If we're looking for a solution to a problem, we say things like, "Let me sleep on it," which means, "Let me open to it." Let the deeper dimensions of the creative mind go to work. Creative impulses are always wanting to pop up, but because of all our daytime distractions, we keep slamming them back down. Waking consciousness is like a blunt hammer that smacks down the subtle impulses of the unconscious mind, like a crude Whac-a-Mole strategy.

What's peculiar about this strategy is how we (the ego) fear these creative impulses, our own power, and reject the imaginative gifts constantly being sent up by the gods that lurk in the darkness of our own mind. In dark retreat, you come face-to-face with these gods and unveil the creativity within. You're returning to the origin of things, so it's no surprise that originality is a natural consequence of that retreat. Creativity is a topic of such importance that we'll explore it in depth in chapter 5. As we'll see, the main reason for the flood of insights is the breakdown of the boundary between the conscious and the unconscious mind. Novelist Arthur Koestler writes, "The capacity to regress, more or less at will, to the games of the underground, without losing contact with the surface, seems to be the very essence of the poetic, and of any other form of creativity."[7]

Problem-Solving

Some people enter the dark to answer a question or solve a specific problem. The questions can range from NFL superstar Aaron Rodgers wanting to figure out if he should stay with the Green Bay Packers, all the way to solving the problem of samsāra, the conditioned world of suffering. You can go into the dark to focus your mind, open your heart, or reflect deeply on your relationship (should I stay with him or leave?), your job (should I quit or try for the promotion?), your career (should I get that degree or move to that town for employment?), or life itself (what should I do with my life?). Any question is fair game.

How you ask the question is important. Remember that if you're interested in what you should do with your life, it could be more fruitful to ask, "What does life want to do with me?" Physicist Werner Heisenberg said, "What we observe is not nature itself, but nature exposed by our method of questioning."[8] In other words, reality as it responds to the way we ask our questions. Ask questions of the dark, the answers to which would change your life. Philosopher Bernardo Kastrup writes, "For as long as the right questions aren't asked by the intellect, the ultimate answers of life and reality will remain elusive . . . ask the questions that will evoke the deepest transcendent answers."[9] And Clarissa Pinkola Estés, author of *Women Who Run with the Wolves*, shares, "Asking the proper question is the central action of transformation . . . The key question causes germination of consciousness. The properly shaped question always emanates from an essential curiosity about what stands behind. Questions are the keys that cause the secret doors (of the psyche) to swing open."[10] In my experience, "how" or "what" questions are more useful than "why," "who," or "when" questions.

If you're religious, you can view it as praying for guidance or supplicating for greater powers to help. It doesn't matter what you call it. What matters is how honestly you ask the question and how much heart you put into it. These two ingredients generate the second element of a successful question: If the question is feeble and half-hearted, you'll get a feeble and half-hearted response or none at all. If you throw your entire being into it and cry out from the bottom of your heart, "Help me!," it's amazing what you can receive. But then you have to be open and willing to receive. Sometimes the answer may not be what you expect or even want. Part of the deal is that you're going to accept whatever darkness has to say. Don't violate that contract.

The best way to maintain your part of the bargain and increase the flow of communication is to pay close attention to what you *feel* the moment a message is delivered. The answer always brings an emotional wallop, however nuanced it may be. Stay with that. Trust that. That's how you can tell the difference between priority mail and junk mail. Your gut reaction, no matter how subtle, signals priority mail. Notice how fast your thinking mind barges in to run commentary about the message. That's the junk mail. Those second thoughts manipulate the somatic or emotional hit into a more digestible form for your ego. Don't listen to that second voice. Trust the first hit. Put more faith in your intuition, not your intellect.

The message can come in the form of a dream, a vision, or a sudden unexpected insight. "Aha! Now I see!" It might arrive in a moment of coincidence or synchronicity, which are intimations of coming into alignment with the nondual. What makes synchronicity so impactful is that something in the outside world is aligning with something inside. It's another manifestation of the dissolution of dualities that occurs in the dark. Pay attention to these magical moments. Sometimes the responses come back without you even knowing you sent out the query. In other words, spontaneous "teachable moments" arise in the dark that can guide you, answering questions you didn't even know you had. I've taken these moments to be the result of my general intention with every dark retreat: Show me what I need to know.

Here's an example of the type of event that often occurs. In my last retreat, I found myself stuck in a ruminative loop for way too long, a classic "think-hole" that I kept falling into. I went to the bathroom as usual but noticed that I didn't hear the normal flush. I fumbled around for the plunger, worked it into the toilet bowl and heard a successful outcome as the toilet finally flushed. Being sensitized to any unusual occurrence, I immediately got the message: My thoughts had become constipated. The plugged toilet was an outer manifestation of my plugged mind. Loosen up! Let it go! Was this an accurate interpretation of a common event or an imputation? Was I deriving meaning or projecting it (the definition of paranoia)? I touched into the first hit I had on the experience, what meditation master Trungpa Rinpoche called "first thought, best thought," and trusted the stroke of insight. It rang true.

Intention is the key to incubation. Setting a heartfelt intent is like sending a FedEx letter deep into your unconscious mind. The letter will be opened in the dark, processed, and then returned to sender to be read by your conscious mind. You can set the intention before you even go into dark retreat (which could be part of the "set and setting" process), then restate it as often as you like while in retreat. This will perfume your mind before the retreat and while you're in it, creating the atmosphere for insights to arise. If the letter of intent is stamped with your heart, it will also reach up to the gods, or whatever word speaks to you in terms of higher powers. Whether snail mail directed in or air mail directed out, set and send your intention in all directions. Does it really matter where the reply comes from? If you're more scientifically oriented, the answer will come from your unconscious mind. If you're more spiritual in nature, the answer will come from higher powers. I aim in both directions.

How often have you gone to sleep with a question on your mind, only to have the answer come to you in the middle of the night? Dark retreat extends the night. It allows for more answers. In order to fall asleep, you have to open and relax, otherwise the result is the constriction of insomnia. You literally have to stop thinking. Once again, cessation and negation, two key players in dark retreat, come back into play. To solve a problem often requires the cessation or dissolution of thought itself.[11]

We often think we can think our way out of a problem because we give too much credit to rational thinking. But as Nobel laureate physicist Brian Josephson said, "We think that we think clearly, but that's only because we don't think clearly."[12] And Einstein famously admonished, "We cannot solve our problems with the same level of thinking that created them."[13] It helps to step outside of the box to solve a problem. In yet another irony, one of the best ways to step outside the proverbial box is to go into a literal one. Step into a dark box to get out of your boxed-in ways of thinking. What often boxes us in is overthinking and distancing ourselves from the innate wisdom of the body. Clark Strand writes, "Claim your place in the dark and the body takes over, solving problems the mind could not, making all things simple that are made complicated by light. The bad choice. The false ambition. The things society would compel us to value which, absent the thousand-watt voltage of an artificially illuminated world, are revealed for the destructive illusions they really are."[14]

As you fall asleep, you're temporarily falling apart, and the porosity of that dissolution allows for the infiltration of the light of insight. To find the solution, put yourself into solution. Allow the solvent of darkness to dis-*solve* the boundaries that keep you from solving a problem. The words *solve, dissolve*, and *solution* share the same root, which means "release, loosen." Nothing is insoluble once you liquify. Once a solid (ego) releases, loosens, and melts into a more fluid state of consciousness, that liquidity allows you to flow around, and even dissolve into, a problem. New perspectives bring the answers.

Finally, I've also discovered that if I ask a question in the dark, *of the dark*, on behalf of someone else, with the intention that the answer will benefit others, it's like priority mail.[15] Dark retreat then becomes a gateway into the world of the shaman. As with creativity, I never went into darkness to practice shamanism, but I have discovered that I've stepped into experiences that resemble that role. Because I remain open, I'm constantly surprised at how much darkness has to offer.

Divination

For some people, dark retreat approximates a form of divination. You become the oracle, the seer, by aiming your sights deep into the unconscious mind and opening yourself to "outsights" arriving from higher dimensions. I've had many precognitive dreams and intuitions in dark retreat, times when it felt like I could see into the future. It's akin to climate forecasting. The absolute silence and stillness of darkness invoke exquisite sensitivity and amplified awareness, allowing you to detect which way the inner winds are blowing and what weather patterns are developing at the most refined dimensions of your being.

Dark retreat gets extraordinarily subtle, which invites the detection of extremely rarefied energies and feelings. Subtle doesn't mean ineffectual. Everything in your gross life is driven by subtle thoughts and even more subtle unconscious processes. In Eastern karmic theory, a view echoed in the West by psychologist Carl Jung, karma first develops at the level of the unconscious mind before manifesting in life. Seeds germinate underground before popping up into the light of day. Karmic seeds (bījas in Sanskrit) germinate in the underground mind and can manifest for the diviner in the form of dreams, fleeting visions, or flashes of insight. Dark retreat makes the border between the conscious and unconscious mind more porous, allowing unconscious sprouts more opportunity to pop up between the cracks of the conscious and unconscious mind. This not only gives you a preview of coming attractions (in the form of premonitions and precognitive dreams) but provides the opportunity to purify the karma underground, preventing unwanted experiences from ever manifesting in your life.[16] You can pull out the weeds and water the right seeds. Cleaning things up at root levels can save you tons of time and trouble. It's like working with the DNA of your being, the stem cells of life, the blueprint of your existence, and this is yet another reason why dark retreat is so transformative. You're going right down to the source. But the path is steep, and you have to get down and dirty to do this level of inner work. You must be willing to go underground and soil yourself before you can purify yourself.

Divination in the dark also takes place because the borders between past, present, and future become porous and eventually dissolve. All polarities and dualities dissolve in the dark. Without a proper understanding, you can have trouble at the border, an immigration issue, as contents of the unconscious mind migrate into consciousness The past surges into the present as you're served up undigested unconscious material, and glimpses of the future can drip into awareness as you continue to open and relax. Space and time are constructs, a truth proclaimed by scientists, philosophers, and mystics alike. Dark retreat deconstructs these constructs, eventually delivering you to the timeless and spaceless dimensions of reality, where the shamans dance. If shamans don't dance with you, how about gods and angels? Hosts of unemployed angels are waiting for work. Hire them. Speak to them. Take them off the unemployment line and work them into your life. Countless traditions and sensitive mystics and philosophers throughout history proclaim that the universe is saturated with nonhuman intelligence. Philosopher William James, often called "the father of Western psychology," famously wrote:

> Our normal waking consciousness . . . is but one special type of consciousness, whilst all about it, parted from it by

> the flimsiest of screens, there lie potential forms of consciousness entirely different. We may go through life without suspecting their existence, but apply the requisite stimulus, and at a touch they are all there in all their completeness . . . No account of the universe in its totality can be final which leaves these other forms of consciousness quite disregarded.[17]

Dark retreat removes that flimsiest of screens, and the emphasis on touch allows you to make contact with these angelic forces.

To Experience Altered States

Many people are exploring psychedelics these days, for as many reasons as people are exploring the dark. The parallels between the two journeys are uncanny. *Psychedelic* derives from the roots *psyche*, meaning "mind, soul, spirit," and *delos*, meaning "to manifest, make clear, make visible, or reveal." Dark retreat is all about the concentrated manifestations and revelations of mind, soul, and spirit. This is what makes dark medicine and plant medicine rewarding and challenging, and why "set and setting" are critical for both journeys. Preparation and integration are also key to both adventures. The promise and peril of psychedelics equally apply to dark retreat. Several of the scientists I'm working with in our research on dark retreat also study psychedelics and comment about the similarity of both journeys. Future studies will likely reveal deep neurological and physiological connections.

Sūtra-level dark retreat is more psycholytic in nature (*lytic* means "to loosen"), while tantra levels open to more psychedelic experiences. Psycholytics are not about trippy experiences or self-transcendence, but the experience of nonordinary states of consciousness while staying in touch with the present. This allows you to work with what loosens at unconscious levels and eventually arises in conscious experience, but from a new vantage point.

While the similarities are striking, there are important differences. In dark retreat, *you* become the medicine. The only thing you're ingesting is your experience, unmediated by any drug. One retreatant shared, "With plant medicine, you rely on the medicine to do the journey for you. With the darkness, you are the medicine. You're not dependent on the medicine, or any outside substance, to get you anywhere. The medicine lies within. That's very profound—to realize *you* are the medicine." Dark retreat is completely natural and utterly organic, with fewer side effects. You have much more control over your trip in the dark and can end it at any time. The onset of any altered state is easier in the dark, and coming out of the experience is gentler. You also have much more time to explore your mind in the dark. I don't know of any psychedelic that lasts more than a day, while a dark retreat can last for weeks. You can also "microdose" dark retreat in the blink of an eye, or when you sleep and dream (with the aid of the nocturnal meditations). Big pharma is not involved, legislation and governmental regulation aren't needed, drug cartels will never be interested, and it's legal around the world. It's a legitimate, sober psychedelic.

At deeper levels, dark retreat reveals our so-called normal reality to be the altered state. Waking consciousness is actually the altered state. It's only because we've been tripping on it (double entendre intended) for so long that we take it to be the natural state. Dark retreat provides the contrast medium that allows us to step back, get aligned, and see the truth. It breaks through the façade of wake-centric, sight-centric, and light-centric consciousness to reveal deeper and truer *unaltered* states. When we access these natural and open states in dark retreat, we come to realize that everyday consciousness is the most contracted and, therefore, altered state.

Dark retreat has also shown me that we're always on drugs. Our baseline prescription includes the neurotransmitters serotonin, epinephrine, norepinephrine, glutamate, dopamine, oxytocin, acetylcholine, and over one hundred other agents in a complex pharmacology that would make any scientist's head spin. That's just for starters. Throw in more than fifty hormones, like testosterone, estrogen, progesterone, and melatonin, and you have a cocktail of consciousness that correlates to consensual reality. Scientists will one day study how dark retreat alters these endogenous drugs as it "alters" our consciousness back to its natural state.

Trungpa Rinpoche said that psychedelics are "super samsāra," which is usually interpreted as a pejorative statement. Dark retreat can easily become super samsāra and be similarly misinterpreted. Both methods are nonspecific amplifiers, which again is why proper set and setting are so important. Everything is amplified in the dark because experience is no longer diluted by the distractions of external light. If it's related to properly, super samsāra is a good thing.

Every morning, I recite this brief liturgy: "Grant your blessings so that my mind may be one with the dharma [truth]. Grant your blessings so that dharma may progress along the path. Grant your blessings so that the path may clarify confusion. Grant your blessings so that confusion may dawn as wisdom."[18] I always interpreted the third line as "Grant your blessings so that the path *will get rid of* my confusion." But you can translate *clarify* to mean "to heighten, articulate," a small change with big implications. Grant your blessings so that the path *may amplify and clarify* my confusion. This injunction resonates with alchemical and tantric approaches (dark retreat and psychedelics are alchemical and tantric in spirit) that transform psychological lead into gold and poison into medicine, respectively. But you have to know what the lead and the poison are before you can transform them. You can't solve a problem you don't even know you have, so "clarifying" a problem helps you solve it. The obstacles that arise in dark retreat and psychedelics then transform into blessed opportunities. French author and political activist Jacques Lusseyran writes, "The special merit of blindness is not that it creates a different experience, but that it leads us by necessity toward a heightened experience."[19]

Finally, dark retreat is allied to a synonym for psychedelics, or entheogens, "the divine within." When you drop into the deeper reaches of the unconscious mind, archetypal gods and deities are waiting for you, ready to bless you with clarifying insight. Perhaps this is why there's so much enthusiasm ("the state of being inspired by a god") for both methods, and why so many people come out of both experiences divinely inspired. At the deepest level, dark retreat acts like a thanatogen (Thanatos is the Greek god of death), an agent that simulates the experience of ego death.

To Come to Your (Other) Senses

Many people in these stressful times have a longing to go into silent retreat. The place without words is the place of the soul. Or as Rumi put it, "Silence is the language of God, all else is poor translation." Silent retreat curbs mindless speech, obtunds the dualistic sense of hearing, and invites us to turn within. Dark retreat goes further by also silencing *the* most dualistic sense of sight and virtually demands that we turn to the divinity within. It transcends but includes silent retreat. Darkness invites sensual intimacy, which includes becoming intimate with who we really are. Our most dominant sense of sight entails little intimacy. About 70 percent of sense receptors are concentrated in our eyes, an allocation of sensory resources that keeps us literally out of touch with deeper realities. Sound invites a bit more intimacy but still yanks us away from ourselves. In dark retreat, the most distracting, diluting, and dualistic senses of sight and sound are removed, invoking the deepest possible silence, and eventual communion, with your God.

You're entering a sensory deprivation chamber. Dark retreat is a nonsensical practice, at multiple levels. But what's really being deprived is the ego and its lust for dualistic stimulation. Unlike the fleeting experience of a flotation tank, you can bathe in the revelatory silence for days or even weeks. As darkness divests your most dualistic senses, experience becomes more and more nondual. Outside of mealtimes, when you can briefly smell and taste, the only sense that is fully operational in the dark is feeling. By reducing everything to the most foundational sense of touch, our most grounded sense, you can finally make contact with what really matters. On this, Barbara Brown Taylor writes,

> The problem with seeing the regular way . . . is that sight naturally prefers outer appearances. It attends to the surface of things, which makes it an essentially superficial sense. We let our eyes skid over trees, furniture, traffic faces, too often mistaking sight for perception . . . Speed is another problem. Our eyes glide so quickly over things that we do not properly attend to them. Fingers do not glide . . . To feel a table is a much more intimate activity than seeing it.[20]

Think about it, or better yet, feel into it: You don't really change when you think about things. You change when you *feel* things physically and emotionally. A talking head won't change you, but a feeling body will. In this information age, we once again confuse information for experience. We mistake the menu for the meal and muddle the map for the territory. Experience is what moves or touches people, and dark retreat is the most experiential—and, therefore, the most moving—practice I've ever done. Among the many ironies that surround this practice is how complete physical stillness becomes the very condition for the most profound inner movement. What really moves the needle in my life is putting myself in situations where the needle can't move.

Dark retreat virtually forces you into feeling things more and, therefore, experiencing things more. I've never been so fully in contact with myself—with my feelings, with my body, and with reality—as in the dark. One retreatant shared, "It's as if I was getting into my body for the first time. I'm a bit old to be just getting to know my body now, but that's what it felt like. It felt like I was getting to know parts of me for the first time. And all of that felt so good." You learn more about yourself in the dark because you can no longer get away from yourself. Wherever you go, there you are. If silence is for bumping into yourself, dark retreat is for slamming into yourself.

I can't see my way around in there or hear, smell, and taste in my normal way. But I can feel my way around. Whether it's standing up with arms outstretched so I don't walk into something or being brought to my hands and knees as I try to find my way around without hurting myself, dark retreat forces me to feel my inner and outer worlds in a dramatically heightened way. Through this most intimate and nondualistic sense—the one that is most in contact with reality—I *feel* exactly where I need to go, not just in the dark but in life. By depriving myself of my physical senses, I ironically "come to my senses." Jacques Lusseyran writes,

> All our senses, I believe, join into one. They are the successive stages of a single perception, and that perception is always one of touch . . . what we call *attention* could be the psychological form of this fundamental contact, a form based on feeling . . . A blind person is in a room; a man enters, sits down, and does not talk. Can the blind person come to know him? . . . He can open himself to such an extent that this unmoving person comes closer. By and by, quietly and without moving, he can remove all the inner obstacles that separate him from the other until he begins to absorb the man's appearance . . .

> With the help of the spirit has he transcended the normal conditions of perception? I believe one should simply say: He touched.[21]

When the Buddha attained his enlightenment, he was challenged by Māra (the Buddhist version of the devil) to prove his awakening. The Buddha reached down to touch the ground and said, "The earth is my witness." Known as the bhūmisparśamudrā, or "gesture of touching the earth," it symbolizes nondual contact with reality. Māra tried to dislodge the Buddha by attacking him with his minions and seducing him with his daughters, which manifested in the assault and seduction of the contents of his own mind. Māra tried everything to distract him, to get him to move. The Buddha's immutable contact with the earth, his grounding in reality, foiled Māra. By some accounts, when the Buddha touched the earth, he was calling on the goddess Sthāvarā to bear witness to his awakening. Sthāvarā, whose name means "immovable," is the goddess of the earth. She responded by causing the earth to quake. Māra finally gave up, the temptations to move (distract) fell away, and Siddhārtha became the Buddha.[22]

For me, no practice is as earthy, as grounding, and as immovable as dark retreat. For the movement-addicted ego, it can feel like being buried alive. But what's being put to rest is the ego itself. Relate to that feeling as the compression that presses you into diamond-like nonduality. When dark retreat feels crushing, recognize the claustrophobia as the ego kicking and screaming for more leg room. Relate to that feeling as the necessary stretch into the growth zone, an uncomfortable stretch that ironically takes place when the ego can no longer stretch.

To Find Meaning

Because of the concentrated nature of dark retreat, you can use it to focus the lens of your mind to find meaning in life, and perhaps even the meaning of life itself. Many people are looking for meaning in a world that appears increasingly devoid of it. Young people are trying to find their way in life, to figure out who they are, what they should do, or where they should go. Authors Ross Heaven and Simon Buxton write: "Humankind has been searching for reconnection with the infinite and for meaning in life ever since this realization of our aloneness. Most often, if it is serious, this search will take place in darkness, both physical or actual and metaphysical, or 'the dark night of the soul,' as Carl Jung defined it."[23] Because of the sensitivity nurtured in the dark, subtle intuitions normally diluted by daily activity now stand out. As your inner senses come alive, they help you make sense of your world. A hunch can be heard, an insight can be seen, a nuanced feeling can be sensed. You can travel the world, and all the seas, to confirm for yourself that everybody is looking for something, as Annie Lennox reminded us. What exactly is everybody looking for? Dark retreat separates the wheat from the chaff and helps you locate the essence of your longing by pointing you within.[24]

It never ceases to amaze me what you can find in the dark. You only have to make yourself available to the darkness. With this openness, what you're looking for will find you. In a recent retreat, I discovered something I didn't even know I was looking for. It turned out to be a massive missing piece in the ongoing puzzle of my life. Set the intention to find meaning, stay open, and it will come to you.

On a broader level, meaningless experiences are diluted experiences. Experiences saturated with meaning are saturated with presence. Dark retreat demands intensified levels of presence that make everything in the dark meaningful. Darkness does not reward absence. Not only can you find meaning in your life while in total darkness, but you can also find meaning in the present moment by being delivered fully into it, which may well be the meaning of life. As we'll see in chapter 13, to find meaning in life, it helps to lose yourself in the dark.

Return to Origins

Closely allied to the search for meaning is going into dark retreat to return to the origin of things, as we saw in the introduction. Life becomes meaningless when we lose contact with our roots. With so many distractions in daily life, it's easy to get uprooted and whacked out of alignment. Darkness takes us back underground to the roots. Life on the surface of the planet arose from the dark depths of the ocean. Plants germinate in darkness underground. Thoughts and emotions arise from the background darkness of the mind. Religious scholar Mircea Eliade said, “Light does not come from light, but from darkness.” Many mythologies attribute creation to the emergence of light out of primordial darkness, and countless cosmologies describe the end of the world as a return to darkness.

In Greek mythology, Chaos was the first being to exist, a self-arising primeval goddess who symbolized the lack of order at the beginning of the universe. Author Stephen Fry writes, “From formless Chaos sprang two creations: EREBUS and NYX. Erebus, he was darkness, and Nyx, she was night. They coupled at once and the flashing fruits of their union were HEMERA, day, and AETHER, light . . . [These] were primal, elemental principles that were devoid of any real color, character, or interest. These were the PRIMORDIAL DEITIES, the First Order of divine beings from whom all the gods, heroes, and monsters of Greek myth spring.”[25] Darkness represents the irreducible, or reduction base.

In the Book of Genesis, God said, “Let there be light!,” which implies it arose out of darkness. Neuroscientist Matthew Walker writes, “Sleep was the first state of life on this planet, and it was from sleep that wakefulness emerged.”[26] In Hinduism, causal consciousness is associated with the darkness of deep dreamless sleep, from which emerge both dreaming and waking consciousness. In Buddhism, darkness is homologous to emptiness, and everything arises out of emptiness. Zen teacher Joan Sutherland says, “Darkness is not the absence of light but the presence of the very source of everything.”[27] A famous liturgy of Tibetan Buddhism proclaims, “The essence of thoughts is dharmakāya [emptiness] as is taught. Nothing whatever but everything arises from it.” It’s precisely because everything arises from emptiness and returns to it that dark retreat has such extraordinary potential. Darkness-emptiness is the alpha and the omega, the cradle and the grave, the womb and tomb, of all manifest reality, so it’s no wonder that so much—and so little—takes place in this singularity. Sensitive readers will connect to the underlying thread of emptiness throughout this book, and we’ll formally return to this deeper topic in our later chapters.

To Go Deep

Searching for meaning and returning to origins are about exploring depth. In this age of runaway distraction, rampant entertainment, uncontrolled speed, and relentless busyness, we skim across the surface of life. We've been taught countless ways to escape from ourselves, to do whatever it takes to avoid the inner world, which would put us in contact with the underworld. And who in their right mind wants to go there? In the introduction, I said that humanity has been seduced away from the center of itself and as far as possible from the divine. We search for what we're longing for on high, in brilliant light and breathtaking height. We look up toward the heavens instead of down toward the earth. Philosopher David Loy writes,

> The secular world that we now understand ourselves to be living in was originally one half of a duality, and it remains haunted by the loss of its other half. Modernity developed out of a split that developed between God's transcendence and a de-spiritualized material world. Until the modern era, God was believed to be the source of meaning and value, so when God eventually disappeared up into the clouds, we were left to cope as best we could in what was left: a desacralized mechanistic universe.[28]

Depth and divinity are tucked into the darkness within, but like so many other things inside of us, we deny those riches and project them outside, creating golden shadows. Not all shadows are projections of negativity. Golden shadows are projections of the positive within, which are often plastered onto other people whom we then adulate. When we fall in love with others, we're often falling in love with our projections.[29] If we elevate a teacher, for example, is it because they are special, or is it because we need to see them as special? When we worship something above, we're often venerating something deep within.

The superficial ego is afraid of depth because the profane drowns in the profound. The experience of depth in darkness mandates the courage to face and feel as never before and, therefore, come alive as never before. Experience that is normally diluted in the glare of the light of day comes to life in darkness. People often go into the dark to find what's missing in their lives. What they eventually discover is that nothing is missing "out there." What's missing is in here. We're the ones who go AWOL on reality. Our full attention and participation in life, our willingness to feel fully, are what's missing. But what is lost can be found, and it's often found in the most unlikely places.

To Find Inner Peace

People meditate or go into the dark because they feel that these practices can settle them down and bring inner peace. Being centered means finding that peace. If you surrender to the darkness, you'll find centeredness and peace. If you don't, you'll only find conflict. You'll go to war with the darkness, which means going into battle with yourself. Some people don't fight it directly but think they can outmaneuver, outsmart, or outcontextualize the darkness. If you want to find inner peace, go into darkness waving that white flag. Give up before you even go in.

Retreatants are sometimes surprised when things get stirred up in the dark before they settle down. The word *peace* derives from a root (the Latin *pax*) that means "fasten." Someone who is peaceful is silent, steady, and serene because they're fastened to the present moment. Dark retreat ironically forces you into peace and inner disarmament because you have to surrender to the present moment. The ego is put under arrest and securely fastened in place by the boundary of the cabin, and then darkness itself. Peace ensues from this level of incarceration. Dark retreat acts like a psychospiritual correctional institution, a detention center of the highest order, that serves to rehabilitate the movement-addicted ego. It is movement itself that violates the peace treaty with reality, and every form of movement, every distraction, is arrested and disarmed in the dark.

I talked earlier about meeting the gods in the dark. You don't just meet them; you eventually become them. Peter Kingsley writes:

> [W]hen Greeks wanted to describe in tangible terms the reality of a confrontation between humans and the divine, there was one particular quality that they sensed as characterizing the gods in contrast to people. This was their uncanny stillness . . . Even the most dramatic miracles or displays of power weren't as effective a way of emphasizing the difference between humans and gods as the utter unshakability of divine stillness. It was a method for coming as close as

> possible to the divine world . . . Anybody who was able to maintain a visibly greater degree of stillness than people in general was assumed to be divine: considered someone who's more than human, who belongs to another world.[30]

Stillness has the power to deliver you into another reality, a godlike reality, by ceasing the miscarriage away from this one. Deep inner peace, unshakable stillness, and internal pacification are the fruits of dark retreat that we can bring back into the conflict-ridden world. You go in a mere mortal and come out a god, better able to help the world. And your mere presence can do it.

To Find Your Inner Teacher

Buddhism talks about four types of guru, or teacher: the outer guru as a physical person, the guru as teachings in oral or written form, the symbolic guru (teachings you learn from life experience), and the ultimate guru within. The first three forms of guru are all provisional, meaning that they all culminate in discovering the wiseman or wisewoman within. Dark retreat is uniquely situated to introduce you to the ultimate wise guy within by essentially silencing the outer three voices. Darkness invites you to listen to and align yourself with this deepest inner voice.

I gather myself by meditating in the dark every morning. If I'm feeling scattered during the day, I'll briefly drop back into darkness. I *unplug* to recharge. The same thing happens in meditation, of course, but centering occurs more quickly in the dark. It's often in the dead of night or in moments of silence and solitude that we reflect most deeply on what really matters. In the busyness and distractions of daily life, we forget. Darkness helps us remember.

Meta-Meditation

As we venture into deeper reasons for doing dark retreat, enhancing your meditation is near the top. Meditation is about inner work, and dark retreat is inner work on steroids. Can you imagine getting any more inside of yourself than in darkness? Jesuit priest, paleontologist, and philosopher Teilhard de Chardin suggested that evolution hasn't stopped; it's only moved indoors. If we don't violate the natural embargo of the night, this is precisely where we move when it gets dark. We can, therefore, accelerate our evolution by heading inside with daily meditation and even deeper inside with dark meditation. As Gregory Shaw writes, "The soul's ascent, therefore, is not a literal going up but a going in."[31] In a nondualistic view, higher is replaced with inner. Therefore, the highest practice you can do is the one that takes you most deeply within. Trungpa Rinpoche taught that there is no way out. The magic is to discover that there is a way in.[32]

Dark retreat can be viewed as a meta-meditation, where *meta* means "after or beyond." A meta-meditation ideal for the metacrisis. In terms of the five nocturnal meditations, meta refers to "after hours" practices done while we sleep or dream. In terms of dark retreat, meta refers to meditation that is beyond anything done during the day. At sūtra levels of dark practice, we go inside with the noble motivation to find ourselves. Many people say, "I want to find out who I really am." "I feel lost." "I feel disconnected from the real me." Finding yourself in the dark is a beautiful thing. But at tantra levels, we go even deeper inside to lose ourselves (we'll explore this in depth in chapter 16). I heard Buddhist teacher and humorist Wes Nisker say that "enlightenment is the ultimate getting over yourself." Don't try so hard to leave your mark on the world; otherwise, the world gets all marked up. Don't try to be somebody. Try to be nobody. And one of the best ways to do that is to step into the dark and stop trying altogether.

As our mind's eye gets used to the dark and we continue to dilate our consciousness, we eventually see that below that beautiful (relative) self we found at sūtra levels, there's absolutely nobody there! There's no self to be found. No self is your real Self. In Buddhist language, that's the discovery of emptiness, egolessness, or selflessness. In Hindu language, it's the discovery of the true Self. Dark retreat as a meta-meditation is a central narrative in our journey, so we'll return to this theme repeatedly.

In the Words of Dark Retreatants

People are sometimes surprised by all the reasons one feels called to experience a dark retreat—and what they hope it will offer. Below is a sample of responses from a variety of people interested in participating in a three-day dark retreat.

"I had a very challenging childhood, and I have spent a lot of energy trying to soften my heart and reprogram my mind from that conditioning. I love the idea of sitting with myself and stripping away everything to renew and deepen my sense of awe and love for being alive. I'm seeking the next level of opening myself up."

"As I'm getting older, with marriage, a child, then divorce, it is getting harder and harder to cope. I've been in and out of therapy, medications, and countless 'journeys,' but nothing has really helped. I want to go into the darkness because I feel I am currently in darkness and cannot break through to the light. I so desire to show up for myself and my young son."

"I have a deep past that has been pushed down. It pops up occasionally, and I understand that I need to do the work to become at peace. This process scares me a bit because I know that there is a transformation to be had within. I am a business owner, a mother of three, a wife, but I feel like I'm lost. I am very interested in doing the work and experiencing this therapy."

"I am a twenty-five-year-old and have been very interested in this experience. I have struggled my whole life with anxiety, stress, depression, lack-of love for myself, PTSD, and feelings of inadequacy. I am currently researching and practicing different methods to help with my daily struggles so I can live my life the way I know it is meant to be lived: to the fullest, instead of feeling like a slave to my own mind."

"This summer I celebrated my seventieth birthday. For the past few years, I have intensified my spiritual practice, especially meditation focused on the inner darkness, so that I may eventually part from this life with ease and grace, my affairs ordered, and my vision consciously toward the next adventure."

"My why is to go deep within myself and not have any distractions. I have done plant medicines—ayahuasca, mushrooms, cannabis—and they help, but I seem to be missing a piece of the puzzle. I feel going into darkness will help me go deep within where not even the medicine can take me. I want to stop chasing the quick fix and do the work within myself."

"I can't fully explain it, but I feel a powerful calling to do it. I believe it is rooted in my drive to explore both my physical and mental preconceptions. As a tech entrepreneur and an explorer of the mind, I take on challenges, like sailing across the Atlantic, or running 250km through the Sahara Desert—not just for the challenge, but to gain deeper insights into the true nature of the world and myself. I believe the darkness will offer a new pathway to further these insights."

"Cancer showed up in my life and has since caused me a great deal of loss and suffering. For some reason, dark retreat keeps coming up in my awareness. How would darkness serve me in a time of immense grief?"

"I want to sit still in the darkness and know my worth when I am doing nothing. Why does my worth always have to come from doing? Accomplishing? Can I just be? Who am I when I am just being? This is what I want to feel into in the darkness."

"As far as my interest, I have been pursuing various avenues to improve myself and to address past trauma over the last several years, all in an effort to be a better husband and father. I spent about twenty years in law enforcement,

SWAT teams to be specific, and it took a toll. I've been doing a lot of inner work, using several modalities—somatic work, insight meditation, silent retreats, some medicinal journeys. Dark retreat resonates as an opportunity to get deep in there and discover some things."

"I am twenty-four years old and fortunate to have a beautiful life in New York, with fulfilling relationships, work, and creative endeavors. However, I often feel disconnected and struggle to find emotion and beauty in the mundane of my life. I want to go into darkness to understand better who I am when everything else around me is stripped away. What is important to me? What have I been suppressing? I feel as though I'm at a crossroads of what I want to change or reframe in my life, and I believe that this experience will help me on this journey."

"I am experiencing a lot of grief navigating the collective state of humanity and am concerned for our longevity as a human race. I do not know how to process what I am feeling. I would like to remain in dark silence for a few days to calm my concern, come back to what my soul knows as truth about Buddha nature, reconnect with God and the beauty of the human state, and hear the teachings of Jesus within me as guidance and solace. I hope to leave the dark room with a tether to the beauty of life in all its manifestations and forms, even if that may be expressed in chaos and rajas."

5

Why Is Dark Retreat So Transformative?

The light which puts out our eyes is darkness to us.
—Henry David Thoreau

You're under no obligation to be the same
person you were five minutes ago.
—Alan Watts

What makes this practice so evolutionary, even revolutionary? Why is the return on investment so high? You can go into the dark for just a few days, and the insights last a lifetime. The preceding chapter suggested a number of reasons for the transformative potential, and future chapters will reveal more. This chapter rounds out the picture. Understanding why dark retreat is so transformative can inspire you to engage in this unusual practice and stick with it when the inevitable challenges arise.

Mind Only

Let's begin by exploring what's really going on in the dark, and in life altogether. If you look closely at your experience, you will discover that experience is all you ever have. On one level, this is so obvious we don't see it. Pause for a moment to see if it's true. Is there anything but experience? Another way to say this is that the only thing you ever encounter in life is your mind. Is it even possible to talk about experience without a mind? Whether you know it or not, you're always working with your mind. If you don't think so, point me to something that is not an experience. Can you show me anything that is not experienced by the mind? Don't take my word for this. Look. Test what I'm saying against your own experience. Find out for yourself. If this doesn't land just yet, hang in there as we go through this chapter.

What makes dark retreat so transformative and challenging is that mind becomes reality in the dark. Dark retreat is like lucid dreaming in this regard. When you fall asleep tonight, your senses will withdraw from the physical world, but your experience will continue into the dream world. Similarly, when you enter dark retreat, your senses withdraw from the outside world, which allows inner mental experience to stand out. The point is this: If you're always working with your mind, why not work with it directly?

Inner work in general and meditation in particular are about cultivating a heightened relationship with your mind, which is why any form of introspection, deep reflection, or soul-searching is transformative. But dark meditation is even more transformative because it invites you to work with your mind in the most focused way. There is nothing more reflective and "in your face" than the mirror of darkness.

Daily life is a classroom for learning about your mind and heart. Meditation accelerates the education, and dark retreat is like an institute of higher education. Inscribed above the Temple of Apollo at Delphi was the exhortation "Know Thyself." Joseph Campbell said, "The privilege of a lifetime is to become who you truly are."[1] This is the highest form of knowledge, a knowing that arises from direct acquaintance, and darkness provides the precious opportunity to make your acquaintance face-to-face. If Janus could greet you at the entrance to your dark room, I imagine he might say, "Welcome. It is my privilege to introduce you to yourself." You have no choice but to face yourself at entirely new levels and learn who you really are when no one is looking.

Meeting the Unconscious Mind

Not only do we get to meet and greet the contents of our conscious mind, but darkness quickly introduces us to the deeper dimensions of the unconscious mind. The magic begins here. After three days in the dark, one retreatant said, "This was a rescue mission. I rescued this part of me I never even met before. It was like freeing a baby bird." Some researchers estimate that at least 95 percent (!) of what we do is dictated by unconscious processes.[2] Let that sink in. This brings new meaning to Christ's comment in Luke 23:34: "Forgive them, Father, for they know not what they do." Operating from this inner darkness is what it means to be in the Degenerate Age at psychological levels. The massive forces of the dark side, the unconscious mind, rule our seemingly conscious lives. Paraphrasing Carl Jung, until you make the unconscious conscious, it will control your life, and you will call it fate.

This is also what it means to be asleep at spiritual levels. We spend our lives sleepwalking, unaware of the subterranean forces controlling our lives. The Buddha was literally the "Awakened One." While his name is applied to Buddhism, "awakened ones" appear in every authentic tradition. Through deep inner work, these noble beings were able to wake up to these unconscious processes, bring them into the light of consciousness, and be liberated from the (lower phase) darkness. Jung wrote, "People will do anything, no matter how absurd, in order to avoid facing their own souls . . . One does not become enlightened by imagining figures of light, but by making the darkness conscious."[3] The Gospel of Thomas proclaims, "If you bring forth what is within you, what you bring forth will save you. If you do not bring forth what is within you, what you do not bring forth will destroy you."[4] Going into darkness accelerates this process of emergence. Depth psychologist Robert Johnson writes:

> The disaster that has overtaken the modern world is the complete splitting off of the conscious mind from its roots in the unconscious. All the forms of interaction with the unconscious

> that nourished our ancestors—dream, vision, ritual, and religious experience [or dark retreat]—are largely lost to us, dismissed by the modern mind as primitive or superstitious. Thus, in our pride and hubris, our faith in our unassailable reason, we cut ourselves from our origins in the unconscious and from the deepest parts of ourselves . . . We act as though there were no unconscious, no realm of the soul, as though we could live full lives by fixating ourselves completely on the external, material world. We try to deal with all the issues of life by external means—making more money, getting more power, starting a love affair, or "accomplishing something" in the material world. But we discover to our surprise that the inner world is a reality that we ultimately have to face.[5]

Dark retreat takes you down to the tectonic plates of your experience. Relatively minor shifts in these subterranean plates have massive repercussions on the surface of life. You can really shake things up in one retreat, triggering personal earthquakes that will alter the landscape of your life. In the language of chaos theory, by working with primordial levels of being, you're taking advantage of a principle called "the sensitive dependence on initial conditions," better known as "the butterfly effect." A tiny change in the foundational state of a nonlinear system can result in massive changes in a later state. The image is given of a butterfly flapping its wings in the Bahamas that results in a hurricane on the Eastern seaboard.

My experience after every retreat verifies that butterflies abound in the dark. Even a few days in darkness can alter my life for months. The experience is akin to the radical changes that occur with *one* near-death experience or *one* hyperlucid dream. These experiences are so foundational, so hyperreal, that one event can shift an entire life. In Hindu language, as we've seen, dark retreat drops you into "causal consciousness." It's called "causal" because every other state of consciousness is an expression of this root. Change the root of things, and you can change everything.

Psychoanalyst Sigmund Freud divided consciousness into the conscious, preconscious, and unconscious levels, with each level related to the id, ego, and superego. His student Carl Jung added the deeper level of the collective unconscious and gave birth to depth psychology. Integral theorist Ken Wilber describes six types and levels of the unconscious mind: the ground-unconscious, archaic-unconscious, submergent-unconscious, embedded-unconscious, emergent-unconscious, and emergent-repressed unconscious.[6] These levels are not tidy sedimentations but oceanic currents of the underworld—always shifting, interpenetrating, constantly in flux. They don't abide by crisp conscious principles. Like the basis of physical reality itself (as described by quantum mechanics), think of them as inarticulate probability waves. It's beyond our scope to explore the levels of the deeper mind in detail, and don't worry about having a comprehensive understanding of them, but knowing about the general landscape of the unconscious mind helps you orient to what's happening in the dark as the conscious mind relaxes and the contents of the unconscious mind bubble up or erupt into consciousness.

We've discussed dark retreat as the practice of emergence, but it can also be looked at as the journey of submergence. In the topsy-turvy world of darkness, are things coming up, or are you going down? When the mind submerges, or falls into itself, in dark retreat, it doesn't do so in a crisp linear fashion. Nothing is crisp and linear when it comes to the unconscious mind. The descent that occurs in darkness, the journey of "waking down," is more like the haphazard tumble of a pinball, which sometimes get flicked back up, definitely gets pinged around, and occasionally gets stuck. This nonlinear and often disjointed journey takes place with any kind of deep inner work. If you find yourself stuck on the path in general or on the voyage of dark trekking in particular, inserting therapy or other Western methods can be invaluable in getting the pinball moving again.

Dark retreat, or any single method, is not a cure-all. Engage darkness in cooperation with other authentic approaches to transformation. Flick the pinball over to psychotherapy, or somatic work, IFS, EMDR, or whatever keeps the game of growth going.[7] To counteract the bad reputation of lower-phase darkness, I'm emphasizing all the benefits of higher-phase darkness. But we must be wary of what sociologists call "single-action bias," or putting all your eggs in one basket. It's easy to want a silver bullet, but none have yet to be found. And you won't find one in the dark.

While my annual dark retreats exhibit some level of cohesiveness and a semblance of orderly progression, they are just as much jerky journeys that seem to give me exactly what I need at that time. That's why a "beginner's mind" attitude of openness and radical acceptance is so helpful in this endeavor. Don't be afraid to be tossed around a bit, and trust darkness to do its magic.

Once you start to submerge, you'll quickly see how much is going on internally. Diving below the surface into the deeper waters of the unconscious mind puts you in touch with this turbulence, which is only interpreted as such by the closed, uncreative, conscious mind. For an open mind, turbulence can be the gateway to creativity. Trungpa Rinpoche famously said, "Chaos should be regarded as extremely good news."[8]

Where Does the Creativity Come From?

As we saw in the last chapter, one of the reasons dark retreat is so transformative is that it opens you to the realms of creativity. The traditional texts make no reference to this possibility, so I was delightfully surprised when creative insights burst forth in my first retreat. I wrote the insights down (it takes a little practice), but I now take a voice recorder with me to keep up with the creative flow. Because the torrent of insights became stronger with each retreat, I began to explore why. One insight about the flood of so many insights was that the creative dam burst open because the border patrol between the conscious and unconscious mind goes off duty in extended darkness. I'm usually so protected in daily life, shielded against the relentless onslaught of so much information, that armored plates have formed around me and *within* me. It's a defensive maneuver, a fortification that shields me from the barrage of sensory impact, the endless bombardment of exteroceptive and interoceptive data. In terms of exteroceptive assault, Barbara Brown Taylor writes, "Sight and sound both come at me with such velocity every day that I have learned to defend myself against them. If I do not limit their access to me, I will grow such thick calluses that I am no longer capable of seeing or hearing things that really matter."[9] The same applies to interoceptive assault, or the endless arising of impulses from the unconscious mind. When I'm in the dark, I no longer have to protect myself against this blitzkrieg. I can finally let my guard down and relax, allowing the calluses to soften and eventually disappear.

I don't have the courage, nor the stupidity, to suddenly step into the full light of day even after just a few days in darkness, let alone a few weeks.[10] I suspect that if I did so, I might go into shock. The sensory impact would be too much. I would feel such a violent contraction, born of self-defense, that I could pass out from the sensory punch. I, therefore, always end my retreats at night, take my first steps into the nighttime sky, and tiptoe back into the light and my normal life, very slowly. Even then, I often recoil when I make contact with the light and have to return briefly to the dark, bracing myself before stepping back outside. The calluses are slowly slapped back on. It is only then that I realize how open I have become in the dark and how contracted is my normal life. As we'll see in the upcoming chapters on preparation and integration, a gentle off-ramp and an even more gentle on-ramp are keys to successful retreat.

What does this say about where we are today, how thick our calluses have become, how insensitive we are, how solid and impenetrable our perception boxes have become? Is this why people act with such callousness to others, to animals, and to this world? Once again, dark retreat is about letting the darkness tenderize us. It's about becoming an open-hearted, open-minded, and open-bodied being who is truly in touch with others and the world because they made the effort to get in touch with themselves.[11]

Darkness is both diagnostic and prescriptive. It will show you how painfully contracted and hardened you have become and what you need to do to open up and soften. One retreatant, after three days in the dark, shared, "I thought the darkness would be scary. But it was like this warm cloak. It was like a grandma came and took me in her warm cloak. If everybody could come home to themselves in this way, it would be a different world. We would be so much more loving to each other. If we could all just touch this part of ourselves and see how we are protecting ourselves, we'd be so much kinder; we'd be so much gentler. We'd be so much more loving to ourselves and to everyone around us." Another retreatant, after five days in the dark, said, "I have never been with myself that thoroughly. And I learned that the body is so much more sensitive and subtle, and the heart is so much more tender."

While there are many truly wondrous events and advances happening around the world, there are an equal amount of really challenging things taking place. Doesn't it feel like this crazy world is beating you up? The battering ram of so much bad news is bruising. Social media is literally killing people. Political divisiveness is ripping the world apart. We're struck by social injustice, assailed by gender inequality, hit by world poverty, and pummeled by the effects of global warming. The storm of pettiness, culture wars, literal wars, crime, and ecological devastation generates the friction and defensive thickening of our skin. Solitude and darkness shield us from this assault and allow us to open up. The openness then dissolves the boundaries that generate all the divisiveness. When you're no longer trying so hard to create the illusion that you've got it together, you can finally relax and let everything fall apart. A natural consequence of this relaxation and healthy disintegration is that things come up. Whenever I have a new crack in my concrete driveway, it doesn't take long for life to emerge through those cracks.

Dark retreat is a boundary buster. All manner of concretization begins to crack, which can sometimes be registered as the feeling that you—your ego—is about to crack. The concrete border between day and night breaks down, between inside and outside, between self and other, between the literal and metaphorical (which makes for rich wordplay when writing about darkness). *Between* literally means "be two." Dark retreat is, therefore, a "be two" bomber, or duality decimator, that manifests in increasing experiences of unity. The fall of the Iron Curtain pales in comparison to tearing down these walls. At tantric levels, duality altogether collapses into nonduality in the experience of ultimate unity, or enlightenment.

Remember that darkness is the color of nonduality. Lusseyran writes, "To cease seeing with one's eyes does not mean entering a world in which light has ceased to exist... The light is neither within nor without, but encompasses the whole being and wipes out the barriers we have created out of habit. The light is here! . . . I had the same experience with space. When I became blind, I found out that an inner space existed."[12] One could also argue that white light is the color of nonduality before it's fractionated by the prism of ignorance into multiplicity. If it's bright enough, white light can be blinding to duality as much as darkness.

Author Tess Callahan, in a TEDx Talk called "The Love Affair Between Creativity and Constraint," says: "We all admire people who think outside the box. But how do they do it? What if the key to thinking outside the box is to create a box to think inside of? . . . What if limitations aren't just a nuisance; what if they're essential? What if we're meant to put boxes around ourselves so that we can push against them? And the friction of that struggle becomes the flint, the spark, that allows us to create."[13] Callahan is not referring to dark retreat, or otherwise going into a literal box, but her comments apply to dark practice. Go into the dark, rub up against yourself, and watch the creative sparks fly.

I did my three-year retreat before I started doing dark retreats. This long retreat was defined by one constraint after another. We were walled off in a compound on the cliffs of the Gulf of Saint Lawrence, each of us put into a room the size of a walk-in closet and spending some eighteen hours a day in a meditation box. This box was a roughly four feet by four feet square, with a high back, open front, and tapered sides. We even slept sitting up in this box (you get used to it). I came to call it "ego's coffin." In addition to these physical constraints, we spent most of our time in silence and engaged in meditations that invited stillness. The distraction upon distraction that defined my normal discursive life was replaced with retraction upon retraction, forcing me into the confines of the present moment. I was placed in a straitjacket of sanity, and the level of insight and creativity that emerged from that confinement was only surpassed by my time in the more constrained environment of dark retreat. We'll return to the importance of constraint in chapter 12, when we explore some of the reasons why darkness gets challenging.

Solar Addiction

Understanding the transformative potential of dark retreat mandates an enhanced understanding of the unconscious mind. A more refined way to look at the unconscious mind is to view it as the obscured, concealed, or obfuscated mind. What is the source of obfuscation? What is it that conceals the contents of the unconscious mind and blinds us to the treasures within? A few factors are at play here, but first and foremost is light! At the levels of mind and reality that we're diving into, *light doesn't reveal, it conceals.*[14] We're blinded to the transformative contents of the unconscious mind because of our sight-centric, light-centric, and wake-centric ways. These three centricities are all in the service of the mother of all centricities: ego-centricity. Each centricity acts as a contraction that restricts access to all things dark, including the darkness of the unconscious mind. And each centricity serves to confine us to our comfort zone.

I interpret Thoreau's cryptic epigraph to this chapter, "The light which puts out our eyes is darkness to us," to mean that something which appears positive on the surface, in this case light itself, can in fact be so overwhelming that it blinds us.[15] Once again, appearance is not in harmony with reality. That which seems to illuminate can actually obscure. By contracting our pupils, and eventually our mind, light ironically prevents us from seeing the whole picture, fundamentally acting like darkness despite being perceived as light. This is not to categorically dismiss the power of light, of course, but to put it in its place. It's a question of balance. Things that appear to be beneficial can have destructive consequences if taken to extremes. We're talking about metaphysical sunburn here and the shadow side of preternatural solar power. As essentially photosynthetic beings, we need light to live. We eat it to survive. Animals feed on plants, plants feed on the sun, and we feed on them all.[16] But when our appetite for light is taken to extremes, it burns us on multiple levels.

During the day, our solitary sun obscures countless other suns. If you're reading this on a sunny day, step outside and look up. There are innumerable stars up there, but they're all hidden by the light of one domineering sun. When that sun sets, other stars now have the chance to shine. The conscious mind is like the sun, and the unconscious mind is like all the other shrouded stars. These inner light sources may appear to be faint and distant when you first step into the dark, but the longer you keep your inner eyes open, the closer and more radiant they become.

Insights begin to appear out of the darkness, and eventually an entire universe unfolds before you. It's the difference between setting off Fourth of July fireworks at noon, which would be barely discernable and therefore unremarkable, versus doing so at midnight, which would be spectacular. This sort of eruption is what happened in a recent retreat, when this entire book burst into my mind. Lusseyran, who was blinded at age seven, writes, "Inside me was everything I had believed was outside. There was, in particular, the sun, light, and all colors. There were even the shapes of objects and the distances between objects. Everything was there, and movement as well."[17] In the Neoplatonic world, the microcosm is a reflection of the macrocosm, the human soul reflects the World Soul. As within, so without. Hence, all the planets and stars can be found inside. Renaissance philosopher Marsilio Ficino wrote, "These celestial bodies are not to be sought by us outside in some other place; for the heavens in their entirety are within us, in whom the light of life and the origin of heaven dwell."[18]

As discussed earlier, the obfuscation is due to contraction. In our wake-centric culture, with so much artificial light, everybody is so contracted. Stepping into the dark allows your outer and inner eyes to open and relax, and eventually your entire being follows suit. Dark retreat opens the aperture of somatic awareness, psychological awareness, and spiritual awareness. The light-bloated ego may initially contract in self-defense when it encounters the dark (some people feel a jolt of anxiety or fleeting panic when they first step into total darkness), but eventually darkness dilates your consciousness to the point that you see through the ego and into the deepest dimensions of your interior. In *The Symposium*, Plato wrote, "The mind's eye begins to see clearly when the outer eyes grow dim."[19]

Movement Addiction

As blinding as light can be, it doesn't work alone in the genesis of obfuscation. The other central player that walls us off from the unconscious mind is movement. Our relentless busyness, what Lakhar Rinpoche calls "active laziness," keeps us browsing on the surface of life. We're like a stone skipping across the water, hop-skipping along points on the surface of consciousness with the speed of our minds and the relentless activity of our lives. And then we wonder why something is missing. What's missing is within us, or below us. What's lost is a recognition of the vast spectrum of our being. Depth has been stolen. Interiority has been taken. Soul has been pilfered.

Identity theft is a big problem today, and the most damaging thievery is when we don't even know we're being ripped off. This level of identity theft occurs when awareness moves out of itself and is consolidated at the outermost levels of gross material form. Ego is the result of this criminal action because ego is exclusive identification with form. This is a crime that occurs in broad daylight because it's facilitated in broad daylight as we're seduced outside of ourselves and kidnapped by shiny external objects. Pay close attention to your experience and you will notice how movement steals your awareness, and the recognition of that movement is highlighted in the full light of day.[20] The word *steal* has a revelatory double meaning: to "take without permission" and "to move quietly or surreptitiously," as in "She stole down to the basement." The surreptitious movement of awareness from inside to outside is where we lose our identity as we attend almost exclusively to the "great outdoors."

Water is frequently used as a metaphor for consciousness, and being underwater often manifests in dreams to symbolize the unconscious mind. A common name for spiritual masters in Tibet is Gyamtso, which means "ocean." When you slow down and stop skipping, you can finally drop into the depths of your being and recover your true identity. Freud offered an iceberg model of consciousness, where the conscious mind is just the tip of the iceberg. The bulk of the berg, the true scope of your identity, lies below the surface.

Remember that reality is what you attend to. If you're drawn to the surface of mere appearance by the dominant sense of sight, you will spend your life there, attending to your *outer* body, identifying with form, skating on top of things. Lusseyran writes, "Our eyes run over the surface of things. All they require are a few scattered points, since they can bridge the gap in a flash. They 'half see' much more than they see, and they never weigh. They are satisfied with appearances, and for them the world glows and slides by, but lacks substance."[21]

The Sanskrit word *guru* means "heavy." In the West, the colloquialism "That's heavy!" suggests the profundity of something. *Profound* itself means "to go to the bottom, to get to the base." Profundity is associated with depth. If there's one thing you can say about dark retreat, it is deep. Going underground into the cave represents this depth and profundity, and going into darkness itself represents a descent into the unconscious mind. In dark retreat, you're no longer surfing on the surface of this planet. Now you're getting into it. You're diving down into what really matters and getting in touch with deeper truths.

Remember the four types of guru, the most important of which is the ultimate guru within. As long as you're flitting about on the surface of things, infatuated with outer appearances, living in the comfort zone of "life-lite," you'll never make contact with your deep inner wisdom. To meet the guru within, do something heavy. Do something that will take you down to the bottom of your being, where the ultimate guru abides. If movement is central to obfuscation, pick up something heavy and try moving around. Pick up the weighty practice of darkness. Stop seeing and start feeling. Allow dark retreat to put you in contact with the heaviest and most profound sense of touch. In dark retreat, you "come to your senses" by removing the most superficial and distracting senses. One retreatant, after three days in the dark, said, "Oh my gosh! That was not what I expected. Having that kind of power, to just feel again. I haven't felt in a long time. Darkness created the space to be really comfortable and safe. I think I've dissociated my entire life. In there, I could finally feel."

Both light and movement, detected by sight, conspire to draw us away, yanking us away from the center of ourselves. When the sun is shining, we want to go out and do something. When it's dark, we tend to move inside, slow down, and eventually stop. *Light combined with movement leads to distraction.* Distraction is the real culprit. It's virtually antitransformation. To dis-tract literally means to "pull apart." As we'll see in the next chapter, distraction is what pulls us apart from everything that is wholesome or deep. It's at the heart of duality, disease, and suffering. Distraction is how we unwittingly evict ourselves from the Garden of Eden moment to moment. The Degenerate Age is the distracted age, and it's only getting darker as distraction is made more available. This lower-phase darkness is spreading across the globe, largely because of artificial light.

The Degenerate Age stepped up its menacing creep with Thomas Edison. He's not to blame, of course, because artificial light has many benefits. But the dark side of his invention is taking a massive toll in the many forms of light pollution. Author Clark Strand writes, "We believe the modern world rests on a petroleum platform, but it really rests on light. Petroleum merely drives our cars; light drives our consciousness. And what it drives it to is mostly excess—in all its myriad forms."[22] Strand continues:

> Ninety-nine percent of all Americans today live in areas that are officially "light polluted," which means that the night is at least ten times brighter than it should be. The world gets more light-polluted by the second, and that means that our bodies are polluted with it, too. At this point, we're actually addicted to that pollution . . . When everyone is addicted, there is little logic in recovery.[23]

Artificial light pulls us out and away from the natural light within, what Buddhism refers to as the Clear Light Mind, a synonym for the ultimate guru within. A traditional Buddhist teaching talks about "Buddha in the palm of your hand," which suggests the immediacy of awakening. Awakening is right here, right now, in the palm of your hand. In the Kali Yuga, the Buddha has been bumped by Māra. Now, it's "Māra in the palm of your hand," in the shape of smart phones driven by artificial light. Nowhere has distraction taken on more deadly force than with these weapons of mass distraction. To see what's in your future, do a psychic palm reading. What's in the palm of *your* hand?

In dark retreat, both light and movement, the two central players in the deformation of the Kali Yuga, are removed. Your inability to see in the dark makes it hard to move, which arrests the distraction and ensuing deformation. Stop the deformation, and reformation naturally ensues. Countless people come out of the dark feeling centered, aligned, balanced, healed, and reformed simply because they're no longer being deformed. Darkness allows the natural transformative and healing powers of your being to emerge. Dark retreat is viewed as a transformative experience, but it's more accurately reformative. The transformation is essentially restoration.

Cessation of Movement

Everything about dark retreat invites, and eventually demands, simplicity. Minimalism rules the day. The dark cabin or cave offers bare-bones trappings. The confinement radically reduces physical activity and rewards minimal mental activity. Your entire life is put on hold. After three days in the dark, one retreatant shared, "So much gratitude. So much love. Overwhelming love. And appreciation for this space, for the process, for the darkness, for the silence. And for my breath, to be able to guide me when it was difficult. And for my body for being able to tell me what it needed and what it didn't need anymore. It's like, 'Get rid of this for sure. I've carried this for fifty years, get rid of this one!'"

Dark retreat is the complete opposite of the excesses that dominate normal life, especially a so-called successful life. Compared to the extravagant lives of the rich and famous, life in dark retreat is extremely impoverished. Darkness redefines and therefore realigns our definitions of genuine wealth and poverty, even notions of conventional success and failure.

The notion of "holding" is central to dark retreat and Eastern spirituality. The Sanskrit word *dharma*, one of the most important terms in Buddhism and Hinduism, is a multivalent term with at least ten meanings. Dharma essentially means "factor" or "element" and derives from the root *dhr*, which means "to hold" or "to maintain." *Hold* also has a number of meanings, including "to contain" and "to stop." As we'll see in the next chapter, holding is integral to healing, to "whole-ing," and to many of the benefits of dark practice.

The holding environment of dark retreat transforms you from a "human doing" back to a human being. That's where the transformation occurs. Darkness virtually commands cessation, and cessation is at the heart of spiritual liberation. The many words for liberation are mostly terms implying cessation or holding: *nirvāna* ("to extinguish"), *nirodha* ("cessation"), *nirvikalpa* ("nonconceptual"), *nirveda* ("renunciation"), *nirodha-samāpatti* ("equipoise of cessation"), *nonduality* ("not two"), and the like. In Hinduism and Buddhism, to attain liberation means to purify karma (habit), and karma means "action." To cease all action in the dark is to cease the creation of new karma, which allows for the opportunity to purify old karma. The spirit of holding is so central to our journey that I will frequently italicize the word, and its synonyms, to remind you of this key concept and its role in *holding* the main points of dark retreat (we'll return to the second definition of *dhr*, "to contain," in chapter 7).

Emptiness and Infinite Possibilities

Let's conclude this chapter with a brief look at tantric levels of transformation. In Tibetan Buddhism, dark retreat was designed to prepare one for the bardos, the groundless dimension of the after-death state. According to the bardo teachings, everything is exaggerated seven to nine times in the bardos. Why the exaggeration? Because mind becomes reality in the bardos, just like in a dream, or just like in dark retreat. The bardos are sometimes referred to as "the dream at the end of time." Tenzin Wangyal Rinpoche is one of the few meditation masters who teaches on dream yoga, bardo yoga, and dark retreat. Rinpoche says that one fruition of dream yoga, which also applies to dark retreat, is to realize the fluid or dreamlike nature of reality. This realization results in the liberating discovery: This is a dream. I am free. I can change. You're not as solid as you think. The world is not as hard as you think. This allows people to come out of dark retreat feeling lighter, freer, less encumbered, and more en-lightened. Look at the soft faces, the supple body language, the flexible demeanor of someone coming out of dark retreat, and you will witness the embodiment of openness.

Imagine a huge tree stump on land, unmovable by a dozen men. Now imagine that tree stump in water, where a single person can move it. The fluidity creates the environment for moveability and, hence, transformation. Whether you sink or swim in these waters depends on how you relate to the liquidity. As Joseph Campbell said, "The psychotic drowns in the same waters in which the mystic swims."[24] Those who open and relax in the dark stay afloat and swim gracefully. They go with the flow of whatever arises. As one retreatant said, "I am of the same essence as the darkness." Those who thrash about, resist, or fight the darkness are more likely to drown. It's your relationship to the darkness, to your own mind, that determines if you sink or swim.

At the deepest levels of transformation, we dip into the waters of emptiness. The fluidity and groundlessness that manifest at these depths is a taste of this core Buddhist principle. Those who engage in tantra-level dark retreat plunge into the dark to have a direct experience of emptiness. This is where the transformative potential really shines, for as the teachings proclaim: Without emptiness, nothing is possible; with emptiness, everything is possible. Remember that darkness is homologous to emptiness, so darkness returns you to the domain where everything is possible.

6

Where Does the Healing Come From?

We find ourselves ill at ease in modern society, caught in recurring cycles of dis-ease and depression. We might ask ourselves whether our discomfort comes from compromising the sacred and balanced partnership between light and dark. What healing might be available to body and soul if we would turn off the lights and invite the powers of the night into our lives?
—Malidoma Patrice Somé

Deep in their roots all flowers keep the light.
—Theodore Roethke

Dark retreat exhibits remarkable abilities to heal a spectrum of physical, emotional, and spiritual dis-ease. While some data is available from experiments done with sensory-deprivation tanks and the REST method, studies on formal dark retreat are not available yet. Plenty of anecdotal evidence exists, however, and I can speak from extensive personal experience about the restorative powers of dark practice. Malidoma Patrice Somé shares, "The tribal person knows that there are certain types of wounds that can find healing only in the nighttime and only in the hands of the ancestors who show up for work after the last candle has been extinguished."[1] The explanatory models in this section are still speculative, but they offer frameworks that support the curative capacities of this practice.

The healing comes from multiple directions. One immediate source is the ability to relax at such deep levels. Many retreatants, myself included, catch up on a lot of sleep during retreat. I know some practitioners who regularly spend up to sixteen hours a day in bed. They may not be sleeping that entire time, but just resting to this extent is restorative. When we're in deep sleep, human growth hormone is released, stress hormones decrease, and countless restorative processes occur. There's a reason we're forced into bed and into the darkness of sleep when we get sick. The body knows when it's time to shut down the stressed-out mind. In a certain sense, illness, like dark retreat, is a forceful method of liberation. Getting sick forces you to relax and realign by keeping you in bed.

When I do my daily sessions in the dark, I feel the stress fall away. Stress is arguably the greatest contributor to disease, and while certain healthy stressors and challenges accompany dark practice (you are stretching into the challenge zone after all), in the end, darkness is a journey into tranquility. My dark room feels like an invisible healing sponge, absorbing all my dis-ease. In turn, I also feel like a sponge, absorbing the medicinal qualities of darkness through every pore. I step into the dark and drink it all in, like a good patient following the doctor's prescription.

Stress and inflammation work together. In today's overheated world, unchecked inflammation leads to chronic fatigue, infection, insomnia, depression, mood disorders, anxiety, myalgia, arthralgia, acid reflux, constipation, diarrhea, weight issues, and even cancer.[2] Inflammatory processes are not only physical. A highly reactive, volatile, irritable, combative, and explosive mind is an inflammatory mind. Meditation in general and dark retreat in particular are powerful anti-inflammatories at multiple levels. Darkness puts out the flames. Look at the faces and demeanor of those coming into dark retreat, compare that body language to what comes out of retreat, and you'll see the release of stress and almost feel the reduction in emotional inflammation.

Heightened Interoception

Another avenue of healing is the heightened ability to tune into what's happening in your body. As you "wake down" in the dark and make greater contact with your feelings, this includes getting more in touch with your body. This amplified interoception allows you to tune into parts of your body that may be out of tune. You're in such a still and silent environment that you can really listen to what's happening, not just in your mind but in your body. Most of the time, there's just so much static in our lives that we can't tune into our body. In Eastern medical theory, with systems like Ayurvedic, Tibetan, and Chinese medicine, the outer body is a physical representation of the subtle inner body, and both of those bodies are expressions of the innermost very subtle body. By withdrawing from the relentless activity and noise of the louder physical body, we can hear the whispers from the subtle body and then the barely audible utterances of the very subtle body. The silent voices of the deeper body-mind finally have a chance to be heard, heeded, and realigned. One retreatant, after five days in the dark, said, "Part of me anticipated an out-of-body experience. Perhaps I didn't really know what to expect. Or a dissolution of the body. But my experience was a much more profound and intimate connection to the body, much more embodied. Every little vibration, every little feeling, every little ache or pain—in the dark it's the most exciting thing you have, so you can't help but become very curious."

Philosopher Baruch Spinoza suggested dual-aspect monism, a philosophical mouthful that suggests that the body and mind are two ends of one spectrum, creating the body-mind matrix. Body can be viewed as a gross form of mind, and mind can be viewed as a subtle form of body. They work in a bidirectional way, which means that what you do with your mind works in a "top down" way to affect your body, manifesting as psychosomatic disease or good health and ease. Every health-care provider knows this, which is why they always ask about a patient's level of stress. The body also works in a "bottom up" way to affect your mind, which manifests in countless organic and nonorganic ways. Organic ways (literally) include organs affecting the mind when things are off: from uremic (kidney) toxins that lead to cognitive disorders and dementia; to lung problems leading to issues with attention, concentration, memory, and executive functioning; to organ transplants (especially the heart) transplanting memories of the donor into the mind of the recipient. Nonorganic "bottom up" effects include getting drunk on alcohol, buzzed with caffeine, or taking any of the countless psychotropic drugs that work on the mind (biochemistry is a subtle form of body).

In dark retreat, you're withdrawing from external to internal, from outer gross body to inner subtle body to innermost very subtle body, and eavesdropping along the way. You then come back up from very subtle to subtle to gross, carrying the messages back with you into ordinary life. It's like hacking into previously restricted domains of consciousness and getting the access codes to subtle states of your body. Everything you do in the gross material world starts with a subtle thought or emotion. In dark retreat, you're retreating to the origins of your body-mind, which is irreducibly mental. It's what makes dark retreat so effectual. Your physical health is the external appearance of your mind, an outer re-presentation of an inner state. By tuning into the foundational state, you have the opportunity not only to detect early forms of disease but to access the pre-physical mental states that will eventually manifest as full-blown disease if they're not recognized. You can get a glimpse of this process when you slow down at the end of the day or lie down to sleep and notice a new sensation in your body or a subtle somatic impression in your mind. It was with you during the day, but the busyness and distractions prevented you from noticing anything. Magnify this sensitivity, and you'll get a sense of the diagnostic opportunities in dark retreat.

As we've seen, karma starts to ripen at the level of the deep unconscious mind first. Karmic seeds are stored in these depths and eventually work their way up into manifest reality, where they scream for attention at the loudest physical level. This is why many people have precognitive dreams predicting physical problems, myself included. Some serious prostate issues appeared in a precognitive dream I had several years before they made their physical appearance. You may find yourself having such dreams in dark retreat or feeling intuitions portending a disease, a product of getting in tune with your deeper body-mind. When you get so silent and still in the dark, there's no need to scream. You can hear (or feel) your subtle body calling out for attention at less jarring levels and get the message before it reaches the surface. If these inner voices are attended to, you could prevent a disease from manifesting at physical levels.

One near-enemy of this heightened interoception is conceptual proliferation, or even paranoia. You might feel something in the dark that you didn't notice in the light of the day and immediately catastrophize, "This might be lung cancer!" You've gone from a legitimate embodied experience to an illegitimate out-of-body (conceptual) experience. You touch into a subtle somatic sensation, only to get lost in gross discursive thought. For the distraction-starved ego, any form of entertainment is welcome in prolonged darkness, even if it's a self-scripted horror story.

Amplification comes with risks and rewards as awareness of both body and mind are magnified in darkness. It's easy to create the proverbial mountain out of a molehill. The instruction, as always, is to notice everything without judgment or commentary. If you find yourself obsessing or catastrophizing, smile at that and return to the thread of embodied experience. Be a mole and dig back down. Moles are adapted to a subterranean lifestyle. Get back underground, into your body, and remain there. Stay with what you're feeling, don't stray into what you're thinking. As Mark Twain put it, "Some of the worst things in my life never happened."[3] Most of the disquieting sensations are self-limiting, which means they settle back down if you just leave them alone. If a somatic sensation does continue, then trust your intuition, not your paranoia, and go see your doctor after retreat.

In summary: The first healing modality in dark practice comes from the potential for early detection. But there's a difference between detection and diagnosis. Don't rush to any diagnostic conclusions. I do not recommend that you go into the dark with the intention to do a full-body scan, especially if you're a hypochondriac. With nothing to distract you, you can drive yourself crazy with every little sensation that pops up. As always, keep things open. See what comes up. But don't let it go all the way up into your catastrophizing head.

The Health of Nonduality

The third avenue for healing goes much further. Up to a certain point, one that varies from person to person, the deeper you go into the dark, the more transformative the journey becomes. While depth is correlated to duration to a certain degree, some people can drop deep in just a few days. Don't think you need to spend weeks in the dark to harvest all the riches. Quality is much more important than quantity. Regardless of how long it takes, the deeper aspects of dark retreat give you access to the nondual dimensions of your being, which changes everything. It returns you to the primordial darkness before any division.

According to the nondual wisdom traditions, the root of every problem in your life, the primary cause of every physical, emotional, or spiritual disease, is duality. Philosopher David Loy writes, "The very impetus to philosophy may be seen as a reaction to the split between subject and object: philosophy originated in the need of the alienated subject to understand itself and its relation to the objective world it finds itself in."[4] Radical nondual teachers proclaim that if you solve the problem of duality, there's little need for philosophy, or psychology, or spirituality. More integrally informed scholar-practitioners (I would include myself in that population) find this proclamation somewhat dismissive of the messiness of the human condition. Just like with dark retreat, don't put all your eggs in the nondual basket. But with this said, is it possible that the wholeness of nonduality leads to natural healing and less need for medicine?

The first thing to understand is that duality, archetypal misalignment, which is virtually synonymous with samsāra, is not "out there." Duality is not a preexisting world that you are born into. It's a construct. It's something you make up moment to moment. Samsāra is a state of mind, not a state in reality. Nonduality, or nirvāna, is equally a state of mind. This is why the wisdom traditions say things like, "Grant your blessings so that I realize the inseparability of samsāra and nirvāna." They're "not-two," or nondual.

Because duality is a construct, it can be deconstructed. Nonduality is then dis-covered to be the natural state. If there were an instruction manual for how to "build" your dark retreat, it would begin with the words, "Some *disassembly* required." The result of disassembling duality and dropping into the nature of mind and reality is irreducible wholeness, health, and sanity. One retreatant shared, "It was just such a beautiful gift. I wish I could share it with everybody. I just want everybody to experience that. Because it's such wholeness. If everybody could just experience it, it would be such a different world. People would be so different." It's the discovery of a truth "too exalted to be divided into knowledge."[5] Religious scholar Jeffrey Kripal writes:

> Reality only appears to be divided into mind and matter, into consciousness and cosmos, or into a past, present and future because *you* experience it as such. *You* are the splitter of the real and the creator of linear time . . . The social ego does not want to hear it. It actually *cannot* hear it, since this human subject is precisely what is splitting reality into a mental and a material dimension, neurologically creating the arrow of temporality and suppressing or denying the deeper unity of everything and everyone.[6]

Dark retreat is uniquely situated to deliver you to this nature, not because it adds a magical step toward nonduality, but because it removes all the steps that take you away from it. It's physically, and metaphysically, difficult to take any steps in the dark. Everything comes to a grinding halt, and in that very cessation lies liberation, as we saw in the last chapter. As Meister Eckhart says, "The soul does not grow by addition but by subtraction."[7] To arrive at the truth, just subtract whatever is false. Similarly, the body heals by removing stress, pollution, trauma, anxiety, worry, tension, bad food, bad habits, or any of the countless toxins that cause us to fracture away from the natural state. This is why we're forced into bed when we get sick. Stop breaking away, and the innate healing properties of the body-mind naturally manifest. Dark retreat is a seriously healing hard stop. One retreatant shared, "What a deep breath of relief. Learning about that part of you that is whole, rediscovering that part, and just sitting with it. And realizing that, 'Of course, you're not broken! How could you forget? You've been whole this entire time!'

It's almost like a new language that you learn in feelings and emotions that I didn't have before."

Glorious Deconstruction

Ego is the world's fastest construction company. In the blink of an eye, it creates the illusion of a dualistic world. Neuroscience and modern physics tell us that there is no preexisting depth or dimensionality out there, no colors waiting for you to passively perceive. Perception is not passive representation but an active construction. Perception *is* creation. John Wheeler, esteemed physicist and student of Einstein, says that there isn't even an "out there" out there. There is no independent duality. Erwin Schrödinger, one of the founding fathers of quantum mechanics, said, "The world is given to me only once, not one existing and one perceived. Subject and object are only one. The barrier between them cannot be said to have broken down as a result of recent experiences in the physical sciences, for this barrier does not exist."[8]

These insights come clearly into view in the dark and become your direct experience. While you continue to blink in the dark, it doesn't have the same "constructive" power in there. Darkness frustrates the world's most efficient construction company, and things start to fall apart. As we'll see later in the chapter, the mind starts to fall into itself, and ego implodes. Because of the sensory deprivation, there are no building materials in the dark. All the normal data coming into the five sensory ports is boycotted. You can't patch an external world together if there's no raw material to patch.

John Wheeler shares another adage about the construction of reality from a seminal paper on quantum mechanics delivered in 1989. From the abstract: "Every physical quantity, every it, derives its ultimate significance from bits, binary yes-or-no indications, a conclusion which we epitomize in the phrase, it from bit."[9] If there are no bits, there are no its. Playing with this concept at the deepest level and connecting this insight to Wheeler's previous maxim, *it's* not even out there; duality can't be effectively constructed if there are no incoming bits of sensory information delivered to the assembly line.

Our five senses evolved to put us in touch with something *other*, something outside of ourselves. When those senses are deprived of "other" in darkness, when there's nothing out there to contact, "other" gradually disappears. And because you can't have self without other (they coemerge and define each other), self and other eventually collapse into each other in the dark.[10] Inside and outside "lean" on each other, so if one or the other is kicked out, they fall into each other in a nondualistic embrace. The dualistic mind (sem in Tibetan) falls into itself (rigpa), a process known as rangbop ("self-falling") in Tibetan, and duality collapses into nonduality.[11] What's left after this collapse? Nothing. Or more precisely, no-thing, which is what emptiness means. Emptiness is not nothingness; it's no-thingness. One particularly sensitive retreatant, after three days in the dark, said:

> It really trims down all the fat, allowing you to get down to your core nature. All we need to do is be the space in which everything arises and watch it all happen. It then runs its natural course. Be in that timeless space, it's a beautiful space to be. What remains is so vast, so deep, so limitless, so timeless. It's infinite; it doesn't have a bottom. In the day, there's so much data coming in. Darkness helps you focus on what matters. When you ask the questions, "Where are all these thoughts and feelings coming from? Who's producing all of them?" and rest in that answer, you find there is nobody! You're left with this vast, limitless space. There's no right or wrong answer; there's just the exploration. Peel the onion, go deeper and deeper, until you're left with space, awareness. I allowed it to go as deep as it wanted to go. Who's the real me that's in charge of all this? There's nobody. I didn't really like it because I wanted to have control. I wanted there to be a me . . . [on another level], it does feel good to be exposed to the truth, to go deeper.

But we're getting ahead of ourselves. We'll return to these deeper waters in the last chapters.

The most amazing thing is that all this demolition happens naturally when you simply stop. You don't have to bring in any wrecking balls, excavators, cranes, or jackhammers for this deconstruction project. You just need to do absolutely nothing. *Hold*, and watch your entire dualistic world fall apart. As your relative self falls apart in the dark, your absolute Self comes together. Absolute integration is the result of relative disintegration. Healing and wholing are simply the natural result of the cessation of splintering. This is why so many people, if they don't resist the demolition, come out of the dark feeling so together. In Eastern language, it's the feeling of samādhi, which means "to collect or bring together." You've finally collected yourself, gotten your act together, not because of the effort in gathering, but because of the cessation in breaking. To get yourself together, just stop pulling yourself apart. All manner of dis-ease is naturally remedied when you return to the primordial state of ease. Dis-ease is literally "not at ease" or "lacking ease," an "impairment of ease or comfort." Stop impairing and you start repairing.

Duality itself is multilayered, which is why there are so many forms of disease. For every level of splintering, there is indeed a splinter. Once the "original sin," the primordial cut, of splitting reality into self and other takes place, secondary, tertiary, and quaternary fractures reverberate from this ruptured core, giving rise to the infinite iterations of duality. The state of the world is the result of the state of our minds. The fractured state of the world is the result of the fractured state of our minds.

Complexity theory proclaims that the diversified display of this vast complex world can be reduced to foundational tenets. Fractals, like the famous Mandelbrot set, are a visual depiction of the reiterative nature of reality. As the esteemed neuroscientist Christof Koch writes, "The world is awash with recurrent motifs at multiple levels of scale."[12] A fractal is basically a never-ending pattern, generated by repeating a simple process over and over, in an endless feedback, or recursive, loop. The complex patterns display the property of self-similarity across scales (connected to the principles of universality), as iterated in the Hermetic adage "As above, so below," or reiterated in the tantric maxim (Kālachakra Tantra) "As within, so without."

Complexity theory, and dark practice, engage in healthy reductionism to radically simplify things to irreducible principles, showing that things above are copies of things below. By descending into the dark, we're dropping below all the superficial appearances above, "The Ten Thousand Things" in Taoism. We're dropping beneath political divisions, cultural divides, social schism, gender inequality, and racial discrimination and plunging into our common origin. We're finally getting to the bottom of all these iterations, discovering solutions to never-ending problems by returning to the naturally wholesome reduction base.

Samsāra is like a perverted fractal, dazzling in its recursive depth. Imagine a big rock falling onto a sheet of ice, generating countless cracks that radiate from the point of impact. Samsāra is one massive fault, generating fault upon fault, all radiating out from the primordial fault line of self and other. As we'll explore later, metafracturing is what gives rise to the metacrisis. Philosopher Ken Wilber writes,

> [O]ur normal or typical awareness is driven by a fundamental avoidance, a primordial fear, a contraction. In each moment, there is something *that we don't want to look at*—some idea, thought, perception, impulse, sensation, thing, or event. We therefore turn away, look away, move away—and that fundamental avoidance [distraction] is the cause of the entire misery of humankind. In a chain reaction, it creates one dualism after another, one fragmentation after another, one brokenness after another—and a synonym for *brokenness* is *suffering*.[13]

Glorious Healing

It may seem dismissively facile, but bear with me in this chapter, then go into the dark and see for yourself: Dark retreat is so transformative, so healing, so wholing because it has the ability to cure the countless cracks in duality. Darkness takes you down, fracture by fracture, to the primordial rift.[14] Instead of leaving wreckage in its forceful wake, this bulldozer into sanity leaves healing in its wake. Splinter upon splinter is reached and then removed until the final wedge that splinters reality into self and other is accessed and excised. The more distant the level, the more seemingly insoluble the problem. But if we can retreat, step by step, level by level, we can work our way down from every dualistic problem and return to the nondual solution. It's like Hansel and Gretel following breadcrumbs back home. Every crack leaves a crumb and points the way to the cure. Greek philosopher and mystic Iamblichus writes,

> The more we ascend [descend] to the heights [depths] and identify with primal entities in form and essence, the more we raise [lower] ourselves up [down] from particulars to universals, the more we discover the eternal union (*heterosin aidian*) that exists there and behold it as preeminent and dominant, containing around and within itself otherness and multiplicity (*heteroteka kai to plethos*).[15]

The bracketed words replace his path of ascent with our equivalent path of descent. Ascent implies effort, while descent conveys relaxation, which is consistent with our theme of the mind falling into itself and the journey of "waking down." Higher, once again, is replaced with inner. After listening to several hundred people come out of dark retreat touting its transformative power, I kept hearing variations on the same curative theme. Wholeness. Integration. Unity. Completeness. Harmony. All synonyms for various experiences of nonduality. Philosopher David Bentley Hart writes, "All *final* answers are in some way monistic, or they aren't final. The many must become the one, the dual must become the single, the complex must become the simple if reason is to reach the answers it seeks."[16]

One person after another talked about some level of finding themselves, healing their anxiety, mending their trauma, integrating a loss, restoring a relationship, recovering an insight, repairing a broken heart, curing one disorder after another, each one an echo of the narrative of unity, each one a step on the path to the primordial health of nonduality. "I've never felt so complete and whole" is a common response. Nondual teacher Rupert Spira says that you know you've touched into nonduality when you experience beauty in relation to objects and love in relation to beings. Many people come out of the dark to look at the world and proclaim, "It's so beautiful!" Even more people come out and share experiences of unconditional love.

You may not drop this deeply into your broken being and repair every fracture in your first dark retreat, but darkness eventually takes you all the way down to the irreducible essence of your existence. The brokenness that is your relative self disappears in the dark and is replaced with the wholeness that is your absolute Self. Theologian and poet Thomas Merton writes:

> Then it was as if I suddenly saw the secret beauty in their hearts, the depth of their hearts where neither sin nor desire nor self-knowledge can reach, the core of their reality, the person that each one is in God's eyes. If only they could all see themselves as they really are. If only we could see each other that way all the time. There would be no more war, no more hatred, no more cruelty, no more greed . . . I suppose the big problem would be that we would fall down and worship each other.[17]

United States

Physical health is the result of our estimated forty trillion cells working in harmony with each other. Mental health is the result of a less articulated number of sub-selves working in resonance, or in alignment, with each other. Whether it's at the cognitive level with computer scientist Marvin Minsky writing about his "society of mind," Richard Schwartz with his Internal Family Systems, Carl Jung's work with complexes, or Walt Whitman's poetic rendering "I contain multitudes," our mind is a composite of countless mental "cells."[18] Neuroscientist Michael Gazzaniga writes, "But what of the idea that the self is not a unified being, and there may exist within us several realms of consciousness? . . . the new idea emerges that there are literally several selves, and they do not necessarily 'converse' with each other internally."[19] When these mental cells, or sub-selves, are in alignment, the result is a chorus of sanity. The body-mind presents a united front, and every cell or every self works together for the greater good, resulting in wholeness, health, and happiness. When the sub-personalities don't listen to each other, or turn against each other, or splinter apart, the result is mental dissonance, ranging from an innocuous lack of ease to full-blown mental disease. The society of mind collapses. Internal family feuds ignite. The multitudes rise up against each other.

In my experience, dark retreat, as meditation "concentrate," is an unusual form of liberation and healing because it almost forces the issue of reconciliation and integration. It's like being trapped in a packed elevator for hours. You'd better get along with each other, or you're going to kill each other. The confines of dark retreat force the splintered aspects of your being to talk to each other, to reunite, to heal. Disease takes place with dissociation. When detachment, separation, disconnection, disengagement, alienation, or any iteration of dis-traction from wholeness occurs, ease is replaced with dis-ease, and resonance is replaced with dissonance. The misaligned wheel of duhkha, or suffering, is born. We don't have the data yet to confidently state this type of process occurs with everybody who engages dark medicine, but I can confidently assert this is the way darkness has worked on me.

A functioning society of selves is one way to talk about how our sub-personalities work in harmony with each other. The parts of me that manifest as a son, husband, brother, boss, employee, athlete, musician, scholar, meditator, entertainer, joker, etc. all work in cooperation to generate some semblance of balance and mental health. "We" all associate with each other in a cordial and harmonious way. But sometimes my internal "associates" can dissociate, and the result is mental imbalance, stress, and eventual pathology. You feel this when life gets out of balance. One "associate" or "subordinate" tends to dominate the others, who no longer have an honored voice. The healthy differentiation of one subordinate slips into dominating dissociation. A "coworker" gets bossy, and collegiality is tossed into the waste bin. In the "company" that is my life, when the writer in me takes over executive control and I don't get enough exercise, have the time to meditate, play the piano, or relax in nature, I get out of whack and eventually get sick. Others in the ranks of my psyche rise up to revolt, and I'm forced to retreat into some semblance of unity, which sometimes means I'm forced into bed and into balance as I get ill. I'm centered, balanced, and healthy when all my associates have equal footing in the business of my being.

If the process of dissociation gets extreme, you can slip into pathologies like dissociative identity disorder, previously called multiple personality disorder. There's no more order in the assembly, and the psyche splinters. Workable levels of dissociation reify into clinical pathosis. It's just a matter of degree. Stay humble, be grateful, and always remember, "There but for the grace of God go I."

As we saw in chapter 1, if dissociation, detachment, disconnection, disengagement, disenfranchisement, and dissonance are the problem (all synonyms for duality or distraction), then reassociation, reattachment, reconnection, reengagement, and resonance are part of the solution (synonyms for nonduality or retraction). By going into retreat, especially dark retreat, you're entering a healing environment, an intensive *holding* environment, where retraction into unity, wholeness, and nonduality are not merely optimized but enforced. You're being forced to associate and integrate because the opportunities for dissociation and disintegration are gone. This, once again, is why dark retreat is considered a forceful method of liberation.

Like being stuck in that elevator, if you don't cooperate with yourself in the dark, you're going to strangle yourself (metaphorically speaking). If you're not kind to all the manifestations of your being that are coming up to be held and healed, you're going to give yourself a hard time. Just like in a bad dream, when nightmarish experiences arise in dark retreat, recognize them as rejected voices of your being that are calling out for a hearing and, therefore, a healing. It's a call you may not have heard in the cacophony of daily life but that comes screaming out to you in the dark. This doesn't mean you need to indulge these voices but that you hear and acknowledge them. Let them come. Then let them go. Make the elevator of your mind, which is dropping into the basement of your being, big enough to properly *hold* whatever arises.

When you stop dissociating (or otherwise trying to get away from yourself with the distractions of daily life), the process of re-associating (or getting to know and befriend yourself) naturally ensues. You begin to heal. The "dissociates" are returning to be integrated. It's as if *they* feel safe in the dark because they can't be seen and related to in the usual way. These rejected and ugly aspects of your being feel like they can make an appearance because, once again, appearance doesn't matter in the dark. They no longer feel so ugly and unwanted because they can't be seen in the same old way. You're forced to relate to yourself, to the previously rejected aspects of your being, in a new way because you can no longer run away from yourself. In the most magnificent fashion, all the repulsive aspects of the repressed dimensions of your unconscious mind come up to reveal their inherent shine.

When those disenfranchised aspects of your being come home to roost in the dark, welcome them. Open to them. *Love* them for what they are. Relate to them as the parts of yourself that have been dissociated, rejected, and otherwise thrown into the refuse bin of your unconscious mind and are coming back asking for your embrace. Internal Family Systems is a brilliant way to augment this process of re-association, and dark retreat could work hand in hand with this modern approach to enhance and amplify this level of work.

In one of my retreats, a series of painful images arose about the way I mishandled the end of a relationship. I didn't realize that this psychic material was still percolating and needed some caring attention. These images weren't flattering, but they needed to be seen and acknowledged. Instead of guilt-tripping myself, I made friends with these unwanted aspects and resolved to reach out to the person I had mishandled. Ugly thoughts and hideous emotions are still the children of your mind. Love your mind. That's where you find the light. Jacques Lusseyran writes, "The source of light is not in the outer world. We believe that it is only because of a common delusion. The light dwells where life also dwells: within ourselves . . . There was only one way to see the inner light, and that was to love."[20]

Finally, discovering your multiple selves ironically leads to selflessness. Which one of your multitudes is the real you? They all are. None of them are. The more you understand your multiple selves, the less they seem to be *your* selves. You eventually come to realize that all the aspects of your personality are nothing more than different colorings, different flavorings, different manifestations of awareness itself. The word *person* comes from a root that denoted an actor's mask, and we wear many of them depending on the roles we play in life. Multiple personality disorder, at the deepest levels, only becomes a disorder when you lose contact with the unifying light that shines through all these masks, the "pre-personal" awareness that looks out through all these different eyes. In the light of day, you forget that you're wearing a mask and lose yourself in the act. Dark retreat takes you behind the scenes, stops all the acts, strips off all the masks, and reminds you who you really are. Darkness puts out all the eyes so you can finally see.

You finally see through all the dualistic (formed) expressions as you drop below them and into the reduction base of nondual (formless) awareness. Every expression or form is just a beautiful variation on a simple theme, a formless common denominator.

When everything is re-associated, it all has the same taste, called One Taste in Tibetan Buddhism, which makes even difficult experiences easier to swallow. Because, as Jewish scholar-mystic Zvi Ish-Shalom writes, "It all tastes like God."

Cast Your Mind

We're exploring sūtra-level dark retreat, where the word *sutra* means "thread, weave" (from the root *siv*, "to sew"). Sūtra is a thread that *holds* things together and is connected to the word *suture*. Whether it's working our way down, stitch by stitch, repairing all the higher-level cuts in reality, or dropping all the way down to the primordial gash, darkness has remarkable capacities to heal because of its remarkable ability to unite. If we can heal the primordial fracture of self and other, mending duality at its root, every other fracture that ripples from this primal rupture is eventually healed.

Dark retreat is like a healing cast for your splintered mind and broken heart. It places a big dharmic *hold* on everything. When you break your leg, the orthopedic surgeon brings the fractured pieces back together, then forces them to stay together by placing your leg in a stabilizing cast. Once again, disease is associated with dismembering; healing is all about remembering. Dark retreat is a forceful method of remembrance, a tough love technique for healing at physical, psychological, and spiritual levels. The intense confines of this voluntary cast force you to unite with the broken aspects of your being. You feel the restrictions of the cast and the ego's insatiable desire to fracture everything as the pressure to move or break away from what's happening. Ego resists this cast because it lives on movement and the ensuing fractures. Dark retreat heals the fractures as it firmly *holds* the insatiably outward-bound ego.

This is why some people go stir-crazy in the dark as the healing pressures mount. Part of them doesn't want to heal. The egoic aspect of their identity keeps stirring things up, fracturing things, relentlessly making a mess of everything because the ego knows that if it slows down, stops, and puts a *hold* on itself, it is going to disappear. The ego is duality personified. Distraction in living form. You can't have a self (ego) without dis-tracting into other. So the ego keeps splitting reality into two as if its life depended on it. Because it does. Neuroscientist Ruben Laukkonen says, "Resting in the present moment is annihilation."[21] For the ego, "move it or lose it" is a life and death affair that takes on new meaning in the confines of the dark.

Look at your mind in deep introspection, in regular meditation, or in the magnified meditation of darkness, and notice how it always breaks away from the present moment and how quickly the fracturing is reiterated. Notice how quickly you get distracted from the original distraction and how that secondary distraction is quickly followed by a tertiary distraction, ad infinitum. Let's say you're sitting in meditation and hear the harmless sound of a plane. You start to run commentary on that sound, "I wonder where that plane is going." The first break has just occurred.[22] Then, before you know it, you start a second commentary on the first commentary, "Planes create so much pollution!" You've just broken away from the first break and distanced yourself even further from the present moment. Then, before you know it, you run a third commentary on the second commentary, "Pollution is really the heart of global warming. I need to get an electric car." Duality has split into metaduality. In short order, the plane has carried you multiple orders away from what's really happening, giving you a taste of the origin of the metacrisis.

The intense *holding* environment, the cast of dark retreat, dramatically reduces your options for physical movement. It's akin to falling asleep, when mental movement stands up as your body lies down, giving you a great opportunity to work with that subtle level of movement. In tantric language, thought is referred to as "movement of mind." If movement (and the resulting dis-traction) is our strongest samsāric habit, as Dzogchen Ponlop Rinpoche says, then holding is the greatest antidote. Stay in the dark long enough and the tomb shrinks into a casket, and then into a full-body cast. From the ego's point of view, it's a nightmare. You might as well be dead. But from the spirit's point of view, it's a dream. The portal to eternal life. As philosopher Ludwig Wittgenstein said, "If we take eternity to mean not infinite temporal duration but timelessness, then eternal life belongs to those who live in the present."[23] Right view comes to the rescue yet again, not to save the life of your ego, but to help you relax into death. If you (the ego) understand that the mounting pressures of such intense confinement actually result in freedom and health, you're more likely to hold dead-still as you heal.

The Greeks were onto this centuries ago. Kingsley writes, "Before the beginning of what's known as 'rational' medicine in the West, healing always had to do with the divine."[24] People who were sick would go to a temple, like that of Asclepius, and wait to receive a vision or dream from the Divine Physician. At other times, they would go to a dark space, like a cave, and lie down in stillness. "The stillness is the stillness of death, but that's how the healing comes."[25] Kingsley continues:

> What's important is that you would do absolutely nothing. The point came when you wouldn't struggle or make an effort. You'd just have to surrender to your condition. You would lie down as if you were dead; wait without eating or moving, sometimes for days at a time. And you'd wait for the healing to come from somewhere else, from another level of awareness and another level of being . . . there's no real healing until you come to discover what you are behind the world of the senses.[26]

And if you're a healer, "before you can really heal anyone you first have to know what men and women are in their deepest nature."[27] You have to know who they are before they start to break apart into dis-ease.

Distracted Again

Distraction, once again, is at the root of the entire affair. To distract is to fracture, to dismember, to forget, to split. Distraction is the origin of dis-ease, the lifeblood of samsāra. It *is* samsāra. This pulling apart is the source of so much dissing: disconnection, disease, disability, disagreement, disadvantage, disappointment, disaffection, disapproval, disarray, disaster, disbanding, discomfort, discontent, discord, discouragement, discontinuity, discrediting, disdain, disembodiment, disenchantment, disengagement, disfavor, disfigurement, disgrace, disgruntlement, disgust, disheartenment, dishonesty, dishonor, disillusion, disinformation, disingenuousness, disintegration, disjunction, dislike, dislocation, disloyalty, dismay, dismissiveness, disobedience, disorder, disorganization, disowning, disparagement, disparity, distress, dispersion, dispiritedness, displacement, displeasure, dispute, disqualification, disquietude, disregard, disrepair, disrepute, disrespect, disruption, dissatisfaction, dissent, dissidence, dissociation, dissolution, dissonance, dissuasion, distancing, distaste, distortion, distraughtness, distrust, disturbance, disunion, and dysfunction. "Dissing" is the heart of duality, and culminates in the metadistraction we know as the metacrisis.

Cut off the blood flow by cutting off all distraction, and samsāra withers away in the dark. To end distraction is to end samsāra. Moment to moment, we're splitting reality into two, generating the crises of duality every single time we break away from the present moment. Fracture upon fracture, samsāra is a mansion of the broken and bruised, all of it reducible to the primordial fracture of self and other, all of it an echo of the Big Crack at the core of our being, and all of it dis-covered in dark retreat. We no longer hear the Big Crack at the core, not because it happened so long ago, but because it's buried so far down and because we've piled on distraction upon distraction that muffles the painful sound.

So many people feel ill at ease, out of sorts, edgy, misaligned, anxious, apprehensive, unsettled, or deeply troubled, and they're not sure why. Even when you have it all together with a great job, a wonderful home, a loving partner, and terrific kids, in the dead of the night, something doesn't feel quite right deep down inside. You're feeling the quivering core of duality. Maybe that uneasy feeling in the silence of the night will lead you further into the deeper silence of dark retreat, where you will discover that by simply staying with this quivering core, you start to heal it. You will notice the healing process has begun as the quivering stabilizes and eventually fades away, and you find yourself more centered, balanced, and aligned.

Part 2

Entering the Dark

7

Keys for Successful Dark Retreat

Let this be my prayer . . . For by unceasing and absolute renunciation of oneself and all things, one shalt in purity cast all things aside and so shalt be led upwards to the Super-essential Ray of Divine Darkness.

—Dionysius the Areopagite

We need instruction in the art of seeing. Then the invisible becomes suddenly visible.

—James Hillman

This chapter is intimately connected to the upcoming chapter on how to prepare for dark retreat. Proper "set and setting" are at the heart of a successful journey in the dark. But let's start with what success really means. Dark retreat is so unconventional that our normal notions of success often don't apply. On one level, a successful retreat would be one where your preretreat aspirations are realized and you achieve everything you set out to achieve.

On another level, a successful retreat would be harvesting insights you never expected. The darkness ends up answering questions you didn't even know you had. On yet another level, what you deem a failed retreat can also be seen as success. You could be having a difficult time, wrestling with demons, facing the eruptions of your unconscious mind, and wondering how you got yourself into this situation. But with the right view, failures can be seen as success because they show you where you're stuck. It's not just beauty that is in the eye of the beholder but the notion of success. Opening your eyes and beholding dark retreat with a broader vision will help you actualize success.

Right view, or mindset, is everything. Imagine that you're on your way to a yoga retreat in Hawaii, expecting the time of your life. But when you arrive, you discover that you mistakenly signed up for a more advanced retreat than you expected. What to do? You reserved your spot, paid for the flights and room, and can either beat yourself up for not being more careful or have a curious attitude and see how things go. An open and playful attitude changes everything. With the right view, you might say, "Wow, I'm really having a hard time with this pose. Maybe it's showing me what I need to stretch." Your failure flips into a success because you're letting it teach you. If you just keep repeating the same comfort zone postures, you're not stretching into the growth zone.

As I stated in the introduction, don't try too hard to find your way around this practice, literally or metaphorically. You can go into the dark with any of the intentions shared in chapter 4, but you may also discover that you'll find what you're *really* looking for when you let go of any directions and allow yourself to get lost. You can learn a great deal about yourself, as Mingyur Rinpoche did, by putting yourself into a situation where you are unfamiliar to yourself, where all moorings are removed, where you don't know where you are and what you're supposed to do. That type of situation forces you to open and receive whatever darkness may have in store for you. I shared the importance of a properly aligned question earlier and invited you to play with swapping out the question "What should I do with this dark retreat?" to "What does this dark retreat want to do with me?"

Another unconventional aspect to successful dark retreat is realizing that surrender is key to success. Don't go in there with a competitive type A attitude. Don't try to conquer the darkness. Let it conquer you. As the poet Rilke wrote, "Winning does not tempt that man. This is how he grows: by being defeated, decisively, by constantly greater beings."[1] That's the winning attitude. You win by giving in and giving up. Victory is letting the darkness penetrate you. Let it in. As we've seen, a host of gods and deities are waiting for you in the dark. On one level, they are waiting to greet you. But on a deeper level, they are there to lovingly defeat you. At these deeper levels, dark retreat is about transcending the arrested form of development known as ego, which is only concerned with victory. Pema Chödrön writes, "The Tibetan word for pride or arrogance, which is *nga-gyal*, is literally 'me-victorious.' Me first. Ego. That kind of 'me-victorious' attitude is the cause of all suffering."[2]

What's really being defeated in the dark is ignorance. You're not trying to defeat the ego because the ego doesn't really exist. It's just a funny way of looking at things. Inner work is about transcending (defeating) but including the ego. Ego is a necessary stage of development. When you transcend this stage, you still have access to it. It's like growing from age eighteen to age nineteen. You don't defeat age eighteen. You include it while going beyond it. You can still act like an eighteen-year-old when you need to communicate with others at that stage, but you've grown beyond.

Another key to success is learning from your missteps, from all the physical and metaphysical things you bump into in the dark. My teacher Khenpo Tsültrim Gyamtso Rinpoche said, "Erring and erring we walk the unerring path."[3] I have made many mistakes in dark retreat, but each mistake became a teachable moment. Friction creates the pearl. In one early retreat, I was way too tight, trying to do things perfectly, and the darkness had a talk with me about loosening up. In another retreat, I didn't spend enough time honoring my body with yoga and exercise and started to slip into dissociation. At yet another retreat, the processed food I brought quickly let me know this sort of junk doesn't lend itself to mental ease. Many of my missteps have come together in the form of this book, to keep you from making them. If mistakes are so wonderful, am I contradicting myself in writing this book, which has the aspiration to prevent you from making mistakes? Don't worry; I have no doubt in your capacity to make your own mistakes! Perhaps this book will allow you to smile at them and hold them in proper regard. I, therefore, wish you a rich and *bumpy* ride in the dark.

Go with the Flow

Another key to successful retreat is having an open and flexible attitude. Blessed are the flexible, for they are never bent out of shape. Martial artist Bruce Lee said, "Be like water making its way through cracks. Do not be assertive but adjust to the object, and you shall find a way around or through it. If nothing within you stays rigid, outward things will disclose themselves."[4] To "be like water" is an invitation to be fluid and formless. Don't trap yourself in rigid mindsets. Even though "set" is important in the "set and setting" adage, don't be too set in your approach to darkness. Adapt to situations as they arise.

Once again, by putting yourself in solution, you open yourself to solutions. You're more open and willing to receive whatever comes your way. By putting yourself in suspension—by suspending all your outlooks, narratives, and beliefs; by interrupting your life and putting everything on *hold* in the dark—you're allowing insights to arise. Put something into water, into solution, and sooner or later, it dissolves and becomes the solution.[5]

When Bruce Lee was training, he realized that no matter how hard he punched water, he could never hurt it. Nothing in dark retreat can hurt you if you allow yourself to be like water. The blows have nothing to hit and no place to land. Dark retreat, being so elemental, returns you to the elemental nature of things. Water is one of the five irreducible elements, along with earth, fire, wind, and space. These elements are archetypes, and dark retreat eventually returns you to the archetypal nature of everything, including the nature of your own being. In darkness, you'll learn how the water principle of adaptability and fluidity applies to every dimension of life and helps you flow into and out of retreat.

Laughter

Humor, which comes from a root that means "liquid," goes a long way in the dark. One of the best things you can do for a successful retreat is to liquify, and humor expresses that liquidity. Don't take anything too seriously, especially yourself. And don't take dark retreat too seriously either. If you do, it may pull some tricks on you and force you to lighten up. Taking or grasping whatever arises is the only real mis-take, so don't grasp after anything. Releasing your grip is one way to practice being like water. The highest form of liberation is called "self-liberation," which means that if you just leave things alone, they almost always take care of themselves. Self-liberation is like writing on water. You can't write on water because nothing sticks. You can't leave a trace in a liquid environment.

A massive problem in life, which really comes to light in the dark, is taking things so bloody seriously. I am not saying we shouldn't take global warming, political upheaval, social unrest, or any other form of dis-ease seriously, but if we take anything too seriously, we end up taking it literally. We end up reifying things, and that will take us down. Reification is the opposite of liquidity and the essence of "endarkenment." Instead of lightening up, we take ourselves down whenever we solidify things and freeze the flow of life. If that thought that comes up is taken too seriously, you will fall into a ruminative think-hole. If that vision that comes up is taken too solidly, it will freak you out. If that dream that arises is solidified, you'll transform it into a nightmare. Reification, or literalism at any level, is crazy making. The power of humor—of breaking up in laughter, cracking up after a joke, or splitting your gut in hysterics—reveals the wisdom of liquidity and levity, a core feature in the lightening up at the heart of enlightenment. Successful retreat is about developing the vision that allows you to see through the cracks of whatever arises.

I've listened to every post-retreat interview on every dark retreat center's website, and I continue to be struck by how often tears and laughter are the first response, upon coming out of darkness. Reality is touched through tears and laughter. Whether it's breaking down or cracking up, it's the breaking and the cracking that are important. The breaking up of our storylines, the cracking in the armor of our defenses—darkness does whatever it takes to get through to you.

Good Eyesight

Dark retreat nurtures a type of X-ray vision, which can be cultivated in advance to facilitate successful retreat. If we can learn how to see through things before we enter darkness, our experience will be lighter. The notion of "right view" is critical at so many levels of dark practice. Here, it refers to the view of dereification, the ability to see through the solidity of whatever arises. If wrong view is reification, or literalism, the right view is dereification, or deliteralism. Returning to our water metaphor, reification is freezing whatever arises, dereification is the deicing. What does ice melt into? Water, my friend. Something rock-solid and potentially harmful transforms into something nourishing and refreshing.

The deicing is part of what makes dark retreat challenging. Until we do inner work, we have no idea how frozen we've become and how stuck we are at outer levels. You may not make this discovery at the outset, but as the temperature rises in retreat, darkness reveals how contracted and iced up you've become. If your fingers and toes are frozen solid on a bitterly cold day, they can hurt like hell when things warm up and start to defrost. If you understand what's happening, you're more likely to tolerate the deicing. The more you reify things, the heavier they get, the more they get you down, and the more it hurts to thaw. Ice is heavy. Part of the enlightenment process is melting things back to their original fluid (or empty) nature.

One retreatant, after three days in the dark, said, "Once I decided that I had the permission to be soft and that I don't have to push through everything, I found a lot of acceptance. I have never been given that permission, and I didn't even know I needed it. I probably haven't accepted anything ever. Probably because of the anxiety, and because of the lack of being able to be soft around things, and to be fluid, I've just fought so hard to not feel things."

The main preliminary practice for tantric dark retreat is called trekchö, or "cutting through." It consists of a set of dereifying practices that show you how to cut through any appearance, no matter how solid it appears. You don't have to do these practices to have a successful sūtra-level dark retreat, but you would do well to take the spirit of trekchö with you into the dark. In the medical world, a good X-ray, seeing what's going on below the surface, can be lifesaving. The X-ray vision nurtured in the dark can save your mental life. When you come out of retreat, you can then use that penetrating insight to help others. X-ray eyes help you see through people and situations—through the folly of samsāra altogether—bringing benefit to others because you finally know what's really going on.

Willingness to Be Exposed

A closely allied ingredient for successful retreat is the willingness to be opened and exposed. It's another beautiful irony of going blind in the dark. You turn that X-ray vision back onto yourself, detecting, diagnosing, and then curing all sorts of fractures (dualities) you didn't even know you had. It's a form of vipashyanā, or insight meditation. Agreeing in advance to be so opened and exposed is part of the dark retreat contract. When you go to your doctor or therapist to be healed, exposing yourself physically or psychologically is part of the deal. That's why I encourage honest reflection before going into retreat. Why are you really doing this? What do you hope to see? Are you willing to accept what you see? It takes a willing attitude to see the full spectrum of your being, including your shadow sides.

Remember that dark retreat is more laxative than sedative. The healing begins when the laxative kicks in and you start to recover what you've stuffed into your unconscious body-mind. This "liquidating" process is why plant medicines like ayahuasca often involve purging. Throwing up or crapping out represents bringing things up and out from the bowels of your being. A successful dark retreat means being willing to have the shit blessed out of you. If you relate to the crap as a blessing, it becomes one.

Willingness to Be Loved

All the battering, deicing, detoxifying, and defeat that accompany dark retreat sounds brutal. Who in their right mind would subject themselves to this? Having the right view is critical in understanding the real victory that comes after all this surrender. What's being defeated is fake news, deception, all the infinite lies we tell ourselves. That's what gets squeezed out of you. You're ultimately heading toward irreducible truth in the dark, the dharmakāya in Sanskrit, or "body of truth," which abides at the center of your centerless self. Deception cannot follow you into your body (a principle that provides the basis for lie detectors), and neither can it follow you into the dark. If it does, that's part of what gets blessed out of you.

It's beyond our scope to unpack the nuances of the dharmakāya; suffice it to say that it's another word for unconditional love. You're ultimately heading into love in the dark, and realizing this will help you handle any difficulty along the way. A central theme of inner work in general and meditation in particular is openness. My favorite definition of meditation is "habituation to openness."[6] Dark retreat, as a meditation accelerator, catalyzes the opening and, therefore, enhances our experience and expression of love. Look below any experience of love and you will find openness, which starts by opening to yourself, learning how to love yourself. One retreatant, after three days in the dark, shared:

> I have so much courage now to feel things. I love every part of me just the way it is. Putting love into all those different parts of myself, I feel like so much more of a complete person. I can turn a new page now. I didn't realize I was waiting for myself to meet myself. Whatever comes in, I'm just going to embrace it. I'm going to allow myself to receive all those parts of me that I had walled off. I'm willing to receive love to all those parts I have cut off from myself. This is what balance feels like: when you let love into yourself.

Look at your own experience. How do you feel when you're contracted? Probably irritable, impatient, aggressive, self-conscious, and not very loving. There's always some level of dissing going on with every iteration of contraction. These contractions range from gross to subtle to super subtle. Gross-level contractions would include feelings like fear, panic, terror, anger, and intense self-consciousness; more subtle contractions include criticism and complaint, reactivity and judgment, stress and tension; and super-subtle contractions include things like gossip, grasping, attachment, and the biggie: distraction. We'll learn about many more in the pages ahead. Once you're sensitized to them, you'll discover contractions everywhere.

Conversely, how do you feel when you're open? If you're like me, you feel more tender, sensitive, caring, and receptive. In other words, you feel the qualities of love. Love is the natural consequence of openness. This is why the practice of metta, or loving-kindness toward yourself, is one of the best practices to prepare for dark retreat, to express toward yourself while you're in retreat, and to work with for integrating the retreat. If you know you're going to fall into love when you release your grip on all the contractions that arise in the dark, you're much more willing to let go. You're more willing to allow yourself to fall apart if you know you're falling into love. Another retreatant shared, "I was so at war with myself. I had no idea. After being in there and being with myself—being on my own side—I felt waves of self-love. I don't think I've ever known that. I don't think I can ever recall a time in my life when I've loved myself that way."

I came out of one retreat so open, so in love with the world, that I had to be mindful of my speech. Before my old habits came crashing back and closed me down, I found myself spontaneously saying, "I love you," to all sorts of people. In hindsight, it was almost embarrassing. Several people, startled by my openness, didn't know how to respond. The deicing that took place in the dark melted my defenses, and I honestly couldn't help myself. Dark retreat, once again, is about emergence. This applies to postretreat, as expressions of goodness, kindness, generosity, and love that were harvested in the dark spontaneously emerge when you return to the light.

On one level, more than anything, we want to be loved and to love. But on another level, we're afraid of it. Because love requires that we open, and openness makes us vulnerable. But from the vulnerability comes the invincibility. Space, after all, is unassailable. When it feels like darkness is putting the squeeze on you, trying to penetrate you, let it in and realize it's just trying to make love to you.

8

Getting Started

And now go, and make interesting mistakes, make amazing mistakes, make glorious and fantastic mistakes. Break rules. Leave the world more interesting for your being here. Make. Good. Art.
—Neil Gaiman

In a dark time, the eye begins to see, I meet my shadow in the deepening shade.
—Theodore Roethke

It doesn't take much to get started. At the simplest and most accessible level, you have eyelids. Just close them. But you can only do that for so long before falling asleep. In this chapter, I'll offer some suggestions for beginning a home practice, then show you how to transition into formal retreat. "Where there's a will, there's a way" applies to engaging darkness at home. Be creative. Think outside the box, which is in resonance with the "outside the box" nature of dark retreat altogether. Don't wait till everything is perfect before you start exploring darkness. If you have a connection to this practice, just do it. But there's also no need to reinvent the wheel, so a few guidelines may help.

While it is beneficial to do retreats at dark retreat centers, there is great value in establishing even brief periods of practice at home. You do not need to go to a dark retreat center to harvest the fruits of this practice. The continuity of daily practice adds up. Not only does home practice stand alone, but it prepares you for formal retreats and helps you integrate your experience after retreat. Those who only do retreats at centers may be relying too much on that approach and shortchanging themselves by not practicing at home. A freestyle approach with a pioneering attitude, mixed with childlike curiosity and humility, is a great way to get started. Establish your own relationship with darkness. Go in, do your own thing, and find your own way. It's like dating. Everybody learns how to do it by just doing it. This playful approach doesn't make dark practice less meaningful or impactful. It makes it more enjoyable. Remember that dark retreat is all about exploring yourself. You're dating yourself. Darkness just provides the most intimate space for getting to know yourself.

Anxiety and anticipation are part of the game. You're courting the unknown. People are always afraid of what they don't know, so take the time to get to know darkness on your terms. Introduce yourself, become familiar with it, and make friends with it. Which means becoming familiar with your deeper self and making friends with yourself. If you just listen, darkness will tell you how to proceed. I, therefore, recommend that you start by doing nothing in the dark. Couldn't be easier. That's ironically what makes it hard. Just open and surrender. Let darkness teach you. One participant said after her retreat: "The dark is like this wise elder. If you ride its wave and listen, you will get everything." *You* are that wise elder. Darkness allows the wisdom within to come out and give you everything you need.

At a certain point, darkness may suggest more formality. A more structured practice might involve things like darkness therapy, yoga nidrā, or liminal dreaming. At intermediate levels, you can engage darkness for lucid dreaming and dream yoga. Those on the spiritual path can bring any of their daily practices into the dark and see how darkness might enhance those practices. And at higher levels, you can step into tantric-level practices like sleep yoga or bardo yoga. The (dark) sky is the limit. You could devote an entire retreat to each of these practices or explore any number of them within a single retreat. It's beyond our scope to unpack the details of all these options, but a number of resources and capable guides can point the way.[1] From doing absolutely nothing to working with all the practices outlined here or in chapter 4, darkness offers an endless spectrum of possibilities to explore.

Duration

The second facet is how long you do it. This is one of the slipperiest aspects of dark retreat, and where this practice shares similar challenges with psychedelics. Recall that *psychedelic* means "mind manifesting." You're turned inside out in the dark. What was inner and hidden in the light of day emerges to become outer and manifest in the dark. How much mind manifestation can you handle? How much of your innards can you tolerate? How big of a dose of yourself can you deal with? You can underdose and overdose with dark medicine just as you can with plant medicine. While rare, I know people who went in for three days on their first "trip," and it clearly wasn't enough. They didn't get much out of it. I know others who went in for the same duration and clearly overdosed. They ingested too much of themselves and got more than they bargained for. Getting the dosage right may require some experimentation. The maxim "not too tight, not too loose" in the form of "not too long, not too short" is a helpful guide. You do want to find your edge, but you don't want to fall over it. If it's too short and, therefore, too easy, you could water your retreat down to the point that you lose the potency and sacredness. Have you ever encountered a rite of passage that was easy?

Start small. Explore darkness in bite-sized chunks. Dark retreat is slow food, which helps with digesting and incorporating your experiences. It's about quality, not quantity. This maxim cannot be overstated. When people hear that I do dark retreat, the first question is usually, "How long do you do it?" I rarely respond to the question because it sets a bar. Bars set metrics, metrics imply measurement, and dark retreat is about the transcendence of measurement. This practice deals with erasing reference points, not creating them. The question "How long do you do it?" is revelatory of how we consciously or unconsciously measure ourselves and each other. The longer the better, the bigger the better, the more the better, the faster the better—none of which applies in the dark. In darkness, less is more. While I understand the question could be motivated by genuine curiosity, it's much more important to emphasize the quality of the experience than the duration. In a related vein, don't compare your experiences in the dark to experiences shared in this book. This book is not a yardstick by which you should measure yourself.

When I introduce dark retreat in a seminar, I play with the Tibetan forty-nine-day model. Let's do our first dark retreat together to show you how this works. Take a nice deep breath, then close your eyes for 4.9 seconds. That's it! You've just done your first dark retreat. Now, close your eyes for 49 seconds. A slightly bigger bite, but easily swallowed. Next, close your eyes and remain silent and still for 4.9 minutes. Somewhere in this time range is when you want to get an eye mask, like the Manta™ or Mindfold™ mask, which allows you to keep your eyes open underneath the mask. This is also when you can start exploring what it's like to step into a dark closet or any other enclosed space at home.

As wonderful as it is to practice with my mask on, it feels different when my entire body is immersed in darkness. Light does penetrate the skin. That's why I created my tiny dark room in the basement. I don't get the "full monty" effect without taking the full-body plunge. The ability of light to penetrate your body depends on the wavelength. Shortwave ultraviolet light penetrates 0.5 to 2.5 mm; green to orange light penetrates 1 to 3 mm; red to near infrared penetrates the most: 1 to 3 cm (10 to 30 mm).[2] Even though these distances are small, they're not nothing, and the effects of light on your body and mind can be felt.

When it feels right, take the next step and do it for 49 minutes. If this is too much, back off. Forty-nine minutes is just a playful guide. It can be whatever duration works for you. I've gone trekking in the Himalayas many times, climbing above Everest base camp to altitudes nearing 20,000 feet. To prevent high-altitude sickness, you have to spend a night or two at lower elevations to acclimatize before working your way up. If you go up too fast, the altitude becomes a serious problem and can kill you. If you feel a headache, the rule is to descend to an altitude you were at prior to the onset of the headache. In this slow and steady way, climbers can reach the summit of Everest at over 29,000 feet. Dark retreat is a high-altitude practice that warrants the same respect. But once again, don't concern yourself with summiting anything, conquering anything, or achieving anything more than spending quality time with yourself.

If 49 minutes (or thereabout) is workable for you, spend some time at that "altitude" before going higher. An exponential approach means that the next steps get rapidly bigger, so this is when you release the model. For some people, 4.9 hours may be doable, but moving to 4.9 days and beyond is usually too steep for most folks. Relax into durations that are not only workable but enjoyable. Then spend time there to build familiarity so this becomes your new "base camp." With time, you can expand your temporal base and slowly but surely climb to new heights—or in this case, new depths.

One reason dark retreat is considered advanced is that you become your own trekking guide, your own meditation instructor. Dark retreat is about getting to know yourself at entirely new levels and increasingly higher altitudes. No one knows your idiosyncrasies, your faculties and foibles, better than you. Trust your intuition. Listen to your body. Heed your heart. While incremental stretching beyond your comfort zone is good, *never push*. Pushing too hard can throw you past your growth zone and into the danger zone. The only time people get into trouble is when they set goals that are too high, then force themselves to reach those peaks.

What to Expect

By this point, I hope you realize that you should temper your expectations. Expect the unexpected. Most of the benefits arise when you drop everything, including all expectations. Open. Relax. And let the darkness do its thing, free of any hope or fear about what might happen. For some people, all hell breaks loose. For others, all heaven breaks loose. Just go with whatever is breaking and relate to it with equanimity. Openness is what allows for emergence, and it is the best way to relate to what emerges. Going with the flow is the best way to go. Emergence only turns into an emergency when you don't relate to the flow of your experience properly, especially when you try to dam things up. This is why control freaks have a harder time in the dark, because so much of what happens is outside their control. Even spiritual types, who think they can manage everything with their arsenal of meditations, can have issues. This is when they need to recall the slogan "Self-liberate even the antidote," which means *drop everything*. Go into the dark naked and let yourself be clothed by darkness itself.

Being so unconventional, dark retreat does not abide by conventional linear and, therefore, predictable principles. What happens in there is literally incalculable. You're stepping into the wilderness of your own mind, taking a walk on the wild side. It's as nonlinear as your physical meanderings around the dark room. As any meditator knows, you will inevitably run into the same old stories, the same narratives, spinning around you as you run into yourself in the dark. It's just a concentrated version of what happens in life as repetitive patterns express themselves undiluted in the dark. It can appear like nothing is happening, but careful observation of this endless circumambulation reveals otherwise.

Patrick Harpur writes: "However much we wish the soul's path to be straight, upward, and ascending, it is more likely to be meandering, full of regressions, downward turns, and backward glances. The endless, wearisome circulations . . . give us hope that the endless obsessive patterns and neuroses we are so often trapped in may be resolved by the simple act of repetition itself."[3] Every time something comes around and you simply witness it, you're exhausting the habit, or karma, that spins this not-so-merry-go-round. Eventually, you discover that "soul needs no goal, center, or rest for it is always at home on the winding road."[4] In other words, the journey itself *is* the goal. That's pretty unconventional.

Location

While a steady home practice is a complete path unto its own, and arguably the most important form of dark retreat, for many people, the next step is deciding where to go for formal retreats. I've done a day or two of retreat at home and know a few advanced practitioners who have done forty-nine days of in-house retreat. If multiple days of home retreat works for you, that's great. But a big part of dark retreat is complete sensory deprivation and withdrawing from as many habits as possible. Try as I might, I cannot achieve these levels of isolation at home. The noise of planes flying overhead, barking dogs, or emergency sirens all reach my dark room. The sounds and smells of normal household life also reach me, seducing my mind into all manner of habitual commentary. I find that dark retreats in specially prepared cabins or caves are a big step forward.

As of this writing, there aren't many options for formal dark retreats in the United States, but this will change as the word gets out. There's a center in Oregon, another in Vermont, two centers in Colorado, and one in upstate New York. Retreat centers in Norway, Germany, and the Czech Republic tend to emphasize darkness therapy. Bali has a center. Australia has a few centers, there's one in South Africa, and there are several in Costa Rica.

Dark retreat once again abides by the principles of "set and setting," which means a good physical location is important. A proper setting allows you to relax and surrender to that *holding* environment. Darkness is an incubator, and incubators require high maintenance.

Here are a few questions to consider when looking for a retreat setting. How dark is the cabin or cave? Light leaks are a common issue in ill-prepared rooms. Don't be shy to ask pointed questions about the center and the caretakers before you arrive. Can you look at reviews? Are there people you can talk to who have done a retreat there? Is it quiet? Is it 100 percent safe? I've talked to people who have gone to retreat centers where external sounds and smells were an issue. Is there good ventilation? The first time I did a dark retreat, there was very little air flow in the cabin. The lack of ventilation, on top of the weight of the darkness, felt suffocating at times. Can you control the temperature, and how long does it take for the temperature to change? Is there a fan in the space? What kind of food is delivered, by whom, and how often? For retreats of a week or more, a refrigerator and microwave are helpful. These are not needed if you arrange to have all your food delivered. In my first retreat, I had lunch and dinner delivered. I wanted human contact, even if it was just a brief "How are you?" In my second retreat, I cut back and had one meal a day delivered in the evening, with Tupperware containing breakfast and lunch for the next day. Food issues (which often tip into food neurosis) are something you can explore on retreat and work to release.

Anything Else?

In addition to food delivery, what other support do you have? Is there someone you can talk to, or are you totally on your own? Does the center have any preparation protocols and follow-up integration? Is there someone you can reach in an emergency or if something happens to the room? In one of my retreats, an external light-blocking panel came loose from big winds and banged for hours till my food was delivered and I could get help. How quickly can someone respond? What kind of plumbing do they have, and what happens if the toilet plugs up? Who can help you, and how quickly, if a flying insect gets into your space when food is delivered or if a rodent enters the ventilation duct? Is the mattress okay? Do the sheets smell mildewy (a problem I had in one retreat)? I now bring my own pillow and a light comforter when possible.

Some of these issues are grist for the meditative mill and give you the opportunity to work with irritation and impatience. Some can be quite humorous. But other issues aren't so funny. You don't have to be neurotic about getting everything perfect. A rugged pioneering spirit does help. But you also don't have to endure situations that could detract from your experience. Many centers have yoga mats and meditation cushions in the dark room; a few places offer stationary bikes or other aerobic equipment; and several places have a bathtub instead of a shower, which I always prefer.

In terms of what to bring, keep it as simple as possible. You can always find ways to distract yourself with various accoutrements, so do a gut check and bring the absolute minimum. In addition to loose-fitting clothes, I bring a voice recorder, a backup journal, my eye mask, and elastic workout bands. That's it. I've found that sticky notes work well for jotting down insights. A bullet point or two is enough to jog my memory when the lights come back on, and writing legible notes is easy on a sticky pad. Some level of exercise every day is important to me, so in addition to yoga and basic calisthenics, thirty minutes a day of resistance exercise with the bands is mandatory. Exercise keeps me embodied. I know people who bring their favorite tea, stuffed animal, bedding, and snacks. There's nothing inherently problematic with comfort food and other comfort-zone items, but check your motivation before you pack anything, and remember that dark retreat is a form of fasting. You're in there to detox from as many habits as possible. Bring what you need, but ask yourself, "Do I *really* need to have that?" It may seem a bit extreme, but play with this query: What can I take with me when I die? My mind and my heart. So just take that.

Gray Retreat

The more I guide beginners into dark medicine, the more I recommend starting formal retreat practice with a gray, or mixed, retreat. Instead of a total lockdown into darkness, which can be intimidating, a gray retreat is about weaving in and out of the darkness at your own pace. This is not a lesser form of retreat but a more relaxed way of exploring darkness. A gray retreat allows you to titrate the darkness, consuming as much as you're able to digest. Get acquainted with darkness on your terms. Try it on for size and see how it fits. How does thirty minutes fit your style? An hour? An afternoon? A full day? Gray retreats are also a great way to explore your relationship to all three zones, especially the stretch from your growth zone into the risk zone.

While dark retreat can appear extreme to outsiders, a practice for fanatics, always remember that it's not about being hard on yourself but about being soft on yourself. In a gray retreat you go into the dark, stay in as long as it feels right, then come out or flip on the lights if it gets too uncomfortable. What "too uncomfortable" means will be explored in chapter 14. Dark medicine is truth serum. It's about being true to yourself, honest with your experiences, and above all, gentle with yourself. One retreatant said, "Just being in that much space, to just be everything I am, without anything receding from me or coming for me. Just being there. Maybe it taught me how to be a friend unto myself. Which I then did."

If you start to feel uncomfortable in the dark, I recommend that you feel into the discomfort for a bit. It's like breathing into an intense yoga pose. You're assuming new physical, mental, and spiritual asanas in the dark, and like any new pose, it can take some time to work your way into it. Instead of impulsively alleviating the discomfort and distracting back to your comfort zone, stay with the discomfort. Feel the stretch, but don't feed it with your commentary or judgment. Be curious. Explore the unease in the ways outlined in this book, which will help you establish a new relationship to it.

How long you do this is up to you. It could take a few minutes or even longer. If the unease persists or worsens, do what you need to do to relieve it. In my first retreat, I would sometimes step outside at night with my mask on just to feel the cool air and hear distant sounds. Sometimes, just a few minutes of a break will do it; other times, a few hours or even longer. The notion of "fresh start" is important for any form of inner work. Trust yourself, and *never ever push*. "When in doubt, leave it out" is a healthy adage for beginners.

One retreatant openly shared her experience in trying to do three solid days in the dark: "At first, it was really disappointing. Thinking you have done all this work on yourself, healed a lot of things, and to be confronted with how much more there still was [to work on]. I let softness be there, I let vulnerability be there, I let myself be afraid. Then I let myself turn on the light when I needed it. It's okay to turn on the light. It's okay. Sometimes you need to." It's more than okay! It's a sign of intelligence and an expression of loving-kindness toward yourself.

What Do You Do?

You can engage darkness in many ways, as we have seen. The following are suggestions to get things started at home, tips that also apply for going into formal retreat. If you've never worked with dark practice, I recommend that for the first few weeks of home practice, you don't set any agenda. Go dark and see what happens. One retreatant shared: "I don't know if there are words. It's so wonderful to just *be*. I have such gratitude for giving myself the opportunity to face all of it, all of me, every bit. Every bit I've judged, every bit I've loved, and just be with it. All those things that mattered so much before I got into the dark became so small." If there's a mantra for this practice, it would be "open . . . relax." You can let this mantra perfume your time in the dark, or if it feels right, go ahead and repeat it overtly when you're in retreat. It's similar to the instructions for how to approach a psychedelic session: "trust and surrender." If you can do that, darkness will take care of the rest. (We'll elaborate on this theme in chapter 9, in the sections on mindfulness and metta.)

You can see the irony of providing more instruction. But without some guidance, the instruction to "do nothing," "just open," or "simply be" might be too open, and spaciousness flips into spaciness.

You can see how subtle this gets because even self-observation, or the cultivation of witness awareness, implies that you're witnessing and observing, which is doing something. Trust your experience. Another practitioner shared: "I spend so much time in my life making things happen. And needing to do things, to be perceived as successful, as lovable, as worthy. Not anymore, that's for sure."

Another guideline, always worth reiterating, is to stay embodied. It's easy to get lost in headspace, to spin out in rumination, or to fall into think-holes in the dark. If you find yourself getting sucked into the draft of mental content, smile at that, let it go, and drop back into your body. Trauma therapist Bessel van der Kolk writes, "Only by getting in touch with your body, by connecting viscerally with your self, can you regain a sense of who you are, your priorities and values."[5] A beginner's mind is a childlike mind, playful and inquisitive. And children are very embodied. One thing I often do in my retreats is take an ice-cold shower. I enjoy cold plunges in general, the rush of the dopamine release (some studies noted up to a 250 percent increase), and because I'm so deeply in touch with my body in the dark, a cold shower gets super cold. I playfully challenge you to keep an emotional upheaval alive when you're taking a cold plunge. The intense sensory impact hurls you into your body and out of your ruminating head.

If these open-ended approaches are not what you're after, that's totally fine. Use darkness anyway you like. Set the aspiration or intention for what you'd like to get out of the dark, work with the ancient principles of incubation, and see what happens.

9

How to Prepare for Dark Retreat

> I wish I could show you when you are lonely or in darkness the astonishing light of your own being.
>
> **—Hafiz**

> The visible exhausts me. I am dissolved in shadow.
>
> **—Theodore Roethke**

There are two ways to prepare for dark retreat. The first, which I emphasized in the last chapter, is to do nothing. Go in with a sense of curiosity and see what happens. Paraphrasing the poet Antonio Machado, "Traveler, there is no path. The path is made by walking." There's not a lot of walking going on in the dark, so on one level, there is literally "no path" in there. One retreatant, after three days in the dark, said: "Show up. Forget everything you've learned in the past. Let the darkness teach you. Allow yourself to receive whatever it shows you because darkness will show you the path. If you think you already know the path, you're not going to do well in here. Just have the courage and willingness to receive whatever shows up. I just opened up. When you do that, darkness will do its thing."

The way of "no way" has traditional support. In the East, Kashmir Shaivism speaks of "the path of no path," or anupāya ("without means"), which refers to the spontaneous realization that occurs without effort. Buddhism talks about the highest form of practice in terms of "nondistracted nonmeditation." Advaita Vedanta teacher Rupert Spira says, "The highest teaching is no teaching, no teacher, no effort, no practice."[1] A perfect summary of the spirit of dark retreat.

In the West, Parmenides and Socrates, the fathers of Western philosophy, understood that true knowledge, according to Peter Kingsley, "involved having your whole being turned upside down until you no longer knew if you were coming or going. Socrates used to talk about aporia, or 'pathlessness,' about watching every familiar sense of direction vanish."[2] You already have everything you need. You just need to dis-cover that. After three days in darkness, one retreatant shared: "Everything that I ever look for is already there. It's just I'm always looking for it outside of me. That is so fucking crazy! When I'm there and I tap into it, I know it's there. And it feels so good. I feel I don't need anything else. But then, when I want to leave my body (I guess that's what it is), that's when I start feeling the unhappiness and dissatisfaction and the striving and the needing to feel whole again—which is fucking insane because you know where you need to go! But you so easily forget."

I recognize the irony of offering directions in this book when at an absolute level, getting no direction is the best direction. But who says we can't hold both views simultaneously? This more flexible and open stance is referred to as dialetheism, a fancy word for a nondualistic view where contradictory truths can be *held* at the same time.[3]

When I enter my dark room every day, I drop everything. Every spiritual technique, every meditation I've learned, every teaching I've studied. It's all left at the door. As the guardian of the gate, Janus won't allow anything into my temple. No chants, no mantras, no visualizations, no formal meditations—nothing. While dark retreat is a traditional practice, it could be the most secular and nonsectarian practice you can do. What tradition has a patent about stepping into darkness and doing nothing? By surrendering to the darkness, I make myself available to what it has to teach. I simply sit there, in total silence and stillness, and drink it in. It feels like a spiritual bath, a soaking in sanity. Marination replaces meditation as I breathe a massive sigh of relief and release. Paraphrasing the Taoist tradition of Wu Wei, "By doing nothing, nothing is left undone." One retreatant shared: "The simpler you are, the better. Darkness is simple. That's it. No practice, just show up. Preparation can get in the way. What it wants to do, let it do it." Another practitioner said: "It's okay as it is. There's nothing wrong with me. What a relief!" But it's ironically difficult to do nothing for so long.

While this absolute approach of no approach is arguably the best approach, most people benefit from some idea of what to expect and how to make the most of the experience. Even though I had some sense of what to expect before my first retreat, I wish I had known more and been better prepared. What might I have gleaned with more preparation? Perhaps even greater results. I've never heard anyone come out of the dark saying they were overprepared.

A Buddhist adage proclaims, "Good in the beginning, good in the middle, good in the end." Many of the preparatory tips presented in this chapter also apply when you're in retreat and again when you're integrating the retreat. Conversely, many of the integration tips in the next chapter will help you before you go in and apply while you're in retreat. The instructions for what to do before, during, and after retreat reinforce each other.

Four Pills

Dark retreat invites, and eventually demands, a number of things. You can't move around in a small dark room, so darkness invites and rewards stillness. When you do move, you'll learn that you'd better move mindfully or that unexpected wall will suggest you do. So practice mindful movement now. A successful dark retreat means a silent retreat, so silence is nurtured and remunerated in the dark. The one thing you do want to run into in the dark is yourself, and silence is perfect for that. Spend time in silence now. Practice mindful speech now. Dark retreat is considered a forceful method of liberation because everything is so concentrated, but it doesn't have to be forceful if you're properly prepared.

While your dark room is physically small, it ironically invokes a quality of spaciousness. Darkness invites you into the confines of the present moment, and within this confinement is real freedom. The mind and heart ironically expand when they're pinned down to the present moment. Tenzin Wangyal Rinpoche talks about the "three pills" of stillness of body, silence of speech, and spaciousness of mind, to which I've added the fourth pill of slowness. Adaptation is the key to evolution, and darkness compels you to adapt in order to survive, let alone thrive. To thrive in the dark is to abide by the principles of stillness, silence, spaciousness, and slowness. Start to unplug from the relentless speed, noise, and congestion of your life before darkness forces the issue.

Unplug to Recharge

Depending on how long you intend to stay in retreat, take some time to get into it. If you're going in for an afternoon or a day, you may not need to work your way in, unless it feels like the right thing to do. But if you're going in for three or more days, take a day to slow down and settle once you arrive at your cabin or cave. Otherwise, the contrast can be jarring. I didn't take my own advice on one retreat, and I felt like a speeding Porsche slamming into quicksand. Hitting the darkness at such speed created a whiplash effect. Now I always start every retreat with several hours in the dark, then either go for a mindful walk or meditate back in the light for an hour or so. Then I rinse and repeat. I go back in for a longer stretch in the dark, maybe four or five hours, then take another break. I repeat this sequence as needed as I decelerate into the dark.

The following is just my style. I start to work my way into retreat several weeks in advance. If it's a long retreat of a month or so, I'll begin to slow down several months in advance. This involves spending less time on my phone, backing away from impulsively checking text messages or emails, and freeing up my calendar. I start to unplug at every level. In terms of formal practice, I'll spend more time wearing my eye mask as well as spending longer stretches in my dark room. The idea is simple: Do what you need to do to stop doing so much!

Recall that the Tibetan word for meditation (*gom*) means "to become familiar with." Also recall Mingyur Rinpoche's comment,

"I wanted to put myself in situations where I was unfamiliar to myself . . . to explore the deepest depths of who I really was . . . to test my own capacities in new and challenging situations." To ease your way into darkness and keep the challenge zone from flipping into the danger zone, become as familiar as you can with what darkness eventually forces you to become familiar with. Things get easier the more you become familiar with darkness, which means things get easier the more you become familiar with yourself.

Dark Retreat Hygiene

As part of the family of nocturnal meditation, dark retreat abides by many of the principles of good sleep hygiene. As a former clinician and an active member of the American Academy of Sleep Medicine, I've advised many people on how to deal with sleep disorders (there are over one hundred). And as a teacher of all five nocturnal meditations, I've counseled innumerable people on how to improve their relationship to sleep and dream. The idea of "set and setting" comes into play if you want to have consistently good sleep, and yet again if you want to have a good dark retreat. In terms of sleep hygiene, "setting" refers to your bedroom: how dark it is, how cool, quiet, and clean you make the space; "set" refers in part to how much you honor and respect your sleep, how important it is to you. In brief, what is your relationship to Hypnos, the Greek god of sleep?

In the wake-centric West, where productivity rules the day, many people have a frivolous attitude toward sleep, seeing it as a necessary interruption to the relentless busyness of life. Sleep, after all, is the most unproductive thing you can do. Hypnos responds in kind. Which means he doesn't respond. Why should he? The same applies to Morpheus, the god of dreams. "It's just a dream" is a dismissive comment. Why should Morpheus respond? A proper mindset that unlocks the treasures of the night involves shifting this dismissive relationship. Instead of looking down at sleep and dream, good sleep hygiene suggests we *bow down* in gratitude to Hypnos and Morpheus. Do that and they will respond. You may find yourself sleeping better and dreaming with greater clarity, stability, and lucidity. If the deification of sleeping, dreaming, and darkness doesn't work for you, just elevate your relationship to the clinical importance of these experiences.

If we respect them, many of the gods and goddesses that look over the night will look over us in dark retreat. The Greek god of medicine and healing, Asclepius, can help us heal our relationship to darkness with the aid of his daughter Hygeia, the goddess of cleanliness and hygiene. While Asclepius is associated with curing illness, Hygeia is associated with its prevention. Better to invest in the daughter than the father because "an ounce of prevention is worth a pound of cure." If we clean up our relationship to the night, Hygeia can facilitate the call to Nyx, the goddess and personification-deification of the night. Nyx will then arrive to comfort us in the dark instead of smothering us. If we clean up our act in how we relate to darkness, Hygeia can also put us in touch with Erebus, the Greek god and personification-deification of darkness. Erebus will then respond by gently holding us in the dark instead of squeezing us. A clean mindset before entering the dark goes a long way once we're in it. This doesn't mean we have to supplicate these gods or become cultish, but that we remain respectful, be humble, and elevate the principles they represent. Remember that mythology is ancient psychology, and psychology is modern mythology.

In relation to good dark hygiene, a clean mindset means uplifting your relationship to retreat altogether. Honor it as a precious opportunity to work on yourself in such a special setting. How rare is this occasion! One retreatant shared: "It was an amazing, just amazing experience. You know, some people wait for a near-death experience so they can go into the light and have that life review. And I got to have that life review in the darkness while I'm still alive. There's still time to change and create the life I want to live."

In addition to cleaning up my act before retreat, I do a few more things that I was instructed to do before I went to Costa Rica for a week of plant medicine. I clean up my diet by cutting out all sweets and processed food. Nutritious food before, during, and after retreat supports the journey. I avoid alcohol or other intoxicants several weeks before going in and do more yoga to prepare my body. Dark retreat is truly a temple for me, and I treat it as such.

With all this said, and in the spirit of finding the middle way, I also want to avoid the impression that you're preparing for a marathon or some form of psychospiritual boot camp. If you honestly feel that you can go into the dark without doing any of this, go for it.

Remember that you're preparing to do *nothing*. How do you do that? That's why preparation can appear paradoxical. As with so many aspects of dark retreat, you become your own guide. Look into your own lifestyle and see what helps you come undone.

Lose It Now

Bardo yoga, which comes fully into play in tantra-level dark retreat, can lend a helping hand at sutra levels. For example, try this contemplation: At the moment of death, of what value is your home, your car, your portfolio, any possession, or worldly activity? Isn't that precisely their inherent value now? What seems to help in life can be a hindrance in death, or in darkness. Taking stock of anything that holds you back, anything you're attached to, or anything that weighs you down can help you move forward. You want to travel light in the dark. This means traveling with the lightest possible mind. In the end, what can you really take with you? Have you ever seen a hearse with a luggage rack? Strip down to bare-bones necessities. Leave all your baggage behind.

As we saw in chapter 3, if you don't leave your baggage behind, the psychological luggage you bring into the dark will be transferred onto it. That, once again, is what makes the darkness heavy. You'll feel the load of what you're unable to release as if it were coming from outside. Left alone, darkness is weightless. The weight of the darkness is directly proportional to how much stuff you project onto it. While traveling light is the aspiration, unless you're completely en-lightened, it's also impossible. Don't worry about your ability to travel 100 percent light because dark retreat is about working with what you do bring in and lightening the load. Worrying about your weight only adds more weight. Just keep the aspiration in mind.

The genius of dark retreat is its ability to show you exactly what you're unwilling or unable to release. That's why you're going in there! You want the darkness to point that out. It's like standing on a scale to see how many pounds you've put on.[4] This is another instance of the diagnostic and prescriptive power of darkness. It points out where you're weighing yourself down, how much protective covering you've put on, and what you need to do to drop that weight. One way to know that you're progressing in dark practice is when it no longer weighs on you so much.[5] I've noticed this over the years, as anxiety was gradually replaced with anticipation, and each retreat became lighter and easier. The diet of darkness was working.

With this understanding, you're more willing to deal with the gravity of what's being pointed out in the dark, which allows you to come out of retreat feeling lighter and freer. You can see this "bearable lightness of being" in the open faces and relaxed body language of those who come out. Furrowed brows ease, pursed lips slacken, clenched jaws loosen, and shoulders are more upright. Tension is visibly drained away. Burdens are noticeably lifted. And stress is palpably released. People literally seem to walk lighter upon this earth. One retreatant shared: "Wow! That is major! I didn't know I needed so much permission to feel, to rest, to just be. You don't realize how much armor you put on yourself. Just being here in the privacy of your little bubble in time, and your permission to just take it all off. I don't think I've ever felt my shoulders be so far away from my ears!"

Lighten Up

Traveling with the lightest possible mind has a beautiful, deeper meaning in the bardo teachings. The "lightest mind" refers to the mind of bodhicitta, the "awakened heart-mind." A person who expresses bodhicitta is called a bodhisattva, someone who lives and acts for the benefit of others. Bodhicitta is what gives birth to the enlightened activity of a bodhisattva. Zen master Suzuki said, "Strictly speaking, there are no enlightened beings; there is only enlightened activity."[6] Awakening bodhicitta in your heart is how to travel lightly through life. One of the best ways to prepare for the dark, and help you when you're in it, is to do your retreat for the benefit of others. It's a more advanced motivation that leads to more advanced realization. At tantric levels of dark retreat, bodhicitta is mandatory.

Everything lightens up when you do it with love and compassion. Things only get heavy when you're burdened with the weight of self-centeredness. Things only get dark (lower-phase darkness) when you're too full of yourself. It's natural to think about things like: "How am *I* going to do in there?" "Is it going to be difficult for *me*?" "What can *I* do to prepare?" But don't get too carried away with yourself. Replace self with other, selfishness with selflessness, and watch everything lighten up. When I'm feeling down in the dark, I flash the spirit of bodhicitta to lighten up the space. The breakdown of the duality between self and other is one result of dark retreat and a potent preparation for it. Bodhicitta lays down a red carpet leading into your dark room and provides the softest floor covering when you're in it.

Looking back over my retreats, I've noticed a definite progression in my motivation. I've matured from "I'm doing this for myself" to "I'm not *just* doing this for myself" to "I'm *not* doing this for myself."[7] It's that alignment issue again. This world is not about me, but it can't happen without me. And it's not about you, but it can't happen without you. Suzuki Roshi said that if it's not paradoxical, it's not true.

The evolution of doing dark retreat for myself to doing it for others has been one of the greatest enlightening experiences of all my retreats. Transitioning from self to others was such a massive relief! It's a tiny switch with tectonic implications. Bodhicitta now gets me into retreat, motivates me to keep going while in retreat, and inspires me to keep coming back to retreat. I'm willing to deal with the purification, the fasting, and all the stretching for you. I cannot overstate the importance of this transition for my own journey. Each retreat got easier and easier precisely because there was less and less of me. If you really want to make dark retreat easier for yourself, don't do it for yourself.

Meditation

Having the right view of dark retreat is the best general preparation. With the right view, or mindset, you can handle anything. Next to that, establishing a healthy relationship to your mind in advance can help because the mind lights up in the dark. Look what happens when you turn off the lights and hit the sack every night. Your mind stands up as your body lies down. Dark retreat is "psychedelic," or "mind manifesting," in this regard. The biggest problem in darkness is overdosing on yourself. How much of your mind can you handle? Meditation helps you get the dosage right by inviting you to spend concentrated time with yourself now. You prevent overdosing by becoming familiar with yourself (the very definition of meditation, or gom in Tibetan) in advance. Meditation is the art of getting to know your mind. If you don't like the word *meditation*, replace it with *contemplation*, *prayer*, *introspection*, or any form and term for inner work that help you relate to yourself.

Take a close look at your experience and you will see that you are *always* working with your mind, as we saw in chapter 5. Can you think of a single experience that isn't mediated by the mind? Experience without mind is impossible. Now, take a closer look and you'll see that you're either relating *to* your mind or *from* it. Relating from it is no relationship at all. That's your usual habitual reactivity, an unskilled relationship that yanks you hither and tither through life. Meditation shows you how to relate to your mind, transforming it from an enemy into an ally.

Meditation is like the word *sport*. It's a multivalent term referring to many different practices, just like there are many different sports. Almost any meditation will help you prepare for darkness, but a few meditations warrant our attention.[8] You may not need to formally practice the following meditations to have a successful retreat, but I guarantee you'll be engaging the essence of these practices while in retreat. In other words, if you're not mindful, patient, and kind to yourself in the dark, it becomes oppressive. Darkness squeezes these meditative qualities out of you. Why not cultivate them more gracefully in advance?

Mindfulness

Mindfulness is what people usually refer to when they talk about meditation, and this practice is gold in dark retreat. Darkness forces you to be mindful. If you don't move mindfully, you'll bump into things. If you don't eat mindfully, food goes everywhere but in your mouth. If you don't have a mindful relationship to the contents of your mind, thoughts and emotions will get the better of you. Mindfulness is about being fully in the present moment. If you drift away from the present and into the future, thinking about how much longer you have to go, you'll torture yourself. If you break away from the present and float back to the past, memories will possess you. By *holding* yourself to the present moment, you're actually setting yourself free.

Impulse control is connected to mindfulness and is a great preparation for any form of retreat. Pay attention to your life and you will quickly realize how impulsive you are. If you're buffeted around by your impulses in daily life, you'll be hammered by them in the dark. Sensitize yourself to how often you impulsively reach for your phone, your laptop, your tablet, your TV remote control, the fridge, the snack cabinet, the liquor cabinet . . . and pause before you act on those impulses. Then inquire, "Do I *really* need to do that?" Sensitize yourself to how often you impulsively speak just to fill the space. Then inquire, "Do I *really* need to say that?" Impulses are mindlessness in action, habits on display, and the confines of dark retreat are designed to frustrate both. Make your retreat experience less frustrating by working with your impulses and habits now.

There are countless books and online courses that show you how to practice mindfulness, and many meditation centers offer instruction free of charge.[9] Investing in mindfulness reaps big dividends in the dark.

Metta

Metta is the practice of loving-kindness and a wonderful preparatory practice. You're going to practice metta in the dark whether you know it or not. Metta relates to mindfulness in several ways. Mindfulness helps you establish a more open relationship to your thoughts and emotions, and metta takes this openness a step further. You're not merely opening; you're now fully embracing the contents of your mind and heart. Metta is also perfectly aligned with the spirit of bodhicitta. Thoughts, which refers to any content of mind, are the children of your mind. They're born from your mind and live in your mind. Mindfulness helps you relate to your children better; metta shows you how to love them.

I practice metta with this supporting liturgy: "May all sentient beings enjoy happiness and the roots of happiness. May they be free from suffering and the roots of suffering. May they not be separated from the great happiness devoid of suffering. May they dwell in the great equanimity, free from passion, aggression, and prejudice."[10] *I'm* a sentient being, so metta reminds me that I, too, can enjoy happiness and the roots of happiness and dwell in equanimity. You can practice metta without any liturgical support; just openly and lovingly accept whatever arises. Love arises with openness. Mindfulness and metta are practices of radical acceptance or unconditional love. It doesn't matter what happens in the dark when your mind and heart are open and loving.

Here's the way I practice metta in my daily practice and in the dark. Before I start my formal meditation every morning, I put my right hand over my heart as a way to check in with myself: What's it like inside today? What's the weather like indoors? It's a gesture of unconditional acceptance and loving-kindness to whatever state of mind I'm in. The practice is to feel it but not feed it. I know I'm feeding it when I start commenting about the feeling, so I'll catch that, release it, and return to the feeling. The gesture of putting my hand over my heart feels like I'm giving myself a warm hug and saying, "I'm okay just the way I am." It doesn't matter what I'm feeling. The practice is to accept *whatever* it is and feel it fully.

Swami Kripalu taught, "The highest spiritual practice is self-observation without judgment."[11] Dark retreat showed one person "the need to let go of the need to do, and just be. You don't have to constantly do things. You don't have to be efficient; you don't have to be valuable. Because you *are* valuable. I am worthy. I am loved. Dark retreat eliminated the constant need to do something, to compare, to judge. It's hard to just be. Just letting go of the need to know, the need to do something, and just be yourself. That's the magic in itself."

In addition to doing this every morning, I'll practice metta with my hand over my heart whenever any challenging experience comes up. I welcome it, embrace it, and let it run its energetic course. By *holding* it in the cradle of loving-kindness, I'm taking care of these experiences and, therefore, taking care of myself. In a recent month-long dark retreat, when some challenging experiences arose, I found myself spontaneously putting my other hand over my tummy. This created a wonderful sense of not only holding myself but hugging myself. Over the next few weeks in the dark, as more "interesting" states of mind emerged, instead of trying to divert myself from these dark gifts, I literally embraced them in this tender way. It nurtured an indestructible holding environment of loving-kindness, which generated the confidence that I could handle anything coming up from the depths of my being. Love really is the most powerful force in the universe.

But this is not your conditional, referential, or "contractual" love. This is pure, unconditional, nonreferential love. Indulge me for a brief digression. When you first encounter a loved one, there's only nondual and, therefore, unconditional love. It's purified of the dualistic stain of self and other. In that first instant, you're completely open. It's not transactional. It's not contractual. If you pay very close attention and feel into what happens next, you will notice how quickly that unconditional openness contracts and becomes conditional, stained with duality. There's a lightning strike of pure love, immediately followed by the thunderclap of impure contraction. You'll notice the thunder when instead of saying "love," you contract, refer, and say, "I love you." Simplicity devolves into complexity; the nondual becomes (a) dual. The warmth of unconditional love can then further contract into the heat of lust. If you can feel into this, you can drop the condition of "I"—which drops the condition of "you"—and fall back into unconditional love. It's yet another instance of "first thought, best thought." We'll return to explore how this open relationship to the *unbeloved* experiences that arise in darkness can transform even the most unwanted experiences into nondual love (see step four in chapter 15).

Around week three of my retreat, I woke up in the dead of night after a rare difficult dream. It wasn't a nightmare, but it was unpleasant. These can be some of the more challenging times because you can't get up, turn on the light, and distract yourself. Like it or not—and I did not like it—I had to relate to it. As I lay in bed, I brought my hands up to my heart and my stomach and just held the challenging feeling—I held myself—in this loving way. Because I was in a liminal state, specifically the hypnopompic space between dreaming and waking consciousness, thoughts blended into images, and a memory of the movie *Little Buddha* came to mind. On the night of the Buddha's enlightenment, he was attacked by the distracting forces of Māra. Bernardo Bertolucci, the film's director, depicted this famous scene as a barrage of arrows being shot at the budding Buddha. Because of the Buddha's resolve to stay gently but firmly seated under the bodhi tree, the arrows transformed into flowers. Instead of being penetrated by painful arrows, he was pelted with flower petals. I recorded the experience after I woke up and called it "The Night of Arrows and Flowers."

Nocturnal Meditations

Dark retreat breaks down the boundary between day and night, so learning how to play in the froth of liminal spaces helps you take full advantage of every hour. The five nocturnal meditations introduced earlier help you explore the nighttime mind: liminal dreaming, lucid dreaming, dream yoga, sleep yoga, and bardo yoga. As a devoted student of these meditations, I was delighted to see how they applied in dark retreat.[12] Each of the five practices follows the narrative of *transcend but include*—which means that lucid dreaming transcends but includes liminal dreaming; dream yoga transcends but includes both lucid dreaming and liminal dreaming; sleep yoga transcends but includes all three; and bardo yoga transcends but includes all four. At tantric levels, dark retreat is an aspect of bardo yoga, so it's no surprise that all five nocturnal meditations can be engaged in the dark.

It's beyond our scope to explore these practices in detail, but a few comments will get you started. Liminal dreaming (*liminal* means "threshold") works with the plasma dimension of mind that is not quite awake and not quite asleep, the pre- and post-sleep states that are formally known as hypnogogic and hypnopompic, respectively. You're drifting in and out of sleep a lot in dark retreat, so liminal dreaming comes into play in these borderland states of consciousness. Armed with liminal dreaming, you can surf your mind at the shore, where land (waking consciousness) meets sea (dreaming and sleeping consciousness). You can watch how thoughts morph into images, how those images morph into dreamlets, and how those dreamlets morph into full-blown dreams. Liminal dreaming doubles as a form of dream incubation, allowing you to seed a dream with the thoughts you mindfully maintain as you drift from land to sea.

As we discussed in chapter 4, dreaming really takes off in dark retreat. I always have more dreams in retreat, and they tend to be clearer, more stable, and longer lasting. It's so dark in there that I've had naps where I slept with my eyes open (I could tell because my eyes were unusually dry when I woke up). I have also woken up many times in the dark, in what I guess is the dead of the night (you often just don't know), to have a dream continue into hypnopompic space and then extend further into waking consciousness.

Lucid dreaming, which is when you realize that you're dreaming while still remaining in the dream, is often heightened during dark retreats. Knowing what your options are in lucid dreaming helps you take advantage of this hybrid state of consciousness. Dream yoga uses lucid dreaming as a platform to engage in a series of practices, each one more subtle and advanced. Lucid dreaming is more psychological in nature and works with self-fulfillment; dream yoga is more spiritual in nature and works with self-transcendence. Sleep yoga (also called luminosity yoga) is intimately related to yoga nidrā in Hinduism. It's graduate school level and deals with maintaining lucidity, or full awareness, in deep dreamless sleep. Awareness of absence is not absence of awareness. It's just super subtle (divine) awareness that more readily comes to light in dark retreat. Sleep yoga really comes to life in dark retreat.

All these different meditations may seem to contradict the approach of doing nothing in dark retreat, but it's ironically hard to do nothing for so long. These practices give you constructive options for your time in the dark, as well as ways to prepare for it. Instead of twiddling your thumbs or indulging your ruminating and catastrophizing mind, these meditations help you stay on track. Many other practices can be engaged in dark retreat, but this is more than enough to get you going.[13]

10

How to Integrate Dark Retreat

Some [psychedelic] journeys can be transformational, but the real gold lies in the integration, not the journey.
—Scott Shannon, MD

The human opportunity is to transform flashes of illumination into abiding light.
—Huston Smith

Dark retreat is similar to psychedelics yet again in that a successful trip depends not only on preparation but on integration.[1] What do you do with the treasures that emerge out of darkness? How do you consciously polish them or unconsciously tarnish them? What can you do to prevent yourself from losing your way in the light of the day? How do you enter and then keep going on the path of dark trekking? The distraction and rampant light pollution of our Degenerate Age are like a metastatic cancer eating away at the world. Retreat in general and dark retreat in particular put you into remission. But the cancerous distraction will return if retreat experience isn't integrated into daily life. This chapter helps you stay in remission.

Dark retreat is one of the most experiential practices you can do, but like the retreat itself, experiences always have a beginning and an end. They're unstable. Integration is about transforming those fleeting states into enduring traits. Otherwise, you can become a state junkie, addicted to intoxicating insights and meditative highs, and generally stoned on delicious or unusual states of mind. Buddhism lends a hand with its three-fold pedagogical approach of understanding, experience, and realization. We had a glimpse of this format in the introduction; now it's time to unpack and apply it.

Experience lies squarely in the center, but what you do before (with the stage of understanding) and after (with the stage of realization) an experience is everything. In the spirit of good dharma, how do you properly *hold* your experience so it matures? If you hold it too tightly, you're grasping after the experience. If you don't hold it at all, it slips through your fingers. Several of my colleagues in three-year retreat and many friends who have done dark retreat shared with me how quickly old habits took hold of them after retreat. Recidivism reared its ugly head, and they were swept away by deeply rooted patterns of behavior.

Backsliding is an issue for any level of retreat. Countless practitioners go into retreat to suspend the patterns of their lives, experience life-changing insights, and come out of retreat only to slip back into their old ways. Patrick Harpur writes, "Once the enchantment is broken by the summons of expediency and common sense, the treasure evaporates and the great Secret is forgotten."[2] What happened to the magic of retreat? Where did the insights go? Everybody becomes a repeat offender when the wicked force of karma, or habit, kicks back into gear. When I left my three-year retreat over twenty years ago, I resolved to do whatever I could to *hold* the magic of those years. I knew from many years of shorter retreats that the force of habit is formidable, so I initiated a morning and evening practice that has not wavered. These daily routines continue to serve as a container to hold and nurture my retreat experiences. Discipline, which is almost a dirty word these days, is one of the best methods to stabilize and integrate.

The maxim "not too tight, not too loose" comes back into play, and finding your own middle way is a practice unto its own. One example of being too loose is talking flippantly about your experiences. Loose lips diminish the power of the experience, which dribbles away with mindless babble. Keep your experience concentrated by not diluting it. But if you're too tight-lipped, others may not benefit from your experience. You're being stingy. If experiences are shared properly, with the right motivation and with the right person, they become a gift.

When you have the impulse to speak about any deep experience, pause for a gut check. What's your motivation? Do you want to impress others with the uniqueness or grandiosity of your experience, which only feeds your ego, or are you honestly inspired to share your experience as an offering? Here's a checklist that helps: (1) Is it true? (2) Is it kind? (3) Is it helpful? If it's a "yes" to all three, then say it. If it's not, keep it to yourself. I have worked with these guidelines for many years. For the first few decades, I didn't say a word about my dark retreats. Not because of a lack of truth or kindness but because I didn't feel it was helpful. I now realize that's too tight. After my gut check and seeing the shadow sides of dark retreat appearing in podcasts and the press, it's time to speak my truth and try to help.

We've discussed the many facets of dark retreat: how it first acts as a tomb, then as a womb, and now in terms of integration as an incubator. Many insights are fragile. Without the first hand of proper understanding and the second hand of proper integration, the infant may not survive out in the world. Your habitual patterns will crush the insights, or they will get swept away in the currents of life. Until they have enough strength to take on a life of their own and can stand up to the force of habit, insights are vulnerable.

The first stage of understanding relates to the preparatory phase, while the maturation of fleeting experience into stable realization applies to the integration phase. Many of the preparatory tips apply to integration, creating a thread that you can hold onto before, during, and after your retreat. Without these pre- and post-phases, you can easily become a dilettante, adding yet another experience to your contemplative resume or a new credential for your ego.

My traditional and conservative training is on display here. If you're going to do dark retreat, try to do it right. Otherwise, it can blow up in your face and in the faces of those in your orbit of influence. This doesn't mean that my version of right is indeed right. If you have clarity and confidence in your own version of dark practice, go for it. But there are many ways to do something wrong, especially when you're doing it in the dark. Whether the material in this book is the right way is entirely up to you. My approach may not be your approach. Test what I say against your experience. Follow the truth of *your* experience, not what anybody else feeds you. Dark retreat empowers you to trust yourself and listen to your own inner voice. But in the spirit of "not too tight, not too loose," remember the words of physicist Richard Feynman: "The first principle is that you must not fool yourself, and you are the easiest person to fool."[3]

The Plastic Mind

The first few hours, days, and weeks after coming out of retreat are the most critical and fragile. In the introduction, I stated that in scuba diving, it's important to go down slowly. It's even more important to come up slowly. Decompression sickness, or "the bends," is a very serious matter. We don't have data on this yet, but the scientists I'm working with agree with me that the brain is probably in a highly malleable or neuroplastic state at the end of dark retreat, making it particularly open to transformation—or deformation—by what you do with that plasticity. In other words, the direction you set your mind right after coming out and your ability to hold the course during those formative early days are of paramount importance in sustaining the insights of retreat and molding a new mind. How are you going to shape your malleable mind? Are you going to let your old habits take control and shape it for you, or are you going to take control and shape your life in new ways?

Using our maxim "not too tight, not too loose" when you're in retreat, you want to open, relax, and emphasize the side of too loose. But the minute you step outside, you want to swing the pendulum to the other side and start out being too tight. Tighten your mindfulness, your discipline, and your intention, using all three to create a container that shapes your plastic mind in healthy new ways. These new directions and shapes can occur at any level. For example, during one multiweek retreat, when I was fed the healthiest possible food by a caring cook, I vowed to radically alter my diet after coming out. Being so open and sensitive in the dark allowed me to feel the benefits of eating such nutritious food. I came out, bought a reverse-osmosis water purifier, got rid of all my processed food, and totally remolded the way I ate. This healthy habit has continued, and I have dark retreat, along with my resolve, to thank for this new course of action.

As I've shared, dark medicine expands every dimension of my being, opening my mind, my heart, and my body. With every opening comes a deeper level of peace. I find it painfully revelatory and equally fascinating to witness how the levels of contraction slowly come back after retreat, like layers of armor that simultaneously construct and protect my reemerging sense of self. I notice it as increasing impulsiveness, speed, restlessness, busyness, impatience, and discursiveness kick back into gear and kick me out of the openness. These common expressions of contraction are how I habitually eject myself from the temple of darkness.

A friend shared with me after her retreat that, "before the habit caught me, I caught it. I was able to catch what was about to happen before being swept away by it." For me, the middle of the night "gotta dos" return, stress gradually returns, and distractions take hold as the relentless power of habit (karma) yanks me away from the simple state of human being and back into the complex domain of human doing. My postretreat practice is to pay particular attention to the armoring process and not add insult to injury by chiding myself for falling into old ways. I witness the old habits reemerge with curiosity and levity: "Look at how quickly I fall into these deeply engrained patterns of behavior!"

Here are two techniques that help me "hold my seat," as the wisdom traditions say. The first one is to take a sip of space every time I feel the contraction of impulsivity by engaging in a one-breath meditation. It's as simple as it sounds, but don't let the simplicity belie the efficacy. I often close my eyes as I do this, but that's optional. If I feel the urge to check my phone, for example, which is always driven by some subtle level of contraction, I'll pause and bring my full attention to one inhalation and exhalation. This brief pause is remarkably effective in interrupting the force of habit and keeps me connected to the present moment. Sometimes I'll add the query "Do I *really* need to do this?," a question that is readily extended to many other impulsive and mindless activities. By doing less and less, I find myself achieving more and more. The one-breath meditation is a good habit that acts as an antidote to loads of bad habits. It's a simple way to transform obstacle (mindlessness/contraction) into opportunity (mindfulness/openness).

The second technique is to engage the counteracting power of mantra, which literally means "mind protection." When I sit down at my computer every morning, I tend to carelessly type in my password and off I go. To counteract this mindlessness, I'll recite one mantra, like the famous "om mani padme hum" (the "sound" of compassion), before getting started. I have friends who recite other mantras or aphorisms, like "God is love," before engaging in otherwise mindless activities, which helps them stay grounded in the present moment. See what works for you. The point is to *do something different*. Don't just capitulate to the power of your habits, which will rapidly sweep you away into the world of runaway distraction. Dark retreat is definitely something different, and continuing to do something different in postretreat to upend your engrained habits is a potent way of sustaining your retreat mind. Make the effort to reboot into the life you want to live.

Success or Failure

Transforming unstable experiences into stable realizations depends entirely on what you do with them. Dark retreat is filled with opportunities and obstacles. If you relate to the obstacles properly, they evolve into opportunities; if you relate to the opportunities improperly, they devolve into obstacles. What you think is propelling you forward may actually be holding you back, and what you think is holding you back may actually be pointing the way forward. The criteria for winning or losing in dark retreat is fluid. As we've seen, being so unconventional, dark practice doesn't always abide by conventional standards for success or failure.

If you relate to what happens properly, there's no such thing as failure in dark retreat, as we saw in chapter 7. What defines a failure after all? Who defines your failures? "Failures" often point out where you're stuck, so a properly viewed setback can set you forward. It's another reason dark retreat is considered advanced. You need an advanced attitude in relating to whatever comes up. I attended a graduation address given by the beloved teacher Pema

Chödrön, where she spoke about the importance of failing. The talk became a booklet entitled *Fail, Fail Again, Fail Better: Wise Advice for Leaning into the Unknown*. What's more unknown than entering darkness? Pema's main teacher, Chögyam Trungpa Rinpoche, said that the only real failure is losing heart.

When I first went into the dark, I had to really work with this. Darkness intimidated me. How was I going to do in there? How was I going to perform? Darkness was acting as a mirror before I even went in. *Perform*? Who cares about how I'm going to perform?! Who cares if I need to turn on the light or come out early? My ego was wrapped up in conventional notions of achievement and success. Success by whose standards? I heard a Zen priest once say, "There is no tyranny as great as the tyranny of success." A defeat in the material world can be a success in the spiritual world. Recall Rilke's words, that winning comes from decisive defeat by constantly greater beings. Defeat and chaos as metrics of success are pretty unconventional. When I recognized my performance anxiety, I didn't beat myself up for it, which would only have added insult to injury. I smiled at my immaturity, then worked to replace my performance anxiety with an open beginner's mind.

While a certain level of preparation and understanding is helpful, too much understanding can backfire by coloring your experience. So even the stage of understanding must be properly understood; otherwise, your understanding won't prepare you as much as it will bias you with too much information. In my early retreats, I realized that some of the material I had studied in the bardo literature had colored my outlook. I read numerous accounts of practitioners going into the forty-nine-day bardo dark retreat and having serious problems. But I didn't come across a single account that suggested maybe you shouldn't go in for so long!

It's similar to how people relate to death. We project so many negative things onto it and end up dreading our own projections, not death itself. We unwittingly deform death by how we "inform" it. It's remarkable to witness how children relate to death. Unless they've been taught otherwise by their parents, children don't fear death the way we do. They haven't had enough time to deform it. Colleagues who work regularly with dying children and their families confirm my experience: The younger a child is, the less they fear death. The less they "know," the better off they are.

While a certain level of understanding can inform your experience in the dark, a wrong understanding or too much understanding can warp it. The fine line between misunderstanding and "overstanding" is another challenge I face in writing this book.

Reminding

If the essence of spiritual practice is remembrance, the essence of samsāric practice is forgetfulness. We lose the magic of meditation, retreat, a psychedelic experience, a powerful dream, or any insight when we forget. Integration is all about retention; disintegration is about inattention. Darkness gives birth to magnificent gifts that can be heart-opening, mind-blowing, and life-changing upon delivery, but it's easy to leave these insights behind in the dark. Whether it's remembering to come back to the present moment, to stay fully embodied, to slow down, or to be silent, still, and spacious, integration involves retention.

A near-enemy of healthy retention is unhealthy grasping. It's like trying to put your finger on a bead of mercury. You think you have your finger on it, but if you press down too hard it squirts out the side. Insights occur when the mind opens and relaxes, and grasping involves closing down. So one of the best ways to nurture an insight is to reestablish the conditions that brought it about in the first place. Stay opened and relaxed. But the near-enemy here is if you're too relaxed, laxity creeps in. Once again, you have to find the middle way.

Dark retreat offers several memory aids to help you stay connected. Unlike psychedelics, you can click into the spirit of dark retreat in the blink of an eye. Literally. You can "microdose" every single time you close your eyes. I'll sometimes extend my blink or close my eyes for several seconds throughout the day as an unobtrusive miniretreat. To keep the inner lights on, it helps to turn the outer lights off, and your eyelids can do that in a flash.

When you come out of retreat, it helps to take a day or two before reentering the world. Come out of darkness the way you went in, by dipping in and out for a day or so. Notice how quickly you lose the retreat mind not only when lights draw you out but when you start to move. If light and action cause you to disintegrate, slow down and turn the lights off to integrate. Find out where you tend to get distracted, then apply your efforts right there.

Dark retreat goes against the stream of so many conventional patterns. You'll feel the force of this stream when you go into retreat and wrestle with releasing those patterns, and you'll feel it again when you come out of retreat and your old habits hit you like a tsunami. Instead of succumbing to the familiar flow, now is the time to hold your ground. Be firm in your intention to set out in new directions informed by the insights of your retreat. Don't let others sway you, and don't let your old ways sway you. It takes a warrior's spirit to go into the dark and a warrior's tenacity to stay the new course when you come out. The wisdom traditions talk about "what to accept and what to reject." Accept those conditions, life circumstances, and people that support your path to sanity; reject those that don't. To reject doesn't mean an aggressive stance but a resolute attitude. Be kind but firm. As the antidrug slogan goes, "Just say no."

Reminding yourself is just as much about distancing yourself from distraction. Being extra disciplined for the first few weeks creates new currents that will generate new canyons. Habit and karma can be used in good ways to create new patterns that will then carry you effortlessly in the new and healthier flow. Do any practice long enough, and it starts to "do you." The practice becomes automatic and spontaneous, though it didn't start out automatically and spontaneously.

Rebodying

Remember that mind and body exist along a spectrum and that you can view mind as very subtle body and body as very gross mind.[4] Reminding, therefore, includes rebodying: returning to the natural sanity and ground of your body. Also remember that the inside of your body is pitch-black. Staying in your body keeps you in the black. The power of "re-" comes back into play, reconnecting us via mindfulness and "bodyfulness." In addition to the pedagogical approach of understanding, experience, and realization, Hinduism and Buddhism also engage the "three wisdom tools" of hearing, contemplating, and meditating. These are three steps to ingest, digest, and metabolize any teaching or experience so it becomes fully incorporated and embodied. Anybody can regurgitate a teaching. Talking heads abound. But only those who go through some form of this metabolic process truly walk the talk, or fully integrate what they have learned or experienced into their lives.

Talking is easy and is associated with the conceptual stage of hearing. This includes listening to a talk or reading about something, basically consuming information. But information is not experience. As important as this first step is, we don't really change at this superficial level. We change when we feel things. We're trans-formed when information drops from the head into the heart and we "wake down" into the wisdom of our body. The body truly keeps the score.[5] The body *is* the score, as in the winning ingredient.

Contemplation is the art of working your way down into the body, massaging the information into the tissues of embodied experience. Contemplating is when you start to chew on the information and get it into your system. It's midway between a conceptual understanding and a fully embodied nonconceptual experience. Journaling or recording your experiences before, during, and after your dark retreat helps you reflect upon them and gradually digest and incorporate them. I transcribe every retreat diary and either reread the transcript or return to listen to the original recording many times after each retreat. This allows me to dip back into my experiences and recapture them, to remind and rebody myself. Without that rebooting, I tend to forget, and the experiences are never fully metabolized and integrated.

Some of the most influential philosophers in history, like Heidegger and Schopenhauer, could really talk, and there's no doubt they contemplated deeply. But Heidegger allied himself with Nazi ideologies, and Schopenhauer was a misanthropist, misogynist, and total jerk. Their heavenly thoughts never found their way down to earth. They never truly understood at somatic and affective levels because they weren't willing or able to stand below their superficial concepts.

The third step, meditating, is when you truly get it because your body gets it—and keeps it. That's when your entire being says, "Aha!" You've finally scored! To *score* means "to achieve" and "to etch." The teaching has finally been etched into your body. You've transformed cerebral data into somatic fiber. During a conversation, you can say, "I got it!" when you understand something conceptually (you can talk about it), but you don't really get it until it drops into your body, and you walk away with it. The teaching or experience is then communicated without saying a word. Your very presence expresses it. To *integrate* means "make whole, complete" and comes from the roots *in* and *tag*, which is the base that produced the Latin *tangere*, or "touch."[6] Once again, we return, remind, and rebody to the most embodied and nondual sense of touch, to that which truly makes sense of something because you're finally in complete touch with it. Even Christianity suggests this pedagogical process of integration, incorporation, and transformation when it says, "In the beginning was the word, and the word was made flesh."

A few retreat centers include a session of bodywork before going into the dark, which is a marvelous way to prepare your body by inviting you fully into it, followed by another session of bodywork the day you come out, which helps massage your experiences into your body. This helps you walk away from the retreat fully embodying the experience. To *integrate* means to incorporate, and to *in-corporate* means to embody, literally to "form into a body." Doing your own bodywork with practices like yoga, tai chi, lujong, chi gong, or trul khor (yantra yoga) is very helpful to prepare for retreat, keep you embodied during retreat, and help you integrate after retreat.[7] If you don't engage in any of these contemplative forms of bodywork, regular exercise in the form of stretching, calisthenics, or even resistance training will help you stay embodied. In addition to a forty-five-minute session of bodywork every day in retreat, I'll sprinkle in deep knee bends, walking in place, or stretches to keep me grounded throughout my days in the dark. Some European centers have a stationary bike or elliptical machine in the dark room, which is a wonderful addition. Anything that invites you into the wisdom of your body will keep you in touch with your experiences and help to integrate them.

So many different experiences can occur in and out of retreat. In terms of the body, some people come out buzzing with energy, feeling really high, which can create temporary forms of restlessness and insomnia. This is often a consequence of somatic opening. As we've seen, it's not just the mind and heart that open in the dark but your entire body. In the language of inner yoga, the channels and chakras of the subtle body open with deep inner work, and the result is a release of energy that courses throughout the body. Your body can tingle, vibrate, and even shake at times as the energy, in the form of the inner winds, flows into previously blocked areas. In time, this settles down and incorporates as you learn to receive this energy and distribute it throughout your body. Dark retreat really brings you to life by bringing you so fully into your body.

Silence

Profound experiences are often accompanied with silence. Have you ever had a deep experience while jabbering away? Experiences of depth take place in silence and can be nurtured in silence. The reasoning is straightforward: Integrate your retreat experience by reinstating the conditions that brought the experience about in the first place. If you leave your body and run up into your talking head, you're back at superficial levels and skimming again. You also run the risk of diluting your experience by talking about it. Dropping into the silent wisdom of your body through contemplation and meditation purifies dualistic concepts into nondual experience. If you don't come back up and speak mindfully, you can stain the experience as it gets colored with language and concept. Instead of integrating, you disintegrate. You lose it.

I've written extensively about transforming obstacles into opportunities. This is a two-way street. If you don't relate to opportunities properly, they can transform into obstacles. Decades ago, near the end of a weeklong ritual practice, meditation master Trungpa Rinpoche (who led the spiritual community) checked in to see how things were going. His final words of advice were, "Don't let the siddhis leak." *Siddhi* is the Sanskrit word for spiritual power. Siddhis almost always arise in silence and are nourished by remaining silent. In order for experience to mature into realization, for transient states to transform into stable traits, keep your heart open and your mouth shut. The Taoist tradition admonishes, "He who knows, does not speak. He who speaks, does not know." I interpret this strong statement in softer terms. It doesn't mean you shouldn't share things. It means practicing the golden rules of sharing: Is it true, is it kind, is it helpful? If so, share your experience. If not, keep it to yourself. A Zen master allegedly said, "If I speak, I tell a lie. But if I remain silent, I am a coward." Perhaps the best we can be is brave liars.

Mindful speech, which includes checking your motivation before you do speak, goes a long way on the path of integration. The word *silent* is related to the Gothic word *anasilan*, a verb which denotes the wind dying down. A breath-taking experience settles the winds and is equally a speech-taking experience. According to inner yogic theory, a major problem in the world today is that the elements are out of whack. You can see this with raging fires, howling hurricanes, flash floods, and other physical imbalances. The five elements of earth, water, fire, wind, and space have inner applications. This should be no surprise because you're not merely part of nature; you *are* nature in human form. As Indologist David Gordon White says, "In effect, a yogi's mind-body (or more properly speaking, his consciousness-body) complex becomes virtually coterminous with the limits of the universe."[8] Recall that thought is referred to as "movement of mind," and that movement is driven by the inner winds.[9] If you don't control these winds, they blow you away into endless thinking and mindless speaking. Wind is at the heart of distraction and disintegration. By working with noble silence and mindful speech, you can prevent yourself from being blown away from your retreat experience.

Nightly Dark Retreat

As we've seen, dark retreat is part of bardo yoga, the fifth nocturnal meditation, which transcends but includes the other four. Every night, you enter a form of dark retreat where the practices of liminal dreaming, lucid dreaming, dream yoga, and sleep yoga can help you integrate and stabilize your dark retreat experiences. Even if you don't engage in these practices, you can relate to the darkness of the night in a new way. In this Degenerate Age, when wakecentricity dominates and busyness is rewarded, sleep is viewed as a necessary evil. With this dismissive attitude toward the night, we miss out on a golden opportunity to reconnect to the spirit of dark retreat every time our head hits the pillow. By learning about the nocturnal meditations that we discussed earlier, you empower your sleep and can stay connected to the magic of Nyx and Erebus.

Community

Dark retreat is a solitary practice. You're on your own in the dark, and when you come out, you're still largely on your own. Having like-minded friends to lift you up when the rest of the world is taking you down is invaluable. Even though the community of dark trekkers is growing, not that many people are doing it. Several online communities are available, and there will surely be more. Night Club is an online platform I started seven years ago that supports all five nocturnal meditations and has expanded to emphasize support for dark retreat.[10]

A unique form of community support is available for those with spiritual or religious inclinations. Reaching out for help through prayer or supplication is a powerful way to garner support for your journey before, during, and after retreat. Many people who engage in dark retreat feel that they're not alone in the dark and often report feeling guided and supported by invisible presences. If this speaks to you, don't be shy to ask the spirit world for help. One retreatant shared:

> I felt safe. I never felt safe before in the dark. I felt nurtured, warm, like I wasn't there alone. It's like I was being supported by something bigger than me, that I was surrounded by love. To feel so much love even when I was going crazy on day three; I still felt protected. I felt so much light and love from within. I've felt that a bit on plant medicine, but not for hours, not for days . . . I was able to feel God inside of me. In those moments, I could have stayed there forever. Feeling that light, that warmth. It was the best experience of my life. To go into the dark to find myself. I could almost see in the dark, it wasn't dark anymore. It's a whole other level of transformation. Even when I was resisting so much and wouldn't allow myself to feel, I never felt alone.

Going Back In

One of the best ways to stabilize and integrate the insights of dark retreat is to make darkness part of your ongoing path. Can you truly expect a single experience of anything to effect lasting change? Because dark retreat works at such deep levels, it does have unusually transformative effects, but any practice benefits from repetition. That's why it's called a practice. How do you transform a peak experience in the dark into a plateau realization that manifests in daily life? Repetition. Repetition. Repetition.

Look at how good you are at distraction. You don't even have to practice it anymore. Distraction comes naturally at this point. You may not know it, but that proficiency took some time and a lot of mindless repetition. Do you have any idea how many times you have practiced distraction? And how often you continue to repeat it? Repetition has gotten you into this mess, and repetition will get you out. That's why some of the key points of dark retreat have been stated and restated in many ways throughout this book.

While there is plenty of magic that takes place in the dark, there are also plenty of mechanics. In this regard, dark retreat is no different from any other form of meditation or even conventional disciplines. The more you do it, the better you get at it, and the more you harvest the results. I continue to do annual dark retreats, building on the experiences of previous retreats. Old insights resurface and stabilize; new ones come forth. The mind is immeasurably deep. It takes time to explore this vast inner world, to allow all the light to emerge, and to integrate your inner light with outer life.

While my annual retreats provide the deepest transformation, my daily practice is the backbone that supports everything. Because my tiny dark room is right next to my study, I take ten-to-twenty-minute dips throughout the day to hit the refresh button. It's fascinating to observe how my mind changes during the day, and the mirror of darkness allows me to witness these changes in a heightened way. If I'm on the road, I take my eye mask with me and dip into the dark whenever possible. Nothing centers me more quickly than darkness.

I have never come across instructions for how to establish or maintain a daily dark practice, so everything I'm sharing comes from my own experience. It has not been a journey of trial and error because I don't feel like I'm making any errors. I'm just finding my own way in the dark and learning as I go. It's been a magical journey of endless exploration and discovery. Let darkness show you the way. Open to yourself. Listen to your inner voice. Nobody knows your mind and heart better than you do.

Surprise yourself with your ability to experience the most amazing things. Or to experience nothing at all. Be patient. Allow things to come to light, including the path itself. That fluidity and indeterminacy may be unsettling to some, but it's refreshing for those who stay open. Kay Larson, in her biography of the iconoclastic composer John Cage, writes, "Accept indeterminacy as a principle, and you will see your life in a new light, as a series of seemingly unrelated jewel-like stories within a dazzling setting of change and transformation. Recognize that you don't know where you stand, and you will begin to watch where you put your feet. That's when a path appears."[11]

What does it mean to accomplish dark retreat? How do you know when you're ready to "perform"? It depends on what you want to accomplish. If you're looking for creativity, it goes on forever. If you're looking for emotional or physical healing, that depends on the depth and extent of your wounds. If you're looking for spiritual awakening, it depends on how asleep you are. If you're looking to plumb the depths of your soul, the journey is endless. Heraclitus, the Greek philosopher of flow, allegedly wrote, "You could not find the ends of the soul, though you travelled every way, so deep is its measure."[12]

Part 3

Navigating the Challenges of Darkness

11

Contraindications for Dark Retreat

Someone I love once gave me a box full of darkness. It took me years to understand that this, too, was a gift.
—Mary Oliver

One does not become enlightened by imagining figures of light, but by making the darkness conscious.
—Carl Jung

My aspiration in writing this book should be restated at the outset of this chapter: As much as I want to encourage people to try this practice, I also want to keep people out who could be hurt. When speaking of dark retreat and the importance of healthy boundaries, Namkai Norbu Rinpoche said, "You go in a marmot and come out a marmot."[1] On rare occasions, that's a best-case scenario. You can go in a marmot and come out a slug. You come out worse than before when you went in. This chapter is about making the journey as safe as possible and keeping the marmots out.

Most people who do dark retreat tend to self-select, which means the population that might be at risk of getting hurt have no interest in this practice. Lower-phase darkness provides a healthy service in scaring the shoppers away. But there are people who get past this first type of screening, take the plunge into darkness, and find themselves in over their heads. Some of them wisely step out and say, "This is not for me." It's not a failure to call it quits. Toughing it out to meet a self-imposed goal would be the failure. For some people, it's just not a good fit. As we've seen, many things can grow out of darkness. Dark retreat is a psychospiritual petri dish, a fantastic growth medium where many wondrous things can be cultured. But growth without direction is one definition of cancer. The aspiration of this book is to provide the proper growth medium, or *holding* environment, that ensures metanoia instead of malignancy.[2] The contraindications listed here mostly apply to extended time in darkness, staying in for multiple days or weeks without any breaks. Many of these contraindications don't apply to a gray retreat, or weaving in and out of darkness. Nor do they always apply to supersafe home practice. How much danger is there in closing your eyes?

On the psychological front, with the guidance of a darkness therapist, you could skillfully work with some of the following contraindications as a form of exposure therapy, or desensitization technique, which involves gradual exposure to the challenging situation in a voluntary and controlled setting. But darkness therapists are hard to find. Until studies affirm or deny the indications and contraindications for dark retreat, it's difficult to provide hard and fast rules that apply to everyone.

On the spiritual front, a common maxim in the tantric tradition is "go to the places that scare you." With this tantric view, you might be more inclined to face your fear of physical and metaphysical darkness in retreat. In other words, fear becomes an indication to go into darkness, not a contraindication (chapter 16 explores this in detail). Charnel ground meditations, or other forms of reverse meditation, promote this radical relationship to intentional unwanted experience.[3] If you're a student of such traditions, consult with your teacher on how dark retreat may apply to you.

Father Thomas Keating was once asked about the dangers of meditation. He listed a number of contraindications but then said that there are more dangers in *not* meditating than in meditating. The same can be said for dark retreat. Over seventeen thousand studies have been conducted around meditation, touting its benefits and pointing out its limitations. No studies exist on the risks and benefits of formal dark retreat.[4] Keep that in mind while reading this chapter.

Escapism

As we've seen, dark retreat is a nonspecific amplifier. Whatever state of mind you bring with you will be exaggerated. If you're trying to escape from a challenging life situation or state of mind, dark retreat may only amplify that.[5] You might be able to go in for a day or so to "sleep it off" or "hide under the covers," but you can only sleep and hide for so long. Using darkness as a hideout doesn't work in the end because the practice is more of a "findout." It's about finding out who you really are. Sooner or later, you have to wake up and face yourself. And there's "more of you" in the dark. It's been said that "alcohol makes a man more so," meaning that it loosens you up, lowers inhibitions, and invites unfiltered expression that isn't always healthy. The same can be said for the lubrication of darkness, except that the unfiltered emergence here is in the spirit of health and wholeness. The holding environment is entirely different. But the questions still remain: How much of you can you tolerate? How big a dose of yourself can you take? How much truth can you handle? And parenthetically, if you can't be with yourself, how can you expect others to be with you? Dark retreat instills empathy for your partners, family, and friends.

If you're trying to escape the distractions and busyness of life—if you're going into the dark to escape from your normal avoidance strategies—that's a different story. This form of escape is aligned with the practice of renunciation. You retreat from distraction, busyness, and the toxicity of materialism to advance your spiritual growth, which is an act of courage. Recall Thoreau's words, "I went to the woods because I wished to live deliberately, to front only the essential facts of life, and to see if I could not learn what it had to teach." Or you can retreat to avoid the challenges of life, which is a form of cowardice and a branch of spiritual bypassing.[6] Dark retreat is about running toward, not away. You're retreating from deception to advance into truth.

Remember the line "Grant your blessings so that the path may clarify confusion." How you relate to your clarified (illuminated) state of mind dictates your journey in the dark. With the proper skill set, you'll be able to relate to whatever arises and transform any obstacle into opportunity, which is the work of a good alchemist. But without that skill set, an obstacle can blow up into a bigger obstacle, which is the result of a poor chemist. This serves as a reminder that when you feel like running away from darkness, what are you truly wanting to run away from? Yourself.[7] You want to get away from what's being revealed in such a clarified and magnified way. This escape act is successfully accomplished when we return to the lit world of endless distraction and the unconscious egoic agenda to essentially distract and dilute ourselves unto death.

Dark retreat is designed to break you down, to strip off all the protective outerwear. But breakdown doesn't always lead to breakthrough. If you're not willing to be stirred up and taken apart, to really shake your snow globe, dark retreat can amplify your propensities for reconstitution and make you even more solid.[8] This tends to happen when you're toughing it out and resisting the dissolution that the solvent of darkness, the black acid, is designed to bring about. You'll notice this when you say to yourself during the challenging times, "*I* can get through this!" "*I'm* not going to let darkness defeat me!" "*I* can outmaneuver this!" "*I* can conquer this peak!" Way too much "I" is what makes for a bumpy ride. Your defenses are coming up, not breaking down. That heightened sense of self doesn't result in insight into the nature of the self but rather a fortification of the self. Darkness is designed to put out your "I's." Not strengthen them.

Those who do well in the dark are open, humble, ready to learn, and willing to surrender. They make themselves available to darkness—to themselves, to the truth—and abide by the lessons being taught. It's not an overt contraindication, but hyperintellectuals, or those who think they can outsmart the darkness, may not profit from the experience. The expert, arrogant, or antagonistic personality does not lend itself to being unmasked and penetrated by darkness. The armor of expertise gets in the way. Confidence in your ability to handle darkness (yourself) should not be conflated with the conceit that you can outfox it. The earlier comment "There is no tyranny as great as the tyranny of success" can now be expanded to include "There is no tyranny as great as the tyranny of expertise," or the tyranny of certitude. While some predictable patterns of experience await you, dark retreat is about as predictable as the weather. How accurately can you predict your next thought, emotion, or mood? Dark practice is about "weathering" your mind in this receptive regard.

Don't try too hard to wrap your mind around this practice or attempt to outcontextualize it. And always remember, as Trungpa Rinpoche said, that ego cannot attend its own funeral. Don't go into the dark expecting to witness your enlightenment because you and enlightenment are mutually exclusive. Enlightenment takes place at the moment you (the arrested form of development we call ego) finally give up and "die." This leads directly to the next contraindication.

The Overachiever and the Dabbler

If you're looking for the latest and greatest transformative technique or want to add another exotic practice to your meditative resume, dark retreat may not be for you. This practice is about subtraction, not addition. Dark retreat deals with erasing conventional ambitions, not achieving them. Ambition and achievement can be an issue for spiritual types, or seasoned meditators, or anybody who hears about dark retreat and views it as the next summit to climb. Most conventional overachievers have no interest in meditation or anything that involves surrendering because achievement implies conquest. Most of the achievements in dark retreat arise precisely because you're not doing anything. You're allowing yourself to be defeated. In a space that demands rest, overachievers get restless and head for the door. Movers and shakers have to stop moving and shaking, and that's not easy.

One retreatant shared: "Being an extremist, I always thought I had to blast off to Galactagon and get zapped by this alien. That's how [my awakening] would happen to me. But it was the subtle nurturing that did it. It just brought me back home. Dark retreat is that which brought me back home." No need to go to Galactagon; just open up and realize it's within you. Another retreat participant said, "Oh my God . . . Oh my god . . . I eagerly keep running to temples and mosques, but I've never actually, truly, entered my own home."

People who go in with the attitude of "I've got this down!" will probably be taken down by darkness. While some degree of inner confidence is helpful, the near-enemy of confidence is hubris. Hubris and darkness go together like oil and water. Replace hubris with humility and darkness will reward you. Dark retreat is an acid bath for bloated motivations. Christ said that the *meek* shall inherit the earth. If we define it carefully, *underachievers*, or those who don't want to achieve anything in retreat, do well in the dark. Conventional losers can turn into unconventional winners.

Unreasonable expectations—to have visions, to see the lights, to have major breakthroughs—are not necessarily contraindications but do seem to be indicators for a harder time. Expectation is often premeditated disappointment. Replace expectations with modest aspirations and you won't be disappointed.

Dabblers and dilettantes, or those who scroll through life searching for a quick psychological or spiritual fix, are another contraindication. They might be able to handle darkness for a few hours, then pop out and post it with a selfie on social media, but real dark retreat is not for browsers or window-shoppers. No selfies allowed in the dark. This doesn't mean you need to be a professional, ultraorthodox, or superserious to explore the dark, but that dark practice is not conducive to skimming. The impatient, impulsive, impetuous, or hasty personality will struggle against the restraints of darkness.

As a practice that takes you to the depths, the greater the duration, the greater the depth (at least to a certain degree, one that varies from person to person). You'll probably get more out of a full day in the dark than an hour, or a full week versus a day. But maybe not. Quality is much more important than quantity. At a certain point, you reach the stage of diminishing returns when dark retreat can backfire. That's when having a guide for your retreat comes into play because that point is not always easy to determine on your own.

The Thrill Seeker and the Disembodied

Dark retreat is so unusual, exotic, and esoteric that it can readily attract psychological or spiritual thrill seekers. The practice is getting attention because of its bizarre nature, and ego quickly steps into anything that grabs the limelight or tests the limits. Dark retreat is viewed by some as an extreme sport. This sort of wording is not uncommon as more athletes and high achievers explore darkness as the final frontier, a place to "boldly go where no man has gone before."

From a recent article, we find this account: "[He] upped the solo exploration ante. Following his experience on K2 [the second tallest mountain in the world], he enrolled in what would become his biggest challenge yet—a seven-day darkness retreat." Later in the article, we find this hyperbole, "Meditation is an extreme pursuit . . . Many Navy SEALs have found sitting in stillness more challenging than jumping out of planes or holding their breath in freezing water . . . In some ways, meditation was the first endurance sport." And finally, "It's no coincidence that darkness retreats—of which there are currently dozens worldwide—have drawn the interest of athletes who have gotten to where they are because they're accustomed to finding their edge and pushing past it."[9]

Because it's so radically different, darkness can be thrilling for the first few minutes or hours. But stay with it long enough for transformation to begin, and you'll discover it's much more of a "low" than a "high." Dark retreat is a downer by design. If you're going into darkness to have a K2 peak experience, that motivation often bombs as darkness hurls you into the valleys of monotony and ordinariness. It's the "single tone" (mono-tonus) nature of the night, the drone of darkness, that works to get you in tune with yourself, that leads you back into alignment, into unity, into harmony.

Countless mystical and shamanic traditions use repetition, like endless drumming, chanting, or whirling, to initiate altered states of consciousness. The relentless droning of the dark works in a similar way but with the aim of tuning you into the *natural* state. One retreatant shared: "The hardest thing is just the unrelenting nature of it. Most of our daily life, even in meditation retreats, there's always the next thing. 'I'm going to meditate for an hour and then get up, and then it's the next thing' . . . In the dark, there is no next thing."

This is not to say that you can't have authentic peak experiences in the dark, but if you go searching for them, you're less likely to find them. You'll find the real highs in the lows, in the liberating and extra-ordinary fact that you already have everything you could possibly want. That's a real downer from ego's point of view. In many

Himalayan countries, you're not allowed to summit a sacred mountain. You circumambulate it.

How many times in these pages have we heard about how homely dark retreat is, how it's so utterly simple and grounding? After three days in the dark, one retreatant shared explicitly: "Oh my goodness. It's almost painful! I'm abso-fucking-lutely fine. There is nothing wrong with me. There's nothing wrong with me! [In great laughter] And there's nowhere to go!" Another retreatant said: "The spiritual path has always talked about seeking, like you're seeking something [a peak experience]. I just keep coming back to being. It just feels really beautiful to not be broken." And from yet another, "So beautiful . . . the truth is that all I ever needed is all I've always had." Dark retreat is an incredibly earthy practice, designed to bring your head of out of the clouds and put it smack underground. You must bore (in both senses) to get underground, and that takes the air out of any thrill seeker.

Another population that may be contraindicated, akin to hyper-intellectuals, are people who mostly live in the high altitudes of their heads. Being grounded means being embodied, and dark retreat gets problematic if it becomes disembodied. If you're losing contact with your body or getting lost in disembodied headspace, it could suggest derealization (discussed next) and loss of contact with reality. As we'll see in chapter 14, this is one indication for when to stop.

Psychological Contraindications

The following psychological and medical contraindications only apply to extended dark retreat, which means more than several hours in the dark. If you're exploring darkness at home with your eye mask or dark room, dark retreat is totally workable for many people. Most people don't freak out or have medical issues when they close their eyes for a few minutes or hours. You spend a third of each day in a form of dark retreat when you sleep, after all, so most of the contraindications in this section don't apply to titrated home practice.

In longer formal retreats, several psychiatric conditions could be problematic if they become amplified in darkness.[10] Anyone dealing with the following conditions should consult with a mental health professional before considering longer retreats. Once again, if you're engaging darkness with the guidance of a darkness therapist, that's a different story. Darkness therapy is always done with the frequent and direct supervision of a trained therapist.

The most obvious contraindication is claustrophobia, the fear of confined or enclosed spaces. Nyctophobia, an irrational or extreme fear of the night or darkness, is another contraindication. Being in a small, dark room could be traumatic for anyone suffering from either condition. Anybody dealing with dissociative disorders could struggle, circumstances which the Mayo Clinic defines as "mental health conditions that involve experiencing a loss of connection between thoughts, memories, feelings, surroundings, behavior and identity. These conditions include escape from reality in ways that are not wanted and not healthy."[11] These disorders include dissociative amnesia, depersonalization or derealization disorders, and dissociative identity disorder. Major depression, anxiety disorders, bipolar disorder, extreme expression of personality disorders (including but not limited to paranoid personality disorder, narcissistic personality disorder, borderline personality disorder, and obsessive-compulsive disorder) are also contraindicated. Schizophrenia, schizoaffective disorder, and brief psychotic disorder are probably unworkable as well. While rare, alternative world syndrome (a delusional disorder mostly seen in people who spend too much time in virtual reality headsets or video games) is another contraindication. If there's any doubt, always consult with a mental-health-care professional. "Better safe than sorry" applies to dark practice.

If someone has a previous history of traumatic experience occurring in the dark, like a sexual assault, dark retreat could bring about challenging flashbacks. People with a general history of trauma may not be stable enough to handle the groundlessness of dark retreat. Traumatic contents could surface in darkness, and a person could destabilize during the retreat and struggle afterward. Because of the concentrated nature of this practice, all kinds of concentrated experiences can occur. Those suffering from general anxiety disorder, major depression, or mood conditions like bipolar disorder should check with a mental-health-care professional before considering dark retreat.

There are over one hundred sleep disorders, and contraindications here would include nightmare disorder or chronic insomnia.

Sleep apnea that is managed with a CPAP machine could also be unworkable. Narcolepsy is a contraindication because its adolescent age onset is often coincident with "first break" schizophrenia, or the first episode of psychosis. Hallucinations may be intense from either disorder and could worsen in extended darkness. Consult with a sleep doctor if you have concerns. Once again, these conditions and those in the next section don't exclude you from reaping all the benefits of home dark practice.

Medical Contraindications

Consult with your doctor if you have any concerns about medical issues or medications that may compromise your dark retreat experience. Contraindications for medical issues would include epilepsy, severe hypertension, congestive heart failure, alcoholism, substance abuse issues, severe irritable bowel or inflammatory bowel disease, kidney failure, and diabetes requiring insulin injections or management with an insulin pump. Those predisposed to vertigo could have issues. Colleagues who run dark retreat centers inform me that people dealing with autoimmune disorders may not handle the stressors of darkness well, which can trigger issues like cold sores and headaches. They also share that hypertension and arrhythmia can get exacerbated.

Contraindications in terms of medications would include antipsychotics, antidepressants, benzodiazepines, insulin, and medications for sleep disorders or psychiatric disorders. With the careful guidance of a darkness therapist and the clearance of your doctor (who may adjust or discontinue a medication before going in), you could safely explore dark retreat even if you are taking medications. Prolonged darkness can alter your body's normal reaction to medication. For example, it's possible that your normal daily dosage of a medicine could lead to underdosing or overdosing in the dark. These issues have yet to be studied.

Ophthalmology Issues

It's impossible to cover all the possible adverse experiences in the dark, including unexpected physical situations. I mention the following eye issue only because I was beset by this condition several years ago in daily life, which could have seriously compromised my vision had I not sought immediate treatment. A partial vitreous detachment, which occurs when the vitreous gel that fills the eye pulls away from the retina, requires immediate attention, as do many forms of retinal detachment. Other issues include retinal hemorrhages, tears, vascular occlusion, macular bleeding, or optic nerve problems. Sometimes these conditions are accompanied with flashes of light, which means you could detect this in the dark. But not always. If something like this occurred in the dark, it's possible you wouldn't see it.

The trick here is that many people doing dark retreat report seeing flashes of light or sustained kaleidoscopic displays that have nothing to do with any visual pathology. These entopic visions, or endogenous experiences of light, are quite common in darkness. At tantric levels of dark practice, they could signal the onset of visual displays that have nothing to do with the anatomy or physiology of the visual system. The odds of visual pathology happening in dark retreat are very low. Of the hundreds of people that have done dark practice that I'm aware of, no such occurrence has ever been reported. With that said, be very careful when coming out of your dark retreat and reintroduce light *very slowly*. One dark retreat guide shared with me that she hurt one of her eyes by coming out from a long retreat too quickly. Her eyes "overheated." If that happens, step back into the dark immediately or put on your eye mask. As with every aspect of dark practice, slow and easy rule the day.

Daily life is full of risks and unexpected adverse events. Debris from a falling satellite could hit you. You could be struck by a car or lightning. Do what feels right and what fits within the limits of your comfort and challenge zones, and trust your intuition. The bottom line is that the risk/reward ratio to physical and psychological health leans heavily in the reward category. The one true hazard in dark practice is to your ego health.

12

Why Is Dark Retreat Challenging?

If you can find a path with no obstacles, it probably doesn't lead anywhere.
—Frank A. Clark

Until we have met the monsters in ourselves, we will keep trying to slay them in the outer world. For all darkness in the world stems from darkness in the heart. And it is there we must do our work.
—Marianne Williamson

Dark retreat is challenging for as many reasons as it is rewarding. With the right understanding, the challenges transform into the rewards. Many of these challenges have been hinted at throughout our journey, but this chapter gets specific. Some of the challenges are obvious, while others are not. Let's start with the more obvious hurdles and work our way down to the subtle ones.

The first challenge is that for most people, spending dedicated time in darkness is just so unfamiliar. We're mostly familiar with darkness as it manifests in contrast to light but have less awareness of how we relate to it in *opposition* to light. We fight it with streetlights, motion-sensing floodlights, flashlights, and countless other artificial lights, as if darkness were an enemy to defeat. It only becomes an enemy if we don't relate to it skillfully, or if we're trying to move too quickly, which is precisely what the human race (to where?) is all about these days. Darkness imposes a natural speed limit that we constantly violate in our insatiable desire to achieve.

As a wake-centric culture, we spend so much time obsessed with light that we engage darkness just to go to sleep. Using darkness to "wake up" is a foreign concept. English historian Arnold Toynbee said, "Death is unAmerican." It's not a stretch to say that darkness is virtually unAmerican. In our infatuation with productivity and in a culture where sight, appearance, and action are emphasized, where *distant* goals are valued (because they can be seen), we try to defeat darkness as much as we try to defeat death. Is this because darkness interferes with seeing and, therefore, reaching our goals? In our attempts to defeat darkness, we pollute yet another natural resource.

How many people do you know who have actually sat down with the intention to get to know the dark? Fear is a big challenge in dark retreat, and we fear it because we're unfamiliar with it. We're always afraid of what we don't know, so why not get to know it? Remember that the Tibetan word for meditation (*gom*) means "to become familiar with," which entails becoming familiar with your mind, with who you truly are. As we've seen, becoming familiar with darkness is really about becoming familiar with yourself. Darkness just provides the best mirror for that. The first obvious challenge leads immediately to a more nuanced one: the difficulty of unearthing who you really are and accepting what you discover. Carl Jung said, "The most terrifying thing is to accept oneself completely."[1] But it's also the most rewarding thing.

Vertigo

Dark retreat is also challenging because it's steep. You can make the slope more gradual by doing a gray retreat, but the precipitous nature of the practice is precisely why transformation is so quick.

You can reach the heights of psychological and spiritual development more rapidly in the dark, but because the terrain is unfamiliar, it's also easier to lose your footing and take a tumble. For those so inclined, the rewards are well worth the risk. Personally, I want to extract the essence of every moment and every day. Going into the dark ironically concentrates my experience of life during the day. Life is so short. I'm literally one heartbeat away from death. On my deathbed, I want to feel that I made the most of this precious life. Once again, the rapid rewards in dark retreat are not the result of how much I can do in the dark but how much it forces me to stop doing. You make the most by doing the least.

You can work your way down this sheer slope by titrating the darkness with the methods in this book, but sooner or later, you have to take the plunge and turn out the lights. As an adjective, *steep* means "sheer, sharp, unreasonable, extreme"; as a verb, it means "to soak, immerse, submerge, saturate," as in steeping a cup of tea. Both definitions apply to the dark. Dark retreat is a form of *extreme* transformation, totally *unreasonable* from ego's wake-centric perspective. The rapid evolution is catalyzed by the 24/7 *saturation* in darkness, where you're totally *submerged* in the dark, *soaking* it up like never before.

Concentrated

Dark retreat is, perhaps, the most immersive practice you can do, and therefore, it's one of the most demanding. We live in a world of such rampant distraction, constantly watering down our experience with endless activity, that we're rarely fully present for life. With the relentless distraction of smartphones, "We are forever elsewhere," says MIT professor Sherry Turkle.[2] As it says in the fine print for many lotteries, you must be present to win. We're completely habituated, even addicted, to movement and distraction. When those are taken away in the dark, everything naturally gets concentrated. It's a major reason why this practice is so transformative. Even in daily life, look at how much more you accomplish when you're focused. The concentration in dark retreat is not the same as conventional concentration, but the rewards are even greater. You're not sitting in there with a furrowed brow, concentrating in the normal way (which doesn't mean you can't do that on occasion). You're concentrated by the fact that you can't attenuate your experience in normal ways.

The intense level of concentration reveals our lust for dilution. The bardo teachings talk about facing "the bright lights" after death and resisting the temptation to lower your gaze into the "soft lights." The bright lights represent concentrated experience, or truth. The teachings on the bright lights cultivate a more direct and intense relationship to the truth of whatever arises. "Soft lights" refer to habitual patterns, and one of the most powerful habits is for distraction, which amounts to a "lower gaze" that leads us into the lower realms. Even though it's dark in there, remember the teaching from Janus to face everything head on. Avoid the face (and lower gaze) that looks down or away from what's happening, no matter how intense.

Disciplined

Dark retreat is also challenging because it invites and eventually demands new levels of discipline. Even though entry levels of dark retreat are largely freestyle—you can do whatever you want in there within obvious limits—just staying in darkness requires self-restraint. You can escape into light at any time, and the temptation to do so can be overwhelming at times. Working with that powerful impulse is revelatory. Why is it so hard to be alone with yourself? What are you really trying to get away from? If you can relate to the compulsion instead of acting it out, you'll learn a lot about yourself and how you're buffeted around by your impulses.

With absolutely nothing to do, dark retreat can be insanely boring. You can't check your phone, run to your laptop, or follow your social media feed. French mathematician and philosopher Blaise Pascal said:

> The only thing that consoles us from our miseries is diversion. And yet it is the greatest of our miseries. For it is that above all which prevents us thinking about ourselves and leads us imperceptibly to destruction. But for that we should be bored, and boredom would drive us to seek some more solid means of escape, but diversion passes our time and brings us imperceptibly to our death . . . I have discovered that all the

unhappiness of men arises from one simple fact, that they cannot sit quietly in their own chamber.[3]

If you can stay with the boredom, that's when you start boring deeply within. Relate to it that way and you will dig deep. Capitulate to the boredom, and you will continue to skim across the surface of your life and continue to feel that something is missing.

Discipline is one of the most immediate ways we can get a healthy *hold* on ourselves. Darkness imposes a magnificent set of restraining orders designed to frustrate the machinations of the ego, and of karma (habit), which literally means "action." Until the ego is transcended, it needs to be regulated and restrained. Look at Vladimir Putin, Hitler, or any other out-of-control egomaniac for the disastrous effects of an unrestrained ego. You may not be that out of control, but dark retreat will reveal your desire to be in control. Control freaks tend to have a harder time in the dark, as their ability to dictate experience and express their alleged freedom are taken away. If you have a big ego, you're going to have big challenges as ego is put under house arrest. Dark retreat is one big "time-out." By removing relative expressions of freedom, which essentially amount to the infinite expressions of distraction, you're being invited and eventually forced into real freedom—which can only be found in the confines of the present moment.

Discipline is almost a dirty word these days, but it still facilitates "maintenance of order (necessary for giving instruction)."[4] Discipline keeps the order that allows you to receive the lessons from the dark. As we saw earlier, by putting a *hold* on yourself, you're starting to heal yourself. It can seem punishing at times, like containing the tantrum of an out-of-control two-year-old, but this intensive *holding* environment is a form of tough love. At the deeper levels of dark retreat, you're essentially going to love yourself to death. You're going to restrain the ego, your relative self-sense, your insatiably outward-bound propulsions, to such an extent that ego disappears. When the ego is *held* at such levels by this straitjacket of sanity, it gets psychologically hotter and hotter in there until it eventually melts, like the Wicked Witch of the West. Resting in the present moment is annihilation, after all. And when it melts, all the energy that went into the refrigeration and preservation of the ego is released. I'm often high for weeks after a retreat, flying on all the energy. It borders on a healthy form of hypomania.

Darkness is a powerful disciplinarian. Ask any prisoner in solitary confinement about the challenges of involuntary holding environments or punitive restraints. Dark retreat is voluntary, but it can feel penal. If it feels penalizing, that's your ego feeling. Restraint can be corrective if it's properly understood. Relate to the discipline as psychospiritual rehabilitation and cooperate with the disciplinarian that's there to help you realign the course of your life.

Withdrawing

One of the gifts of meditation is that it creates a new contrast medium that allows the practitioner to perceive in new ways. For example, the stillness of sitting meditation creates the contrast of stasis that allows one to detect previously unseen levels of the movements of mind. The practice of open awareness creates the contrast of spaciousness that allows one to see how contracted we are. These meditations identify our lust for movement and our addiction to contraction, while simultaneously suggesting ways to overcome these unhealthy habits. Dark retreat gets challenging because it provides a number of unique contrast mediums that diagnose a number of uniquely harmful conditions. The backdrop of silence, stillness, and darkness allows us to see and feel things never seen or felt before.

Dark retreat is a magnifying meditation that exposes a number of faults and fractures, as we saw earlier. A host of previously unconscious and, therefore, undiagnosed fractures are brought into the light of consciousness, where a diagnosis can finally be made. It's like going to the doctor and learning that you have colitis, skin cancer, and hypertension. On one level, it's good to know about your condition; on another level, it's really hard. How much truth can you take? But more importantly, how can you cure a condition you don't even know you have? I talked to an elderly friend last week who told me he has inoperable stage 4 prostate cancer. To my surprise, he didn't trust the health-care system and, therefore, never had a single PSA screening. Unless you maintain the flippant attitude, "It's all good until it's not," ignorance is not bliss when it comes to disease. As difficult as it is to hear, early diagnosis is a lifesaver. While these medical analogies may be a bit extreme, you get the idea. To accept the diagnoses that the good doctor of darkness has to offer, it helps to have an advanced attitude in relationship to the advanced diagnostics of dark retreat. If you don't want to learn about yourself, it's better to stay lost in the light.

The enforced stillness of dark retreat exposes our addiction to movement at so many levels. This is not to negate the obvious benefits of movement and the importance of getting things done, but to point out our addiction to relentless activity and how readily we slip into active laziness. As an exercise enthusiast, enforced physical confinement in a small, dark room is always challenging. I express my need for physical movement by exercising every day, and then relate with any enthusiasm that remains after my workouts by inquiring, "Do I *really* need to move so much?"

Even more revelatory is how the restraint of darkness exposes our addiction to mental movement, or distraction. Allow me to take a brief digression into tantra-level dark retreat to show you how subtle and deep this issue of movement is and why it's so challenging to withdraw from it. Remember that in tantric language, thought is referred to as "movement of mind." There's nothing wrong with this level of movement or the natural play of the mind. We need to think to function in the world. But do we need to think so much? Do we need to spend so much time at the "movies"? Our addiction to thought, and the distraction it provides, is another signature of this Degenerate Age. Darkness reveals how we're all thought junkies, addicted to the movies of our mind.

In this context, darkness is a detox center. By withdrawing from all physical activity and sensory stimulation, you're feeling the pain of withdrawal. One retreatant shared: "Being a human hurts sometimes. I guess that's part of it, right? We're here to experience the beauty, the brightness, and the pain. We put all these things on top of it. We don't even know. At times, [the darkness] just feels unnatural. Unbearable. But you don't even know why." I'm writing this book to help you know why.

It's not just physical and mental movement that's curtailed, but sensory movement also comes to a grinding halt. In other words, with nothing to see and seduce you forward, you're less likely to move out of yourself. If movement is our strongest habit, and dark retreat puts this habit under arrest, it's no wonder things get challenging. Darkness is a forceful method of liberation because it reveals the force of habit. It's designed to disrupt things, to turn over the applecart, to flip your world upside down so things can be seen anew. Lusseyran writes:

> Blindness is my greatest happiness! Blindness gives us great happiness. It gives us a great opportunity, both through its disorder and through the order it creates. The disorder is the prank it plays on us, the slight shift it causes. It forces us to see the world from another standpoint. This is a necessary disorder, because the principal reason for our unhappiness and our errors is that our standpoints are fixed.[5]

The prank is also how dark retreat fixes, or realigns, our perception by unfixing or unhinging our reference points. We lose ourselves to find our real Self. Darkness uproots the normal expression of our fixed habits, and when those habits can no longer be expressed (and diluted) outward, they force themselves upon us. It's the only other direction left. Depending on the degree of our addiction to physical movement, sensory distraction, and thought itself, we're going to have challenges in direct proportion to the level of our outward-bound habits. Understanding this also helps us prepare for dark retreat. We can start to withdraw from this unholy trinity (physical movement, sensory distraction, and thought addiction) in advance to make things easier for ourselves in the dark.[6] Reduce the pain of withdrawal by withdrawing and retreating now.

Laxating

A less-than-obvious reason for some of the challenges in the dark applies to any form of meditation. You may not be doing dark retreat for meditative purposes, but many meditative principles apply to dark practice because both ventures involve working with the mind. One such principle is the purifying nature of meditation. Remember that at deeper levels of practice, meditation isn't a sedative; it's a laxative. When you're no longer trying so hard to create the illusion that you've got it together, you can finally relax and allow yourself to fall apart. This breakdown can lead to breakthrough. Gregory Shaw writes, "To recover its divinity, the soul must first honor its corporeality, the mud of human experience. Only then can it become the receptacle of the god. In the theurgic itinerary, it is not possible to skip over corporeality and the darkness of embodiment. Our reception of the god depends on it."[7]

When you open up, things come up. One retreatant summarized his forty-nine days in the dark as a "soul scrub." Recall that by some estimates at least 95 percent of what we do is dictated by unconscious processes, or the massive forces of the dark side. Dark retreat is uniquely situated to bring these forces to light, to allow these energies to break through into consciousness, which diminishes and eventually eradicates their power. That which was previously obscure, unclear, unintelligible, and dictatorial in the light of day becomes ironically clear, intelligible, and readable in the dark. You become more legible to yourself.

Entry levels of the unconscious mind are where the repressed aspects are stored. Out of sight is not out of mind but merely out of the conscious mind. What we refuse in daily life becomes the refuse heap of the unconscious mind. What we don't want to face in conscious experience is thrown into the upper levels of the darkness of the unconscious mind, which tends to be what we initially have to face in the early stages of dark retreat. Parts of my early retreats were a real shit show. I had no idea that just below the surface of my life was all this unprocessed crap. Fear? I thought I had transcended that! Anxiety? That's for people who don't meditate (and I did). Catastrophizing? Not for this evolved soul! We don't want to face the crap in the light of day, but we come face-to-face with it in the dark because that's where we tried to hide it. It's a big reason why the initial stages of dark retreat are often the most challenging. The laxative is starting to work.

Greek gods often have many epithets, or aliases. Dionysus is one of the principal gods in Greek mythology, and you will meet him in the dark in the guise of Dionysus Lysios. Jungian analyst Gary B. Astrachan writes that Lysios is "the 'loosener,' 'liberator,' 'releaser,' the untier of knots and bonds. The name is cognate with the practice which we perform in psycho-ana-lysis. Lysis, lysios. The loosening, dis-solving and dis-solution of the psyche [ego]. Psychoanalysis is seen here as the practice and performance of freeing the psyche, the loosening of the soul."[8] You're not doing psychoanalysis in the dark, but you are being "lysed." Remember that sūtra-level dark retreat is psycholytic (versus the psychedelic nature of tantra-level practice). Look at the before and after countenance of those going into the dark, and you will see the lysis of hard into soft as ego softens into egolessness. On the front end, you'll see the tension and stress of someone caught up in the rat race; on the back end, you'll witness the openness and relaxation of someone who has been loosened and liberated from the race.

Understanding this loosening and purgative process, the "stool softening," goes a long way in helping you deal with the initial crap show. If you know that the repressed elements are coming up to be *held* and healed, you're more likely to *hold* them in the cradle of loving-kindness. The crappy elements are just rejected aspects of your own being calling out for love and integration. If you don't understand this, you'll probably reject the challenging experiences yet again and stuff them back down into your unconscious mind. There, they will continue to constipate and express themselves (symptomatically) as the reactive and shitty experiences of your life.

Emotional upheavals are common in retreat as the mind starts to open and heave. The purging releases the repressed and rejected elements, hurling up the undigested experience so it can be digested in the light of consciousness. Dark retreat is not overt therapy, but it is massively therapeutic.[9] As the practice of emergence, the unconscious mind tends to throw up more in the dark because the opportunities for distraction and throwing things back down are removed. In my experience, it's as if the unconscious mind knows that the mess it makes in there will not be seen by others. You can crap and puke to your heart's content in the dark, getting all that repressed and rejected crap out of you because you're the only one who has to deal with it. Now's the time to let it fly! Nobody else can see it, and nobody else has to clean up after you. It's totally your crap show in there. So give it your best shot—or heave.

I am not endorsing some new form of "primal therapy," also known as "scream therapy," which is not accepted in the field of psychology and is completely absurd from the point of view of karmic theory. Screaming into your pillow in the dark or even beating it up while screaming may feel like the right thing to do sometimes, and if it feels right, go ahead and do it, but don't get into the habit. In karmic theory, the more you do something, the easier it is to do and the more inclined you are to do it again. If you remove all filters and express yourself without reservation, you're not a healthy adult; you're a two-year-old.

It's a delicate dance in the dark, or in life, because if emotional energies don't flow properly, they can get somatized. The energy is thrown into the body in ways that block the natural flow, which could initiate damming pathology. Men who don't relate to anger properly, for example, could end up with prostate problems. Your prostate manages urinary *flow*. It's a matter of finding the middle way between not too tight (repressed) and not too loose (expressive). Using our prostate example, it's a matter of getting pissed off properly. You're too loose if emotional energy sweeps you away, and you either explode or find yourself trapped in emotional loops. You're too tight if you stomp on the emotional energy and either implode or deny your feelings.

At even deeper levels, dark retreat is a form of psychic surgery, an incisive process of cutting through the bullshit, slicing through mere appearance, to discover the underlying reality. One retreatant, after three days in the dark, said: "It was a three-day extraction. Like a slow, methodical surgery being done on myself, by myself, to myself."

Me and My Shadow

Chapter 1 introduced the notion of shadow work. It's time to illuminate the depth of our shadows and reiterate the central role they play in dark retreat. Left alone, darkness is harmless. But as we've seen, we don't leave it alone. Because darkness can hide and store anything, we turn it into a convenient refuse heap for all our rejected and projected experience. We plaster darkness in our own negative image, hurling everything we don't want to face into this metaphysical waste bin. "Garbage in, garbage out" takes on new meaning in the dark, as all the garbage comes out in retreat. In this regard, dark retreat is high-level dumpster diving. You're landing in your own landfill. But in an alchemical way, the refuse acts as psychospiritual compost that we transform into fertilizer for our souls.

Darkness exposes parts of yourself that you may not want to see. In the days when cameras required film, the photographs taken during the day were developed in a dark room. Dark retreat develops the film of all the shots we've taken throughout our lives that we don't want to see or feel. How many shots can you handle? The previously invisible is made visible in the dark, which is one reason many people are anxious about what darkness might reveal. They don't want to get hit with the truth. Like a highly polished magnifying mirror, all the rejected and projected material comes back to smack you in the face, more frequently than that wall you keep bumping into.

In one of my earlier retreats, the lyrics from the Elvis Presley song "Return to Sender" kept popping into my mind. (For some reason, lyrics popping up are a common "teacher feature" of my retreats.) Everything you project onto the dark returns to the sender when you're in the dark. It's almost like there's nothing to project against in darkness, so all your projections pull a wicked U-turn and come home to roost. You're given the painful opportunity to finally own up, precisely because you can no longer project out.

Dark retreat brings the Jungian concept of shadow work to a new level. In both the physical and psychological world, the brighter the light, the sharper the shadow, which means the brightest lights create the darkest shadows. There is no shadow as dark as darkness itself. This darkest of shadows, therefore, contains the brightest of lights. In Tibetan Buddhism, the practice of sleep yoga explores this darkness by showing you how to maintain consciousness in deep dreamless sleep. This is the darkest the mind can get during the night, and where the greatest rest and restoration take place. Sleep yoga is better known as luminosity yoga because it ironically reveals the clear-light mind, the irreducible projector behind all our projections.[10]

The point is that dark retreat is a precious opportunity to engage in the deepest possible shadow work, starting with the conventional projections of psychology and working down to the ontological projections of philosophy and nondual spirituality. In other words, not only do we project all our psychological stuff onto the external world, but dark retreat goes deeper to illuminate how we project the illusion of externality itself—that there even is a world out there. That's the level of light and shadow work we're talking about at tantric (nondual) levels of dark retreat.

At more entry levels, as we saw in chapter 1, dark practice reveals that *you* are the one who puts a squeeze on yourself when things get claustrophobic in the dark. *You* are the one who projects onto the dark, then feels that pressure as if it's coming from outside. *You* are the one who stuffs all your rejected material into the dark, then complains about the crushing weight of darkness. Darkness isn't doing any of this. You are. Darkness simply reflects these painful truths, then leaves it up to you how to deal with it.

Physically, you can't really throw things in the dark. Even if you could, they wouldn't go very far. I think about this every time I look in the sideview mirror of my car and am reminded, "Objects in the mirror are closer than they appear." Things that affect you out there are much closer than they appear, and the mirror of darkness reveals this proximate truth. Remember Jung's seminal statement, "Projections change the world into a replica of one's unknown face." If you throw something in dark retreat, chances are it will bounce back and hit you. If you're not prepared for these hits, you'll keep blaming something or someone else, anything but yourself, for the difficulties of dark retreat. "Why is this room so damn small?! Why is it so closed up?! Why is it so stuffy in here?! Why didn't they give me a softer bed?!" Recall that when something *affects* you more that it *informs* you, when you *react* more than you *respond*, you're probably dealing with a projection.

The prepared (informed and responsive) mind is an unaffected and nonreactive mind that takes ownership when the projections come home to perch. The prepared mind stops projecting and, therefore, hitting itself. As with all good shadow work, you eventually own up to what's happening by taking ownership of your difficulties in the dark. Darkness reveals the real story: "Why is *my* mind so damn small? Why is *my* heart so closed up? Why are *my* attitudes so stuffy? Why am *I* so hard?" Dark retreat forces you to grow up by making you own up. With the right view, you realize that you've asked for it in the dark and are, therefore, willing to accept it. Darkness then becomes the most liberating light show in town. Your shadows are integrated back into the light from which they arose. And everything lightens up.

13

Where Does the Resistance Come From?

It is an axiom for all religions that in order to understand reality, arrive at heaven, or achieve bliss we must die and be reborn. That is, we must "die to ourselves" and be reborn as new selves.
—Patrick Harpur

Obstacles are not things that block our path; obstacles are the path.
—Lakhar Rinpoche

We've seen how darkness, like space itself, is weightless. It's also centerless. Because traditional reference points are taken away in the dark, you can't situate yourself in the normal way. You can't echolocate like you normally do. You literally have no idea where you are sometimes, and this centerless environment is disorienting to the self-centered ego. When it can no longer echolocate, or position itself, in the dark, the ego starts to squirm and say, "I don't belong here."

Because it doesn't. Ego has a very hard time finding itself in the dark. This leads to unconscious resistance before going into the dark and a "This is nuts!" attitude when you're in there. Generally speaking, to echolocate is to *ego*locate.[1] When you're feeling the resistance prior to entering retreat and the pressure when you're in it, you're feeling your ego trying to deter you from exploring the dark, from discovering the truth, and from touching into dimensions of your being that transcend the ego. Ego knows it's going to get lost in there, perhaps never to be found again.[2]

If you're moving around and literally don't know where you are in the dark, the dislocation can generate moments of panic. It's like the feeling we discussed when you wake up in the middle of the night in a foreign country, struggling with jetlag, with no idea of where you are. The trip literally dislocates you. But unlike conventional forms of physical dislocation, dark retreat invites positive (but still painful) mental dislocation. The panic from this psychic dislocation, felt as an intense contraction, is the underlying fabric of the ego that is getting torn in the dark. It's an indication that you're getting closer to the truth. If you understand this, you're more willing to tolerate the tear. We need to take a dip into tantra levels of dark practice to see what's going on here. Every superficial level of resistance is a manifestation of deep underlying principles. Hang in there for this chapter, which is one of the most challenging in the book, and you'll see the extraordinary gifts you're starting to unwrap in the dark. If you find the material too much of a stretch, just skip to the next chapter.

In the dark, there's no sense of "out there." You literally can't see anything out there. Given enough time, this form of intentional blindness allows you to see that there's also no "in here." You see nothing in the dark after all. And that is the best seeing. You're finally seeing the truth of emptiness: that you (ego) don't exist. You're dis-covering that who you think you are (the appearance) is empty of inherent existence (the reality). You can't have inside without outside, self without other, subject without object. "In here" and "out there" lean on each other. Take away one or the other, and they collapse into each other. Darkness kicks away this form of duality by first kicking out the legs from underneath "other," which then kicks out the legs from underneath "self," revealing your nondual (or empty) selfless and egoless nature. And ego resists being kicked out.

After a massive left-hemispheric stroke, neuroscientist Jill Bolte Taylor shared an experience that is echoed by many people who engage in deep meditation or dark practice. It could be an entry from my dark retreat diary:

> I could no longer clearly discern the physical boundaries of where I began and where I ended. I sensed the composition of my being as that of a fluid rather than that of a solid. I no longer perceived myself as a whole object separate from everything. Instead, I now blended in with the space and flow around me . . . the boundaries of my earthly body dissolved, and I melted into the universe.[3]

You don't need to have a stroke to have an experience of egolessness; you only need to be stroked by nonduality. Remember that touch is our most nondual sense, so what's happening here is a profound twofold level of contact with reality (relative and then absolute). First, the panic (of dislocation) means you're finally getting in touch with the ground of your *relative* being. Panic, or intense contraction, is what the stripped down and naked ego feels like at its core. When darkness strips everything away and you get totally exposed in the dark, ego defensively contracts to put on more clothing, and that underwear is felt as anxiety, then fear, and eventually panic.[4] Ego is this very contraction. Your sense of self *is* a self-contraction. Contraction equals self. And you're finally touching that cold and naked truth.

The ground of ego is visceral and emotional contraction that we can experience in the dark as deeply rooted anxiety, fear, or even panic. Given enough time, this unholy trinity starts to loosen and come to the surface (or saying the same thing, as you start to descend into this uncomfortable ground). When you have those challenging feelings on retreat, realize you're getting closer to this ground. That very sense of contraction is what creates the illusion of ground, of someplace for the ego to stand, to position itself, to locate itself, to create itself. Once again, self *equals* contraction.

Anxiety, fear, and panic are among the most contracted and reified of all feelings, emotional energies in their most solidified form. When you feel anxiety or fear in any form of deep inner work, you're feeling your *relative* self-sense at the deepest level. You're touching into the self-contraction. The self isn't only panicking; the self *is* panic. And panic, along with anxiety and fear, doesn't feel so good. Ego just doesn't feel good (in both senses). In dark retreat, this takes on additional meaning when you don't feel so good in there. The sick feeling arises because you're starting to feel into the essence of your relative (egoic) being. You're about to barf. You're about to bring up and hurl out the vomitus at the core of egoic structure. Contraction is about to be released into expansion. Understanding this will help you relate to this necessary purge.

In dark retreat, you're getting two medicines for the price of one. Not only are you swallowing a laxative, you're also gulping an emetic (a medicine which causes vomiting). All manner of undigested material will be thrown up in the dark, and that includes ego itself. And just like conventional forms of vomiting, you'll feel a whole lot better once you get that toxin out of you. Dark retreat is big medicine. Can you handle the diagnostics? Can you deal with the cure?

The resistance to this medicine comes in many forms. In my conversations with dark retreat guides, they estimate that for over 90 percent of people who go into retreat, darkness is perceived as a threat. Many of these people seem to be unaware of the resistance and the many ways they protect themselves from the threat.[5] Instead of opening and surrendering to darkness, they steel themselves against it in unconscious ways. They contract in covert and overt self-defense, resisting the "acidic" nature of this medicine. Sometimes the ecstatic reports shared immediately upon coming out of dark retreat are due to the relief in finally escaping it. Shedding their steely armor, which could have taken place in darkness, only occurs when the retreat ends and they can finally relax. These are the people who express little or no transformation or file tepid reports about their experiences in dark retreat. Is this a missed opportunity? Not necessarily. If they understand this defensive process and observe it with genuine curiosity, they can learn a great deal about themselves and how they actually create and then sustain their very sense of self with this armor. But because these processes are usually unconscious, they are often missed, as is the opportunity that darkness affords.

One of the ways retreatants shield themselves is by closing their eyes in the dark. It's our natural way of experiencing darkness in life and normalizes the experience in dark retreat. But in retreat, it's often a way to dissociate and escape from darkness. When you're in dark retreat, play with this. Don't judge yourself if closing your eyes makes the retreat more workable. Just notice. Then see how it feels when you open your eyes in the dark. Do you notice unease, feel yourself contract, or register fear? Do you feel threatened? Some people report sucking in their bodies, literally contracting their chest or stomach as if bracing for impact. Then close your eyes and see how that feels. Do you open and relax? Do you breathe a sigh of relief? Does your chest or stomach expand? Go easy on yourself and remember that this is all normal. Discovering these avoidance strategies exposes all the gross and subtle ways we contract. Once again, you can't solve a problem you don't even know you have.

Why do you feel this threat and the need to defend yourself from darkness? Because you're starting to lose it. Egoic structure is starting to dissolve in the simple gesture of opening your eyes. As previously discussed, if you can't see, you can't echolocate like you normally do, which means it's harder to ego-locate. It's a brilliant irony: You begin to see through the ego by losing conventional sight. By literally losing sight of things, you may find what you're really looking for. But don't take my word for it. Go into the dark and see for yourself.

Going Deeper

Returning to our earlier analogy, if you can stay in touch with these bad feelings, the very fabric of the ego, you'll eventually tear through it.[6] The ego will dissolve, the contraction will open, the panic will soften, the fear will melt, and you'll drop through to get in touch with . . . nothing. Absolutely nothing. *Now* you're in touch with reality. Now you're in touch with the truth. You're finally in contact with the groundless ground of your being, your *absolute* true nature, what Buddhism calls emptiness. The logic is so elegant: You go into dark retreat to do absolutely nothing, which puts you in touch with absolutely nothing.

Now you can see why ego doesn't want to go here and where all the resistance comes from. Ego is the archetypal thing, the *penultimate* ("last but one in a series") stance, and darkness, which again is homologous to emptiness, reveals the *ultimate* no-thing nature of everything. This is why ego whispers and eventually screams out to you, "You don't belong here! You don't have time for this! This is beyond you! You're too busy for this! This is insane! Get out while you still can!" Ego doesn't belong here because there's no place for ego to take a stand. No defensive stance allowed. There's nothing to press against in the dark. There's no way to locate yourself in this centerless (egoless) space. You're floating in the darkness of emptiness, egolessness, and for the ego, that is terrifying. It's the very fear of death. But for your spirit, who you really are, it's fantastically liberating and spiritually orgasmic because it's the revelation of truth.

These discoveries also reveal why ego is unconsciously invested in conflict, divisiveness, opposition, discord, controversy, confrontation, and endless struggle. In other words, duality. Darkness shows you why ego loves to break things, including reality itself. It feasts on being contrarian and disagreeable and hankers for all manner of dissing. Ego *needs* something to press against; it craves any form of *against*. Ego is the archetype of "anti."[7] You can't have self without other, and once you have other, you have to defend yourself against it. You ironically have to defend yourself against your own bloody creation.

At softer levels, this need to locate oneself manifests as competition and helps explain (for just one example) why the multibillion-dollar sports industry is so successful. If you can't press against something at gross levels, you can at least measure yourself, size yourself up, see how you stack up, or otherwise see where you *stand* against others in a less adversarial way. Some competitive types, as we've seen, even go into the dark with an antagonistic attitude and end up in combat with themselves, a civil war of their own making. The intelligent ones quickly realize that dark retreat removes all metrics. It's the antithesis of competition. This is another reason why I no longer respond to the single most common question: How long do you stay in the dark? People seem to want to size me up by the length of my . . .

Understanding the penultimate and then ultimate levels of discovery, of what you're getting in touch with at relative and absolute levels (and the feelings revealed at each stage), is important in getting you into retreat and keeping you there. In other words, the feeling of contraction, the self-contraction, that's discovered at initial stages of dark retreat just sucks.[8] When you feel anxiety, fear, and panic, it sucks. And if you stay out of retreat just because you don't want to feel bad, you're missing an opportunity to understand (and then transform) a host of bad feelings, all based on the primordial bad feeling, the primordial contraction, that is the bedrock of ego. Feel into *any* of these unwanted feelings and you'll touch into varying levels of contraction. The more unwanted a feeling is, the more contracted it is. But if you can stay with the contractions, they will open and release, and you'll give birth to tremendous energy. Kindness, compassion, and generosity ride on that energy. Everything that feels good rides on that energy because openness feels good. Egolessness feels good. Emptiness feels good. And emptiness, openness, egolessness are different ways to talk about unconditional love.

Understanding this makes all the difference in the world in how you relate to the intensity of dark retreat and its inevitable challenges. Knowing that the unwanted feelings that accompany this practice are part of the firewall that protects, *and constructs*, the very sense of self will help you relate to them properly. It will help you open, relax, and release the painful grip you've placed on yourself—that's created your very sense of self—and its retinue of bad feelings. That understanding then allows you to open, relax, and fall into the abyss of love and bliss that lie below. If you can do this in dark retreat, you're dropping into what darkness really has to offer. The transcendence of death.

Here's how it works. There's no place for personal identity, the ego, in the centerless and egoless space of darkness. Ego goes missing in the dark, kidnapped by the truth. In the bardo teachings, falling into this darkness is exactly what happens at the moment of death, when your body drops away and you're sent flying into infinite space. At deeper levels of practice, you're getting a feel for what it is like to die.

The wisdom traditions offer a number of penetrating investigations that look deeply into the nature of the self because if you can answer the question "Who am I?," you've solved one of the great riddles of the universe. This question was the heart of Ramana Maharshi's entire nondual path. But finding the answer is not your usual finding because *not* finding is the best finding. Not finding any*thing* means you've found it. It doesn't mean there's absolutely nothing there. It means there's no-thing there. What's actually found is thingless, formless, and, therefore, deathless empty awareness. Emptiness is found. The looker is what is found.

Your inability to locate yourself in reference to anything "other" eventually orients you to your selfless (and, therefore, otherless) nature.[9] It may be disorienting to your ego, but it's completely orienting to your egoless spirit. Not knowing where you are in the dark can change your orientation to your very sense of self, how you relate to others, and how you relate to the world. Dislocation matures into translocation as your sense of identity transfers from a localized self into unlocalized selflessness, the infinite field of subjectivity that is who you really are.[10] This translocation feels like coming home. It comes with a tremendous relief. And it feels really good. One retreatant shared, "I felt like I was at home. I never imagined that home would come through darkness." And another practitioner, after three days, said, "That's a lot to take in. I felt a lot of fullness, some softness . . . I'm tearing up . . . it's beautiful. That's what you'll find in the dark. Home."

Darkness challenges *any* form of centricity, especially egocentricity, and eventually overthrows it. As I fumble to find my way around in the dark, this quote often pops into my head: "God is an infinite sphere, whose center is everywhere, and whose circumference is nowhere."[11] Darkness points out my centerless, selfless, and therefore godlike nature.

If there's no center of gravity, no self-center, there's no gravitational pull, and everything lightens up. When you stop referring everything back to yourself, which not only creates the sense of self but adds more weight to it every time you do refer, things get lighter and easier in dark retreat, or in life. When you stop thinking, "What can *I* get out of this person? Where do *I* fit into this? How can *I* profit from this situation? What about *me*?" the gravity of any situation lifts. Everything stops orbiting you. You're no longer the center of the universe because you no longer exist. You've died in the dark and discovered your deathless true nature.

The next time you're having a hard or heavy time in the dark, or in life, notice the black hole at the center of that sucky situation. Notice how everything is centered around the sticky sense of self and expressed in the language of "I, me, or mine." *That's* precisely why things get hard and heavy, and that's how contraction manifests moment to moment. The next time you're feeling down, pay close attention to what's happening, and you will feel how referential the situation has become, how everything is getting sucked into you, and how badly that sucks. We'll take another crack at this material in chapter 16, so don't worry if it doesn't land just yet.

Open Palm

Dark retreat points out everything you're attached to, that burdens you, that creates your heavy unenlightened life. It will then slowly and methodically pry your fingers open. You eventually lose your grip on everything in the dark and can watch it harmlessly slip away into the "nighttime" sky. You're going to discover things you had no idea you were so attached to, and you'll recognize this whenever things get hard. The obstacles in dark retreat transform into opportunities by showing you that every challenge is of your own making. Things only get sticky when the mind grasps and solidifies. That's when you stick it to yourself. A completely open mind would have no issues in darkness because nothing can stick to space. Someone like the Dalai Lama would glide gracefully through dark retreat.

By seeing how you construct your challenges, you can deconstruct them. Dark retreat is empowering in that you learn how to take ownership of your misery or happiness. It shows you how to stop pinching yourself. By bringing unconscious processes into the light of consciousness, darkness shows you how you constantly throw yourself into prison and simultaneously hands you the keys.

Not necessarily in order, because everybody is different, it goes something like this: At introductory levels, darkness shows you how attached you are to comfort, to movement, to entertainment, to busyness, to your routines, to distraction, to light, and to sensory delights when all that is taken away from you. You can, therefore, make things easier on yourself in the dark by lessening those attachments now.[12] It's not all death and destruction in there; otherwise, why would anyone go through this? If the letting go, or "dying," is worked with skillfully, attachment is replaced with appreciation, and grasping is replaced with gratitude. Death gives way to birth. You realize that it's actually possible to love without attachment. Dark retreat is an exercise in simplicity, reducing life to its lowest terms, showing you what really matters and what doesn't. I always come home with a newfound appreciation for the people in my life and the things I have. After three days in the dark, one retreatant shared:

> Primarily, I just realized how much of what I regard as myself is really not myself, is not who I am, not what I am. How much of the weight that I carry around is just not me. The darkness helped me to start to differentiate between me and the parts that are not me. The part that is me needs a lot less. It's a lot less adorned, a lot less needy, a lot less graspy, a lot less striving. I was almost going to say it's a lot more present, but it is presence by definition. I'm more content to be what it is.

It's like the story of the Sufi trickster Mullah Nasruddin. One day Nasruddin is walking along a mountain trail when he encounters a dejected old man, with a face ridden by hardship, carrying a small knapsack containing all his worldly possessions. The Sufi master inquires about his sodden demeanor and learns that the old man retired after a life of hard work to set out on the quest for enlightenment. After years of futile searching, the man fell into a deep depression as nothing he encountered satisfied his longing for happiness. After listening to his sad tale, Nasruddin snatches the old man's knapsack and runs away. Being elderly, the man is unable to take chase. Now he is really despondent because all his possessions have just been stolen. Nasruddin scurries ahead to hide along a bend in the path and places the knapsack in the middle of the path. The old man has no choice but to continue walking, even more miserable than before. When he comes around the bend and sees his knapsack with all his possessions in place, he jumps up and down in joy at his good fortune. Nasruddin then appears from behind a rock and says, "Funny what it takes to make some people happy."

When people come out of dark retreat with tears of joy and gratitude, it's often because a similar event has occurred. The trickster of darkness stole what they took for granted. Coming out of retreat is akin to finding the knapsack in the middle of the path. It's a mini version of a near-death experience, which brings you back to life with deeper appreciation for the gift of life itself. Abraham Maslow, in a letter written while recovering from a heart attack, wrote, "The confrontation with death—and the reprieve from it—makes everything look so precious, so sacred, so beautiful that I feel more strongly than ever the impulse to love it, to embrace it, and let myself be overwhelmed by it . . . My river has never looked so beautiful."[13]

At deeper levels, when you've processed and released some of the intro-level attachments, dark retreat shows you how attached you are to your thoughts, emotions, feelings, philosophies, ideologies, belief systems, even your neurosis. And at rock bottom, darkness will show you how painfully attached you are to your very sense of self. It reveals how stuck up you are, how screwed you are, to yourself. When you're having a hard time in the dark, experiment with "getting over it" by getting over yourself.

These subtle levels of attachment may not come to light in your first retreat, but stay in there long enough and every aspect of your sticky mind is revealed. Dark retreat shows you how you unconsciously torture yourself by feeding painful storylines, ruminating and catastrophizing about all you could have done or shouldn't have done. Why do we do this to ourselves? Because *something bad is better than nothing*. When the pressure starts to build in the dark, when you feel the hunger pangs of withdrawal, you may find yourself saying, "I need something, *anything*, to keep me going in here!" The resourceful ego finds ways to keep it going by finding innovative and twisted ways to keep things moving. It will grasp onto any level of distraction, even when it hurts.[14]

With every day in the dark, new opportunities in the form of new difficulties arise. That's what you're paying for! If you relate to the challenges properly, if you can open to and then release whatever arises, every challenge makes you lighter and freer. Dark retreat gets easier and easier as you get lighter and lighter. What's the result? When do you know you've accomplished dark retreat? When you can relate to whatever arises with complete equanimity. When you no longer dread the dark. When you can say, as the sage Krishnamurti did when he was asked about the secret to his unflappable happiness, "I don't mind what happens."[15]

Initiation

The initial entry into the repressed contents of your unconscious or obfuscated mind serves as a test. In many shamanic traditions, initiates go through challenging rites of passage to access the power of a true shaman. These entry-level challenges are a form of initiation into the depths of our soul. Patrick Harpur writes:

> All rites of passage are "little deaths" in preparation for the last rite of physical death—and rebirth into the ancestral afterlife . . . [because we] participate in a worldview that is radically estranged from the reality of soul, we all need the equivalent of the shaman's initiation if we are to open friendly relations with the Otherworld [Underworld]; or, to put it psychologically, to maintain equilibrium between our consciousness and the unconscious . . . it is common for initiation candidates to see themselves as skeletons—that is, stripped down to the bone before they are reconstituted . . . the pain of initiation is like an operation by soul on the body to free itself from an identification with the body.[16]

The challenges of initiation are an efficient deterrent to keep you away from the treasures that lie below. Lama Govinda wrote, "If, through some trick of nature, the gates of an individual's subconsciousness were suddenly to spring open, the unprepared mind would be overwhelmed and crushed. Therefore, the gates of the subconscious are guarded, by all initiates, and hidden behind the veil of mysteries and symbols."[17] And hidden behind the veils of difficulty. When things get challenging with deep inner work, most people want to return to the surface. They want to get back to their comfort zone and add more bubbles to the bath. But remember that the more time you spend in your comfort zone, the smaller it gets; and the more time you spend in the challenge zone, the bigger your comfort zone gets. With a better understanding of the levels of your unconscious mind, you understand that once you get through the initiation, the radiant riches of the deepest unconscious mind become available to you.

Harpur concludes, "These are the experiences that can transform our lives forever and for better if we can resist the temptation to sedate them and instead use the enormous energies they release to reassemble ourselves—with iron bones perhaps for strength; new eyes for insight; and a new heart for affection."[18] It takes an advanced attitude to relate to the challenges of deep inner work, which is one reason why dark retreat is considered advanced.

14

What to Do If It Gets Challenging?

> [T]he human cannot experience with the senses or its ordinary cognitive capacities the apophatic (unspeakable, unthinkable, impossible) depths of the Godhead, which is known, or unknown, as a kind of brilliant darkness or black light—"black" because it can never become an object of perception. There is a kind of transcendent blackness here. Blackness is ontological.
>
> **—Jeffrey J. Kripal**

Discussing all the challenges of dark retreat does not mean that any of them will occur. It's a disservice to this practice to suggest that you're heading into a hornet's nest. You may go into the dark and have the time of your life. I know people who have gone in for five days on their first journey and had nothing but blissful experiences. Discussing the challenges is challenging in itself because being too articulate can backfire when you're in retreat and nothing difficult is happening. "Isn't this supposed to be hard?" "I'm doing great; am I doing something wrong?" Good for you if nothing difficult comes up, and good for you if it does.

Before I went to Costa Rica three years ago to explore ayahuasca, everybody told me to brace myself for the challenges of purging. Over the course of a week, I didn't purge once. This doesn't quite abide by the maxim "Expectation is premeditated disappointment," but you get the point. I wasn't disappointed when I didn't throw up, but the expectation that I would did color my approach to the week. The last thing I want to do is intimidate anyone by pointing out all the possible challenges of dark retreat. But most people who try ayahuasca do purge, and most people who go into the dark do experience some difficulties. The following remedies are orienting generalizations for finding your way if things get challenging. When you travel to unfamiliar terrain, it helps to prepare for some demanding times.

There are as many ways to work with the challenges as there are challenges themselves. Because we're all different, the remedies that follow are not a one-size-fits-all approach. Use whatever speaks to you. We're going to start with general remedies before getting into specifics. Many of the following suggestions also apply to any form of retreat, any level of deep inner work, or any challenging life circumstance.

Because you're intentionally putting yourself in a challenging situation by going into the dark, the first thing you want to do is embrace the challenge. Don't steel yourself against it. You're asking for it. So don't complain when you get it! One retreatant shared, "It's remarkable. In the dark, you have a choice: to endure or to embrace. That's what we get to choose in life too." When you do get it, relate to the challenge as a gift in ugly wrapping paper. The following are recommendations for how to unwrap and enjoy these gifts.

Care for the Moment

The broadest antidote for any challenging circumstance is this: If you just take care of the present moment, everything else will take care of itself. Playing on the notion of being handed a gift, take care of your present. *Hold* your awareness to whatever arises, without grasping after it or pushing it away, without hoping that it will disappear or fearing that it won't, and everything else takes care of itself. It's magic. But because of our habits for avoiding the present moment in general and difficult moments in particular, this magic act isn't easy to perform.[1] Mindfulness is, therefore, a powerful way to practice this antidote. You may think that distracting yourself from a difficult situation is the better way to go, but you can only get away from things for so long, especially in the dark. In my early retreats, I would often move around my dark cabin in a silly attempt to escape or at least to get a different "view." I even sat on the toilet, thinking that novel idea would somehow improve things. It doesn't take long to realize that wherever you go (in the dark or in life), there you are. Try as I might, I just could not get away from myself, so "myself" got increasingly concentrated.

Remember Ruben Laukkonen's words, "Resting in the present moment is annihilation." Don't sit on the toilet. Sit on the present moment. To rest fully on whatever arises does not annihilate what arises. If you're feeling something painful, it won't get rid of the pain. But it does get rid of the suffering. Pain and suffering are not the same thing. Suffering is an inappropriate relationship to pain, and relationship is something you can change. By *holding* to the painful state of mind without repressing or indulging the pain, you can annihilate your suffering. Dark retreat invites and almost enforces this relationship. Otherwise, you can drive yourself crazy in your efforts to get away from yourself, to escape from the contents of your mind. If you're able to stay fully with whatever arises, it self-liberates, like snowflakes landing on a hot rock.

The secret is an open secret: Let it come, then let it go. The difficult experience may return, but you will notice that it usually has less impact every time it does. It's wearing thin and eventually wears itself out. As Jill Bolte Taylor writes, "The healthiest way I know how to move through an emotion effectively is to surrender completely to that emotion when its loop of physiology comes over me. I simply resign to the loop and let it run its course . . . Over time, the intensity and frequency of these circuits usually abate . . . When I'm in pain, I become quiet, coddle the wound, and consciously surrender into the pain, which helps it dissipate."[2]

Trungpa Rinpoche wrote, "Good and bad, happy and sad, all thoughts vanish into emptiness like the imprint of a bird in the sky."[3] Remember that darkness is homologous to emptiness, so you will see how all experiences—if you just leave them alone—eventually vanish into the darkness-emptiness from which they arose. This is where the core instruction "Do nothing" comes back into play. Bolte Taylor continues, "I shifted from the doing-consciousness of my left brain to the being-consciousness of my right brain."[4] The right brain is always right here and right now. But doing nothing, as we've seen, can be the hardest thing to do. The techniques in this chapter supplement this radical approach to challenging experiences.

According to Jill Bolte Taylor, the biochemical correlates of an emotional upheaval are purified *by your body* within ninety seconds. This means that if an emotional upheaval lasts longer than ninety seconds, *you* are the one keeping it alive. Why do you do this? Because a horror movie in the dark is better than no movie. Having no entertainment, nothing to move you, is the real horror story for the ego. The remedy is to stay embodied. Just do that, and your body knows what to do with everything else. "Wisdom abides in the body," proclaimed the sage Saraha.

After three days in the dark, one retreatant said: "There's the pressure to have a big mystical experience, but darkness showed me that being alive is a big mystical experience. Being part of this is a big mystical experience. You don't have to force things to make it all happen. Just let it all go." Your body is always already present; that's where healing and self-liberation happen. That's why people come out of dark retreat and say, "I never felt so alive in my life. I never felt so fully embodied."

Dark retreat has the capacity to heal a host of emotional wounds, but it should not be engaged at the expense of other skillful means. Use it in addition to, not in lieu of, other methods. And always be kind to yourself. The last thing you want to do is beat yourself up if you pass the ninety-second mark and are still struggling with an emotional upheaval. Sustained emotional release could be the result of unrecognized trauma, which does not necessarily abide by this statute of limitation. I've come to view trauma as a condition of chronic contraction, and deeply rooted contractions take time to open.

Lie Detector

As the journey of "waking down," darkness almost demands embodiment and being true or aligned to what you are feeling. One retreatant shared: "I never thought life could be this good. I became more tender, more open. I'm not going to hide anymore. I am who I am, and I show up the way I am." To find your way in the dark, follow the filament of embodied experience. If that filament frays and you dis-tract from your body, you'll get lost in headspace. Rumination, confabulation, and catastrophizing will stampede over your embodiment and sweep you away. That disembodiment can lead to dissociation. This is why bodywork before, during, and after retreat is so important. Dark practice may appear to be a mental or spiritual journey, but you have to bring your body with you at every step. Otherwise, you'll leave the most critical part of the journey behind. This is a deep *inner* journey, and that means a journey into the center of your embodied self, which ironically leads to selflessness.

What do you do when you lose the filament, and the crap hits the proverbial fan? Get rid of the fan. Don't get rid of the crap. Don't fan yourself and try to chill out in your cool head; stay in the fires of embodied experience. Radical teacher Da Free John taught, "The fire must have its way."[5] And Zen master Suzuki Roshi said:

> When you do something, you should do it with your whole body and mind; you should be concentrated on what you do. You should do it completely, like a good bonfire. You should not be a smoky fire. You should burn yourself completely. If you do not burn yourself completely, a trace of yourself will be left in what you do. You will have something remaining which is not completely burned out. Zen activity is activity which is completely burned out, with nothing but ashes. That is the goal of our practice.[6]

Turn the crappy experiences into manure by allowing yourself to *feel* as crappy as possible, which means being as embodied as possible. Don't try to be spiritual. Don't try to be meditative. Don't photoshop your experience. *Don't be a positivity pusher.* Be human. Be real. Honesty supersedes positivity in the dark. When your retreat guide comes to check in with you, don't tell them what you think they want to hear. Speak your truth. Cry with them. Laugh with them. Scream with them. Something magical happens if you allow yourself to be fully human. If you're in a heap of hurt, feel the hurt fully and watch it heal. Feel it to heal it. If you're crying, cry your eyes out, and you will start to see.

Dark retreat is the most experiential thing I've ever done because it's the most honest and embodied thing I've ever done. Deception cannot follow you into your body, which is a principle used in lie detectors. You can almost say that deception cannot follow you into the dark. If it does, you're going to get slapped around by your own deceits and eventually hit with the truth.

Out-of-Body Experience

When challenging experiences arise, take it slow. Go easy on yourself. "Working out" at the gym has similarities to "working in" at dark retreat. You don't get stronger by lifting ten thousand pounds one time. You get stronger by lifting ten pounds a thousand times. Every time you work with a challenging experience, you're getting stronger, more able to handle a heavier load. We're all different, and you will find your own way in the dark, but when I'm facing a challenging experience, I try to stay with it, embrace it, and see if it self-liberates on its own. If it doesn't self-liberate, I'll engage the following four steps as I work my way in. In the spirit of author Martin Prechtel, "Do not get over it. Get into it." This adds a nice wrinkle to our earlier statement, "Enlightenment is the ultimate getting over yourself." It's actually the ultimate getting *into* yourself. And that's the only thing you can really get into in the dark.

To embrace whatever challenge comes up is to properly *hold* it, or relate to it, which entails finding the middle way between indulgence and repression. Once again, we want to feel it but not feed it. We know we're feeding it and indulging it when the storylines begin, and we know we're repressing it when we contract away from it. We constantly contract away from concentrated experiences in our attempt to dilute them with our commentaries. As Irish author James Joyce said of one his characters, "Mr. Duffy lived a short distance from his body."[7] Contracting away from intense feelings generates a disembodied experience as we leave our sensual body and run into our insensate heads.

The thinking brain *literally* cannot feel. This is why neurosurgeons, once they cut through the skull, can do open-brain surgery on a completely conscious person and not hurt them.[8] It's such a dazzling metaphor from nature: We escape from painful embodied (aesthetic) experience into our anesthetic brain in an effort to distance ourselves from the pain of life. No other painkiller even comes close to this level of distraction, this level of "pulling apart" from painful feelings. It's the most profound form of general anesthesia that has the globe sleepwalking through life.

Ironically, this exit strategy then generates the sense that something is missing in life. Something *is* missing: your fully embodied participation in the pain of life. Because it's so much harder for Mr. Duffy to move away from himself in the dark, dark retreat removes that short distance and forces Mr. Duffy back to life by driving him back into his body. The anesthesia finally wears off in the dark. And as anybody knows who has returned to life when the anesthetic wears off, this is not always pleasant (something I've witnessed thousands of times in my clinical practice as a dental surgeon). *It hurts to wake up.* Or in this case, it hurts to wake down into our highly sensual body.

Dark retreat, therefore, also reveals how much Mr. Duffy loves to break away, to generate all those fractures we talked about earlier, and to create that deadening distance. Ego takes its perverted breath every single time we're distracted. And it dies with every breathtaking aesthetic experience. Ego expires every single time we come to our senses and feel things fully. It takes courage to wake down into your intense feelings, Mr. and Ms. Duffy, but you will find yourself coming back to life if you do. One retreatant shared, "Once I was able to feel through everything, acknowledge the pain, feel the pain, and then release it, I touched a part of me that I never even imagined was there."

Many people in this rampant era of distraction, of runaway general anesthesia, feel lifeless. Empty inside. Out of touch. Even more people are insensitive, unfeeling, and untouchable. Popular songs often lament how icy a partner can be. Why are some people so cold? Because a corpse is cold. Because we put ourselves on ice every time we break away from our warm and broken hearts and from each other. People living a short distance from their bodies are frozen stiff inside. They feel like life itself is cold and uncaring, that it's passing them by. They're narcotized. Numb. The (pilot) lights are on, but nobody is home. Because you can no longer break away from yourself in the dark and chill out, things heat up. The blood starts to flow, life force energy is finally unblocked, and that energy starts to circulate. It tingles and burns as you come back to life, but it's worth the discomfort because you become more sensitive, awake, and alive. The tomb is turning into a womb.

In one long dark retreat, around week four, I woke up in the dead of night with a truly bizarre feeling in my left foot. It felt like I had somehow kept my left foot outside in the bitter cold, and it was starting to thaw. It hurt like hell! I've had lots of weird things happen in my retreats, but this was near the top. I held my toes and massaged them, like I sometimes do when coming inside to warm up on a bitterly cold ski day. This happened three nights in a row. After so many days in the dark and being so open, you can imagine the impact of this somatic message.

Dark retreat turns Mr. Duffy inside out and upside down. It's not just the most in-your-face experience possible, it's one of the most in-your-body experiences possible. One retreatant shared: "Just amazing. I feel like I've been reborn. The gift of darkness is that it delivered me back into life. I never felt at such a deep level before. It wasn't easy, but it feels like I'm actually feeling for the first time. Like I've reincarnated back into a new form, inhabiting my body in a much fuller way."

When to Stop

We need to talk about an elephant that may have entered the room. When does a workable challenge cross the line into an unworkable threat? How can you tell if a healthy stretch is turning into a harmful strain? One reason dark retreat is considered advanced is that it's a "free solo" in there. Even with an onsite guide, you're mostly on your own. That's what makes the practice so empowering but also challenging. It's similar to the risks and rewards of the well-known Outward Bound program, but in our case, the journey is obviously Inward Bound.[9] The maxims "no pain, no gain," "no pressure, no diamond," or "stretching is good for growth" can become problematic if you press or stretch too hard. Always remember the balancing maxim of "not too tight, not too loose." If you're too loose, you'll slip back into your comfort zone and won't get much out of your retreat. If you're too tight, you'll slip into the risk zone and either resent your retreat or have to recover from it.

One way to tell that you're moving from the challenge zone into the risk zone is when you feel like you're starting to endure the retreat. People who settle and connect to their bodies, who genuinely welcome what's happening, do fine. Those who endure, try to insulate themselves from what's happening, or enter a flight, fight, or freeze response, should turn on the lights or step outside. *This is not a failure.* Giving yourself a break could be the most revelatory and successful part of your retreat. Dipping in and out of the dark in a gray retreat could be much more transformative than grinding it out.

Increasing agitation or physical discomfort and unease are a few other things to look out for. If you find yourself physically unstable or shaky, excessively mindless (which is sometimes marked by consistently bumping into things or really fumbling around in the dark) for more than just a few minutes, take a break. A little disorientation and bewilderment are part of the package and can even be humorous, but it's not funny if you find yourself out of sorts and start to panic. As always, give yourself a chance to relate to and befriend these unsettling experiences, but if they don't soften, you shouldn't toughen.

Remember that dark retreat is about letting go of appearances. If you're worried about how you might appear by coming out early or taking a break, welcome that as a legitimate experience, then let that thought go. Stop "shoulding" on yourself—"I should be toughing this out," or "I should be able to do this more easily," or "I should be stronger." Instead of shoulding on yourself, love yourself.

If you're in there pounding it out, what's the point? What are you trying to prove? Prove your intelligence by giving yourself a break. An endurance approach just solidifies your ego as you cross the finish line bruised but victorious. When you're in the dark and having a hard time, follow the softest spots. These soft spots can be in your heart or physically in your room. There were times in retreat when I'd get up off the floor and go lie down on the bed. Approach this practice as the kindest thing you'll ever do for yourself. If you come out a "tough guy," you're doing something wrong. Dark retreat is about becoming a softie.

When I did my three-year retreat, some of my colleagues, who were veteran meditators, had problems when they started to push. Some of the practices we did had metrics for accomplishment. For example, with dream yoga, you either had lucid dreams or not; with inner-heat yoga (tummo), you either had the heat or not; with phowa (transference of consciousness), you either had physical signs or not. In an effort to attain these signs, some retreatants tried too hard and made things hard for themselves.

Another indication for when to stop, or at least give yourself a break, is when you feel like you're starting to dissociate. Differentiation, or cultivating a healthy witness awareness, is fine. But the near-enemy of differentiation is dissociation. When you're differentiating from your thoughts and emotions, you're still fully embodied. When you start to dissociate, you're losing contact with your body. If that continues, you can lose contact with reality. When you find yourself getting lost in headspace, spinning into uncontrollable rumination, tying yourself into mental knots, or solidifying the contents of your mind, come to your senses by flipping on the light. Reconnect to the outside world.

If you stay in sensory deprivation long enough, you might start to hallucinate. But hallucination doesn't always mean dissociation. You can have the most spectacular visions and hallucinations in the dark—truly wild sound and light shows—and witness them in a healthy way. They can even teach you a thing or two about the nature of mind and reality, as French philosopher Hippolyte Taine suggests: "External perception is an internal dream which proves to be in harmony with external things, and instead of calling 'hallucination' a false perception, we must call external perception 'a confirmed hallucination.'"[10] Neuroscientist Anil Seth agrees: "The world that we experience comes as much, if not more, from the inside out as from the outside in . . . Perception is a controlled hallucination. When we agree upon our hallucinations, we call that reality."[11]

Talking Test

A voice test is one way to assess when you're stretching out of healthy differentiation. I often talk to myself out loud in the dark, during my morning and evening prayers, spontaneously when I'm expressing my gratitude for the preciousness of the opportunity, when I'm commenting on silly things that happen, or when I'm briefly conversing with my food delivery person. In my early retreats, when I really felt the weight of the darkness, there were times when I noticed that it sounded like my voice was no longer mine or like I was talking through several panes of glass. Something was off. The mind *falling* into itself and eventually bottoming out into the reduction base of innate wholeness is a beautiful experience marked by profound tranquility and indestructible peace. But the near-enemy of this blissful state is when the mind *implodes* onto itself. This implosion isn't so beautiful and can signal the pathological descent into dissociation.

If you have some retreats under your belt, you can explore this collapse of the mind, transform the near-enemy into a near friend, and learn a few things. Obstacle flips into opportunity. But for beginners or even intermediate practitioners, this loss of contact indicates it's time for a break; otherwise, the obstacle can transform into a debacle. In extreme cases, you could lose yourself in inner space and slip into a psychotic break. This is one reason traditional dark retreat fell out of favor. Overly zealous, unprepared, and unguided practitioners toughed it out to reach their goal of forty-nine days (or whatever) and basically reached madness.

When you take a break, pay attention to how quickly you feel better once your awareness is drawn outside and experience is diluted by visual input. Be a good micro-phenomenologist, and you will notice immediate physical and mental relief that exposes the power of distraction. Distraction is not always a bad thing. If you can distract yourself mindfully (a real oxymoron), pulling apart from the intensity of the present moment can be a lifesaver. I explored this process extensively in one retreat and was absolutely gobsmacked at how I could feel intense pressure and anxiety in one moment and in the very next moment—when the lights were on, and I was pulled out of myself—such instant relief. Sometimes I'd experiment by quickly turning the lights off and dropping back into the darkness, noticing how even a mere *microsecond* of light was enough to release the pressure. The brief flash of light was sufficient to help me relax again. I would then explore the effects of longer light exposure, a few seconds or a minute, and learned a lot about the extraordinary power of distraction to keep my ego (self-sense) alive. Here is the key point: If you're starting to *contract* in self-defense, that's when it's time to *open* the door or turn on the light. Keep this in mind when you're working with the balance between your stretch zone and the danger zone. Explore how quickly you can go back and forth between the two, then use this "two-step" to safely walk the path of darkness.

If you need to take a break, how long should it be? Sometimes a few seconds or minutes is enough to hit the reset button. At other times, an hour or more walk in nature is in order. I always did what felt right, aware of the dance between stretch and strain. In the world of meditation, the notion of "fresh start" is a good one. When things start to feel stale, seem stuck, or just don't seem to be working, step outside, then start afresh.

A more nuanced aspect of the talking test is noticing how you talk to yourself. Is the internal dialogue along the lines of, "I *should* stay in the dark," or "I *want* to stay in the dark?" If it's the former, that could be an indication for a break. Even more nuanced is noticing how you feel. Are you starting to contract, or are you staying open? A little contraction is workable; a continuous contraction suggests you're starting to endure.

Who to Listen To?

What does it mean to say, "Things don't seem to be working"? It depends on your perspective. They may not be working for your ego, but the challenges may be working perfectly for your spirit. The activation of different frequencies in the spectrum of your identity is what creates the roller coaster. Clarifying the confusion means understanding all the different voices that represent each frequency in this spectrum, listening to those at upper (spiritual) frequencies while letting go of those at lower (egoic) frequencies. If the lower frequency voices are in control, you're not even going to consider this strange practice. For most people who enter retreat, those bandwidths are already attenuated. But they're not exhausted. When the wisdom traditions talk about "exhausting your karma," they're referring to releasing the habits—and the voices from lower bandwidths of your identity—that no longer serve you.

A chorus of defeatist voices can arise in the dark: "I can't do this," "This is not for me," "I'm wasting my time in here," "I knew this was crazy." Let them come, then let them go. If they keep coming back but feel a bit weaker and quieter every time, you're doing the right thing by ignoring them and hanging in there. You're not toughing it out; you're "softening it out." With time, the negative voices get softer and softer until they fade into silence. The karma has been purified. One retreatant shared:

> You can't run; you can't hide. You have to sit there with it. All of it. And it can be uncomfortable. A lot of people don't want to sit with their own thoughts, or sit with themselves. But I loved it. I loved to sit by myself, and sit with me. And figure me out. That was the greatest part. Being alone with your thoughts. And you're going to feel all the emotions while you're in there. And it comes and it goes, and it comes back and it goes. But you have to learn how to deal with it. Learn how to deal with *you*. A lot of people were saying, "I don't know how I would do it. Be alone with myself, I can't be alone with myself." Yes, you can. That's where you truly find you.

However, if the voices or heavy thoughts keep coming back and feel stronger and louder every time, it's possible dark retreat is not for you, or it's not the right time. You can hit the refresh button by taking a break, or you can hit the eject button and leave the retreat. If you choose to leave, I recommend taking a few hours or even a day to reflect on your experience. Learn from it. With the right view, everything becomes a teachable moment.

People who do dark retreat tend to self-select, which means they internally screen out most of these egoic voices before stepping into the dark. Something is calling them to do this practice, and that voice is coming from higher frequencies. Unless someone talked you into going, many of the doubts and hesitations are, therefore, worked out before entering retreat. This gives you permission to hit the mute button if they start speaking up in the dark, recognizing them as fading echoes of the lower bandwidths of your identity. But don't mistake the mute button for the off button, which can turn silencing the voices into repressing them.

A few retreat centers have qualified guides that check in with you once or twice a day. Some people may not need this support, but for others, it's invaluable. If no such guide is available, but cell service is, you can arrange to have your food delivery person call an outside instructor for you. Set up a time with this person before going in, share the information with the delivery person at the beginning of your retreat, and be sure to send a teaching gift for the instructor when you come out. The delivery person dials the number for you at the prearranged time, then turns off the phone when you're done. With your eye mask on, you can do all this and remain in darkness. A caring voice can make all the difference in the world.

15

Four Steps for Working with Challenges

You will be miserable to the degree that you are hung up on the notion that things should—must—go a certain way. If you have no fixed view, you remain elastic.
—Alan Watts

Even hell wants to be held.
—Elizabeth Koch

Working effectively with challenging experiences starts with radically accepting whatever arises. Even when it hurts. Our conditioned response to challenging states is along the lines of "Oh no! Not that!," which causes us to dis-tract away from the unwanted experience. To say "yes" to what's happening is to open and accept who you are; to say "no" is to contract and reject who you are. Darkness is a "yes" enforcer. The practice is learning how to accept every dimension of your being—the good, the bad, and the ugly. It reinstates the truth that "the smaller the mind, the bigger the problem," and conversely, "the bigger the mind, the smaller the problem."

If an upheaval is particularly challenging, you can greet it with a glance before fully embracing it. The welcoming look is the first of four steps in relating to a challenging experience. The other three—handshake practice, hugging practice, and full intercourse (explained later)—are progressive stages of intimacy with the experience, which requires more courage but results in more transformation. Darkness invites this intimacy. People are more willing to fully expose themselves, in this case *to* themselves, in the dark. The following four steps offer a progressive method for working with any unwanted experience.[1]

The first two steps, the glance and the handshake, are more polite and reserved ways of relating to the challenging state, allowing you to ease your way in before opening to the experience completely. We're so habituated to contracting away from difficult feelings that it's a big ask to fully open right away. Some experiences are so charged that it takes a while to warm up to them. I am not trained in the new field of darkness therapy, but I have witnessed the therapeutic benefits of dark retreat for myself and dozens of others. Some of the benefits come from progressive desensitization, which involves repeated exposure to a triggering event with the goal of reacting less and less adversely.

It's important to understand that the difficult experience is coming up because it wasn't properly taken down and fully incorporated in the first place. Because it was initially hard to swallow, the bitter experience wasn't fully ingested, digested, and metabolized. If the experience was traumatic, you can't expect to digest and metabolize it in one setting or, in this case, one retreat. While I have witnessed nearly miraculous cures in short retreats, it generally takes time to digest and metabolize big events. Don't put any "quick fix" pressure on yourself. Recognize the power of your habits, but without capitulating to them. Capitulating means doing what you did when the difficult experience first took place: You either repress it or run from it. Running or repressing may have been the best survival strategy at the time, but for healing and integration to occur, that habit must be reversed.

The four stages of increasing intimacy allow you to gradually open to the energy and intensity of the experience, breaking it down into digestible chunks. They will show you how you continually try to "light" your way out of challenging experiences. Being polite, or the first step of glancing, means objectively observing the experience without getting sucked into it. You're interested, in terms of welcoming the experience, but not that interested. Indian sage Nisargadatta Maharaj said, "It is disinterestedness that liberates." But don't let disinterestedness slide into the near enemy of dismissiveness. That's not polite, after all. Step one, dispassionately *observing* the challenging experience, allows you to become familiar with it, to be kind to it. Which means you're becoming familiar with and being kind to yourself.

Step Two

Let's return to our four-step strategy: four increasingly refined ways of relating to a challenging experience. Each of the four steps can be engaged progressively or as a standalone remedy. With some familiarity in all four steps, you may find that one step works particularly well for you. You don't necessarily need all four. Because I've worked with this for so long, I tend to go right to the fourth step. But follow *your* experience and see what works for you.

The first step of observing whatever arises cultivates a witness awareness. It's a liberating state of mind that partially frees you from the contents of your experience, and for many people, that's good enough. No need to work with the other three steps. Witness awareness allows you to view whatever arises like clouds passing harmlessly through the sky; as Pema Chödrön says, "You are the sky. Everything else—it's just the weather."[2] But some experiences are so deeply rooted or emotionally charged that additional approaches may be needed. Just witnessing the experience may not get to the roots of it, and you'll know this when the experience keeps coming back. You politely keep witnessing it, it rudely returns.

A near-enemy of step one is when healthy differentiation slips into dissociation, as we've seen. Instead of passively witnessing a thought or an emotion, you slide into a passive-aggressive relationship to it. You're observing it, but with a tinge of dismissiveness. You're not honoring what's arising as a legitimate part of yourself. Notice that tendency and soften your "gaze." Observe the experience in a friendlier way. On an even more subtle level, the first step is still dualistic. "*I'm* observing *that*." You're keeping the challenging state at arm's length. The second step is to offer the difficult experience a welcoming hand, then pull it in so you can relate to it better. Remember that darkness involves retreating to your most nondualistic sense of feeling. This includes feeling in the physical sense of touch and feeling in the emotional sense. In other words, dark retreat shows you how to feel the contents of your experience fully and properly.

Step two transitions into a less cognitive (observational) approach and into a more tactile or felt approach. You're going to hand off the baton to your body. This step is about *being with* the challenging state, which gives you the opportunity to befriend it. If the energy or experience is charged, this isn't easy. It's like the challenge of being with someone you don't like. Your instinct is to get away. Step two shows you that enemies are really friends in disguise, there to teach you. Being with anything difficult goes against the tide of normal avoidance strategies. When I engage in this step, I notice how my mind flickers in and out of the experience. I touch into it, but because it's so hot, I often recoil and start to think about it, which serves to cool it off. I don't know how to feel it properly, to stay in touch authentically. Remember that your thinking head literally can't feel, so it's a lot cooler up there. Right, Mr. Spock? When I notice my inability to stay with the heat, I don't beat myself up. I note the power of my distancing habits, am kind to myself, and do my best to stay in touch with the unwanted feeling.

This is where we need to take another brief detour into tantra-level principles. Every time I use the word "it" when referring to a challenging experience, you can substitute "yourself." Relating to it—to yourself—as an "it" is to objectify it, solidify it, literalize it, which means reifying it. And reification is precisely what turns anything into a challenge. We unwittingly do this, pinching ourselves in the process, because ego, as the archetype of reification, lives on reification. This is how it puts itself on ice, simultaneously generating and preserving itself. Dark retreat emphasizes dereification, deicing, or seeing into the empty nature of whatever arises. This is why it can feel like a blast furnace at times.

Look into your experience and see if the following is true: You suffer in direct proportion to how solidly you take the contents of your experience. The more you solidify anything, the heavier it gets, the more impact it has, the more it gets you down, and the bigger the challenge. This is the essence of "endarkenment." Everything on the spiritual path in general and dark retreat in particular is about lightening up. How many times have we heard about the irony of going into the dark to lighten up? The four stages outlined here are four progressive stages of dereification or, in Buddhist terms, four stages of emptiness heading toward enlightenment. By the time you get to stage four, you realize the liberating truth that "emptiness cannot harm emptiness."[3] At that point, nothing can phase you. Nothing can touch you in a harmful way. You actually feel things more, but they hurt you less. By stage four, there's more of the feeling but less of you. As we'll see later, the experiencer dissolves into blissful nondual experience.

Dark retreat gives you permission to be with it, which means to finally be yourself. After three days in the dark, one retreatant shared: "This is what matters. Being vulnerable with yourself." With no one else to see you, with nothing to do, you can finally let your guard down and be naked. First to yourself, then to your world. Another retreatant shared: "I found myself excessively vigilant at first, but one day, darkness caught me off guard and consumed me! To my utter delight, the darkness then held me in the most loving way. I had nothing to be afraid of!" And one last practitioner said: "I will sit in total darkness and take off to places I haven't been before. But they're my places. They're me. It's very, very intimate. I realized I could trust myself. The knowing inside of me is true, and I can count on it. So the true test is: Who are you when no one is looking?"

By not caring how you appear to others, you can finally care for yourself. This is where the healing comes from. By being with yourself so openly, you can finally just be yourself. By not caring about how you appear, you finally care for who you really are. If you're like me, you're a screwed-up, confused, messy, hurting, but absolutely beautiful human being. Dark retreat shows you that within your imperfection lies perfection, and hidden within your scrappy humanity is your divinity. Beneath the disorder lies the most sacred order. But to find this deeper order, you have to stay with "it" and look and *feel* even deeper.

Step Three

The third step is to be curious about the nature of the unwanted experience and *examine it*. Socrates said that the unexamined life is not worth living, an ancient maxim with modern relevance. You're not looking to do psychotherapy in step three. You're looking into the *felt* nature of the experience. And you're not doing this examination with your intellect, which would pull you back out to the observation deck. You want to examine the feeling with your body. Step two, being fully with the experience, invites the transition into somatic investigation.

Here's how it works: If a sticky emotional state, let's say fear, comes up in the dark, start looking into the experience with a lead-off question from your head. Ask yourself, ask your *body*: "Where am I feeling this fear in my body?" "What does this fear really feel like?" Avoid therapeutic questions, like "Where is this fear coming from?" or "Why am I feeling this fear?" And stay away from philosophical questions, like "What is the ontological status of this fear?" "What is this fear made of?" While these questions are entirely valid, they can be pursued later. You want to stay fully in the present, with what's happening, and let your body massage the question into itself. Engage whatever experiential question invites you down and in; avoid the heady questions that send you up and out. Resist the temptation to cool off in your lofty head and allow yourself to heat up by staying in your grounded body. Remember that wisdom abides in the body. Let the body go to work on itself. Your wisdom body always knows what to do. Steps two through four almost trick you into staying embodied. Your body is always already present. Let your body take care of you.

Give yourself plenty of time and space for these investigations. What else do you have to do in the dark?! Be curious, and be kind. Don't look for a speedy answer. In fact, don't look for anything at all. Don't expect anything. You're engaging the power of an open question in step three. The practice is to ask the question, send your mind in the right direction, let your body do its thing, and stay open. The "answer" lies in the open-ended question. The answer is openness . . . and embodiment, the acceptance of whatever arises in that open space. That's what opens the ugly wrapping paper. Openness is what peels away all the (ugly) concepts you've wrapped around the experience and reveals the underlying (nonconceptual) gift of purified emotional energy.

If you're like me, you'll find that any unwanted experience is always accompanied by some level of contraction. If you stay with it, you'll eventually discover that *contraction is what makes it unwanted!* Resistance is what makes it unwanted. And what you resist persists. Stop resisting, and the challenging experience stops persisting. It begins to self-liberate once you open to it, once you open to and accept yourself. The contraction and resistance are a deeper level of ugly wrapping paper because this level of packaging doesn't come from the superficial level of concepts but from the body itself. This is not to say that the body is the origin of the contraction, but that the contraction is felt by the body. Once you're quiet and still enough in the dark, the heightened interoception allows you to feel all the tension/contraction in your body-mind. You'll eventually discover that your body is riddled with contraction, and opening to it starts to solve the riddles. Reginald Ray teaches on the importance of accessing and releasing the tension:

> As we become more and more aware of the parts of our body, at a certain point we will notice something else: the tension in each part. The more we explore this, the more we begin to sense that our entire body is actually riddled with tension. We are talking here not about the natural, healthy tension that is part of being human, but instead we are talking about neurotic tension, elective tension, superimposed tension—superimposed by our conscious orientation, our ego. Neurobiology tells us that this kind of pathological tension extends all the way down to the cellular level and is a contributing factor to ill health and disease.[4]

If you stay with it and open to it, you'll gradually feel the tension and resistance melt away. The tension/contraction is the result of all the fracturing. It's not turtles all the way down; it's fractures all the way down. And when you go into the dark, the turtles stick out their heads. You start to feel how broken you are and begin to heal the fractures just by feeling them fully.

By looking and feeling in this way, then staying open to whatever arises, you're almost hoodwinking yourself into the cure. You're inviting an expansive relationship to the fear (or whatever unwanted experience), which completely changes the texture of the experience. Something is still there when the gift is unwrapped, but it's no longer "fearful." That label, that concept, has been peeled back. You could append the word "energy" to what remains. With steps one through three, you're relaxing your grip on the experience, *holding* it in a new way.

Prior to this step, your grip is often so tight that it turns into a fist, and you end up fighting the unwanted experience, which only makes it stronger. This is why conceptually *grasping* what you're feeling isn't part of the inquiry. Your time in the dark then becomes a slugfest, shadowboxing at the most painful level. By stepping closer and closer to the experience, facilitated by step two of being with it, you can't throw nearly the same punch or be clocked by a haymaker. Step two is like boxers getting so entangled with each other on the ropes that the only punches they can throw are harmless taps on the ribs. When they're both exhausted at the end of a long fight, the boxers collapse into each other's arms in the ropes, which amounts to the hugging that stage three invites. It's a hugging that's initiated by properly *holding* the experience in a more open and loving way.

The final question of step three is the most profound and acts as a segue to step four. This last question moves the investigation from the experience to the experiencer: "*Who* is experiencing this fear?" The answer to this question, addressed in step four, can change your life.

Step Four

Dark retreat culminates in the experience of nonduality. Don't worry if this doesn't relate to your aspirations for dark retreat, but a brief dip into nonduality shows you yet again how far this practice can take you. This section reiterates and unpacks some of the deeper parts of chapter 6 and chapter 13. It's difficult, impossible actually, to speak about nonduality using dualistic language. But careful use of language, choosing the right words, can at least point you in the right direction.

Step four invites a nondual and, therefore, spiritual relationship to challenging experiences. For many people, nonduality is an abstract concept. Step four shows you how to make it a felt experience. By asking the first batch of questions from step three, you're essentially kicking the legs out from under the challenging experience—the first half of duality, so to speak. The final question, "Who is having this experience?" kicks the legs out from under the experiencer, the second half of the equation. Step four solves this dualistic equation. Since they both lean on each other—you can't have an experience without an experiencer, a subject without an object—yanking one or the other out causes both to collapse into each other.

The difference between step two, which invites you to be *with* the experience, and step four, which invites you to *be the experience*, is nuanced, as is nonduality itself. Before we began the four steps, there's the unquestioned feeling "*I'm* having *that* experience." Step one begins the process where we repeal duality and replace it with nonduality. We start with, "*I'm* observing *that*," which progresses to "*I'm* being with *that*," which leads to "*I'm* examining *that*." But they're all dualistic. Step four culminates in the nondual realization: "I *am* that." You're transitioning from increasingly refined dualistic relationships to the experience of nondualistic union. David Loy writes, "One does not do anything with that anguish [any challenging experience] except develop the ability to dwell in it, or rather *as* it; then the anguish, having nowhere else to direct itself, consumes the sense of self."[5]

This is subtle, so give yourself time to understand and then experience these claims, which is done by repeating the investigation until it clicks. The query "*Who* is having this experience?" is so resonant with reality that it eventually collapses into reality and leads to a direct nondual experience.

Contraction comes back into the picture at these very subtle levels and can therefore help you *feel* your way into the nondual answer. If you slow down and pay really close attention, feeling deeply into what's happening, you will feel a repetitive lightning-fast contraction away from the unwanted experience. This flickering away amounts to a subtle but constant form of distraction. You're contracting/distracting away from the experience and onto yourself, the experiencer, which creates the illusion that "I'm experiencing that." But you're not. It just seems that way. Stay with step four long enough, repeat it enough, inquire enough, open enough, and you'll eventually make an even more subtle and shocking discovery: You're actually contracting onto nothing! Meditation master Trungpa Rinpoche spoke about how this discovery can happen during the day:

> By relating with the ordinary conditions of your life, you might make a shocking discovery. While drinking your cup of tea, you might discover that you are drinking tea in a vacuum. In fact, *you* are not even drinking the tea. The hollowness of space is drinking tea. So while doing any little ordinary thing, that reference point might bring an experience of non-reference point. When you put on your pants or your skirt, you might find that you are dressing up space. When you put on your makeup, you might discover that you are putting cosmetics on space. You are beautifying space, pure nothingness.[6]

As we explored earlier, the contraction *itself* creates the illusion that there is a self. That's when you realize that the sense of self *is* that contraction. What you take as a given, as axiomatic, your very sense of self, is discovered to be a construct, born of contraction. It's a liberating discovery because this means it can be deconstructed. *You* can be deconstructed. And that demolition is accelerated in the dark, when you come to a hard stop and all your normal reference points are gone. Tilopa, the father of one of the four main schools of Tibetan Buddhism, taught, "When the mind is free of reference points, this is Mahāmudrā [nonduality]."[7] Stop contracting away from unwanted experience, stop referring the experience to an experiencer, stop grasping after wanted experience, stop any form of distraction, and the ego disappears. Because contraction, referencing, grasping, distracting are all that the ego is.

Just stop. And the deconstruction begins.

What's left when you unwrap your experience to such a degree? Nothing. The no-thingness, or emptiness, that we discussed earlier. Something is left, but it's not a thing. It's the same "thing" that was unwrapped above. It's completely ineffable, and trying to "eff" the ineffable is a futile attempt to wrap the experience back up in concepts. You can call it energy. You can call it formless awareness. Buddhists call it luminosity-emptiness.[8] Emptiness is the discovery that there's nothing there, no solid or reified experience or experiencer; luminosity is the nondual or dereified "thing" that is left. (Exploring luminosity is beyond our scope in this book.) Trungpa Rinpoche says, "The essence of this discovery is that you are actually nonexistent. By trying to find out who you are, you might find out that you are not anything at all. Then, although you find out that you are *not*, you discover there is still some glowing brilliance that exists within the experience of nonexistence."[9] And Thomas Merton shared:

> At the center of our being is a point of nothingness which is untouched by sin and by illusion, a point of pure truth, a point or spark which belongs entirely to God, which is never at our disposal, from which God disposes of our lives, which is inaccessible to the fantasies of our own mind or the brutalities of our own will. This little point of nothingness . . . is like a pure diamond, blazing with the invisible light of heaven. It is in everybody.[10]

Let's complete step four and take a breather. Talking about nonduality is not easy! If you're feeling fear, or pain, or anything unwanted, not only do you meet it, greet it, be with it, or examine it—you dissolve into it. You become the solution. In so doing, you'll discover that *by becoming one with your pain, there's no one to hurt*. There's just this sensation to which we append the label "pain." By becoming one with your fear, there's no one to be afraid. There's just this intense energy we call fear. David Loy continues,

> *[T]he way to integrate anxiety* [or any challenging experience] *is to become completely anxious*: to let formless unprojected anxiety gnaw on all those "finite ends" I have attempted to secure myself with, so that, by devouring these attachments, anxiety devours me too and, like the parasite that kills its host, consumes itself . . . The school of anxiety [challenging experience] is the path to true freedom, which is what remains after we have been purged of all the comforting hiding places we automatically flee to whenever we feel insecure.[11]

Now you're in full intercourse with the experience, completely naked to what's happening, embracing your experience to the fullest, and melting into it. The implications are immediate and profound. It's profound because it means that the absolute experience of duality is the experience of nonduality. And it's immediate because the freedom that you're looking for is right in front of your eyes. Hiding in plain sight. These four steps show you that the path is perceptual, not actual. Just like in the dark, you're not going anywhere on this path. Open, wherever you are, and it's all right here.

16

How to Work with Fear

When you turn away from all the substitutes, there's suddenly no future anymore, just the present. There's nowhere to go, and that's the ultimate terror for the mind. But if you can stay in this hell, with no way to the left or to the right or in front or behind, then you discover the peace of utter stillness.

—Peter Kingsley

Still, there were times when the light faded, almost to the point of disappearing. It happened every time I was afraid . . . What the loss of my eyes had not accomplished was brought about by fear. It made me blind.

—Jacques Lusseyran

I love the light and follow it as much as I follow my bliss, as Joseph Campbell famously exhorted. But if I only track the light, I tend to get blinded by it. And if I only follow my bliss, I tend to get lost in it. I have discovered that to really grow in this life, I need to keep one eye on the dark and follow my fear into it.[1] Anecdotal data suggests that about 75 percent of people who go into dark retreat experience some level of fear. I suspect that when formal numbers from our studies come out, it will be higher. The fear can range from mild anxiety to moments of panic. I've never experienced survival-level fear in the dark, but anxiety and trepidation were part of my early retreats. I would be suspicious if first-timers didn't admit to some level of anxiety or fear. We're always anxious about the unfamiliar and fearful of the unknown. Many people are afraid of being alone, and that fear is heightened when you're alone in the dark. We like to be in control, and the only thing you can really control in the dark is your mind, or more precisely, how you relate to it. Unless you're blind and, therefore, already familiar with darkness, spending time in the dark is likely to elicit both fear and anxiety. But as Marie Curie said, "Nothing in life is to be feared, it is only to be understood. Now is the time to understand more, so that we may fear less."[2] That's our aim in this chapter.

Relating to fear is a big part of life, a core aspect of inner work, and central to dark retreat. This chapter is, therefore, one of the most important in the book and one of the deepest. Don't let the depth scare you! Trungpa Rinpoche writes, "Fear arises . . . many times on the warrior's path . . . each time we take a further step, as we begin to discover a further stage or challenge of warriorship, just as we are about to give birth to further confidence, that breakthrough is preceded by a sense of utter fear."[3]

We're going to touch into tantric levels of dark retreat again to help us understand the nature of this fear. Like dark retreat itself, we're going to bring the fear that is buried in the cavernous recesses of the unconscious mind and deliver it into the light of consciousness. This is how we transform fear into fearlessness. We don't become fearless by getting rid of our fear but by going through it. Using the insights from the last chapter, to fear less, we need to feel more. We need to feel into our fear, which allows us to understand it, go through it, and eventually transcend but include it.

The dead stillness, ghastly silence, and terminal blackness of dark retreat sound like entering a tomb. It is indeed a graveyard for all manner of deception and, therefore, terrifying to the ego that lives on fake news. One Tibetan liturgy proclaims, "In the state of nonmeditation, all phenomena subside in that great graveyard in which lie buried the complexities of samsāra and nirvāna."[4]

But the graveyard transforms into a maternity ward, and you come to life in entirely new ways when you step out of the darkness and return to life. After three days in darkness, one retreatant shared a statement that is resonant with this chapter's epigraph from Kingsley:

> I found what is, what always is. If I had to put a word on it, I would call it stillness. And if I had to put a visual on it, it would be like a pool of water that, left alone, will return to stillness. I can't explain what is so desirable about stillness; it just feels like home. There's nothing to gain or lose; there are no flashing lights. It just feels like what is. I'm going to hang out there a lot.

The transformative power of dark retreat is directly proportional to its frightful intensity. You're entering the death space, the plot of negation and cessation. Retreatants may not use this language overtly, but at deeper levels of this journey, you're essentially going into the dark to die. Peter Kingsley writes:

> This is the place that gives access to the depths and also to the world above. You can go up, and you can go down. It's a point on the axis of the universe: the axis that joins what's above and what's below. But first you have to descend to this point before you're able to ascend, die before you can be reborn. To reach there, where every direction is available and everything merges with its opposite, you have to go down into the darkness—into the world of death where Night and Day both come from.[5]

Dark retreat is about letting go. And letting go is a euphemism for dying. Darkness invites you and eventually forces you to drop everything. On a physical level, you have to let go of how you normally move, how you habitually perceive the world, how you routinely go to the bathroom, how you eat, how you bathe, how you brush your teeth, how you speak, how you normally behave. On a mental level, you have to let go of your usual narratives, your storylines, your ordinary distractions, your conventional ways of interacting with day and night, your sense of time and space, your normal way of relating to sleep and awakening. On deeper psychospiritual levels, you have to release your patterned ways of structuring reality, the notion of inner and outer, the concept of self and other, your usual psychological or spiritual strategies for survival, and eventually your very sense of self, or ego. Who wouldn't be anxious or afraid of all that letting go? That's a lot of dying![6]

So give yourself a break, and realize that if you're *not* anxious or afraid, something could be awry. The first thing to understand, therefore, is that anxiety and fear are completely normal. Retreat leaders find that people who admit they're anxious or afraid tend to be more open, receptive, and available to the darkness than those who profess confidence and capability. Disingenuous confidence can create an unconscious armor that doesn't let the darkness penetrate.

The second thing to understand and appreciate is that working with the elemental forces of anxiety and fear at such deep levels is a rare opportunity. Every time I go into the dark, I tell myself how fortunate I am to do this level of inner work. It's not easy. But I remind myself that the difficulty is directly proportional to the profundity, which helps me embrace the stretch out of my comfort zone. Another retreatant shared: "Whew . . . ohhh. It's just so beautiful to feel at that depth. And to know that it's okay, that it's safe. I'm so grateful. I'm grateful that I had the courage to come. It was scary, even thinking about it. I am changed forever."

By bringing you face-to-face with fear, dark retreat gives you the priceless opportunity to transform one of the most foundational forces in life. Kingsley writes, "And they [Pythagoreans] understood that there's no going up without going down, no heaven without going through hell. To them the fire in the underworld was purifying, transforming, immortalizing. Everything was part of a process and there were no shortcuts. Everything had to be experienced, included; and to find clarity meant facing utter darkness."[7]

Integral Fear

Relating to a topic as complex as fear requires an integral framework. From this broader perspective, fear is a tremendous evolutionary ally. If we didn't have fear, we wouldn't be here talking about the nature of fear. We'd be a Chicken McNugget on the Serengeti, easy picking for any predator. The Hindu Brihadāranyaka Upanishad proclaims, "Where there is other, there is fear," which alludes to the omnipresent status of fear in our dualistic world, from physical to psychological to spiritual levels. From a biological perspective, we need duality. We need to be able to separate self from other to survive, and fear comes with the territory.[8]

The issue isn't fear but how we relate to it. The question is how to integrate fear into our lives in a healthy way. Include the healthy fear that keeps us alive but transcend the unhealthy fear that colonizes other parts of our lives as we evolve past basic biological needs. Otherwise, we're physically alive but spiritually dead. We'll remain scared stiff, frozen in our comfort zones. Understanding the evolutionary role of fear helps us realize how formidable it is and the power it continues to exert over our psychospiritual life. Fear is hardwired into our DNA, and because it's so foundational, it readily steps beyond its biological domain. If it's not kept in its proper place, this evolutionary driver turns into a devolutionary retardant when we step onto the psychospiritual path and into dark retreat.

Here's how it works and why an integral approach is critical: Fear protects form. Ego is exclusive identification with form. When you enter the path and aspire to evolve from ego to egolessness, from exclusive identification with form (matter) into a more complete identification with formlessness (spirit), how does the ego relate to this move? As a death threat. And fear barges in to keep the ego alive. When you journey deep into yourself in the dark and drop into transegoic bandwidths of your identity, the ego starts to kick and scream yet again: "You can't stay in here!" "You're going to lose your mind!" "This is not for you!" "You don't have time for this!" "You're not strong enough for this!" or any of the countless survival-level reasons that ego kicks up to keep you away from the egoless truth.

This is why it's so hard to grow up on the psychological path and wake up on the spiritual path. Ego wants to hold you back in territory it's familiar with and with experiences that are nonthreatening. A bubble bath sounds pretty good. Not only do you have fear hardwired to protect your physical body, you also have it encoded into levels of psychospiritual development to protect your ego. These are massive forces of the unconscious body-mind that conspire to keep you spiritually asleep in your comfort zone, and they come to light in the discomfort of dark retreat. It's why darkness is such an incredible opportunity to work with fear, but it's also why this practice can be so daunting. Who really wants to do this? Only those who want to evolve. Understanding this integral approach to fear can illuminate your path in the dark and come to the rescue when fear rears its inevitable head.

Fear Is the Fare

Fear is cognate with the Sanskrit *per*, "to go through," and is linked to the English *fare*, "go," both of which suggest an underlying meaning of "what one undergoes or experiences." It's a small etymological stretch to engage *fare* as a noun, meaning "toll, price, cost." In other words, we can view fear as the fare, the tax, that we need to pay in order to evolve. When experiences get taxing in the dark, you have arrived at the tollbooth for evolution. I alluded to Joseph Campbell's famous exhortation, "Follow your bliss," earlier. That's all well and good, but balance his advice with the more transformative adage "Follow your fear," as this one retreatant did: "I felt a strong drive to do the most terrifying thing in my life: put myself in a cave. I went in where the truth lies. Everyone's truth hides in the dark." This person had a rewarding experience because he had the courage to follow his fear. If you really want to grow in this short and precious life, go to the places that scare you.[9] But tread the middle way. If you only follow your fear, you'll just get freaked out. "Follow your fear" doesn't mean spiritual thrill-seeking or viewing dark retreat as a haunted house. It means finding your balance between the chicken-out zone and the freak-out zone.

We want to follow our fear because fear is the affective expression of ignorance. That's what we're really going after. We want to transform ignorance into wisdom, and dark retreat is uniquely situated to do that. Fear is the minion of ignorance. We're always afraid of the unknown. To transform ignorance, relate to its fearful expression. One reason I entered a three-year retreat decades ago was because nothing scared me more than having to face my mind so directly and for so long. I started doing dark retreats after that, partly because nothing intimidated me more than having to relate to my mind so intensely. In both instances, I was able to relate to anxiety and fear in a highly concentrated way and use them for the deepest psychological and spiritual growth.

Buddhism refers to emotional upheavals as klesha attacks, where *klesha* is the Sanskrit word for "factors [poisons] that disturb the mind and incite unwholesome deeds of body, speech and mind."[10] In order to evolve, the kleshas must be eliminated or transformed. But they first need to be identified. As we've seen, dark retreat is a practice of distillation, one that condenses the complex display of reality down into irreducible ingredients.[11] In terms of emotional upheavals, all our colorful kleshas reduce into the primordial palette, the three root poisons of aggression, passion, and ignorance. Dark retreat takes you down to these poisonous roots, where you can either pull them out or transform them into medicine. It's easy to recognize when you or someone else is having a klesha attack of passion or aggression. But I've never been able to say, "I'm having a klesha attack of ignorance." It's because we're always under attack. Ignorance is so subtle, constant, and unconscious that we don't see it, like a fish unable to identify the water in which it lives.

Ignorance is the root of the three root poisons and, therefore, the root of every klesha.[12] Aggression can be reduced to passion ("I don't want it" is an inverse form of "I want it"), which can be reduced to ignorance ("I want" because I don't know better). This isn't superficial ignorance, like not knowing about a subject, but deeper ignorance of the nature of mind and reality. If you can pull out this root, all the leaves, branches, and even the trunk of samsāra wither away and die. But you have to dig deep, which is precisely the opportunity afforded in the underground practice of darkness.

To get a sense of how insidious and omnipresent ignorance is, pause for a minute and see if you can touch into what it actually feels like. What does this root ignorance literally feel like? Can you contact it? Take a moment and try. (This question is a refinement of step four from the last chapter.) It feels like *me!* It feels like the ever-present sense of self, expressed in the feeling of "I, me, and mine." Let's take this a step further. What else does ignorance feel like? The sense of *other*, or anything external, expressed in the feeling of "it" or "you" or "they." You can't have self without other, inside without outside. They coemerge, or prop each other up, referred to as "coemergent ignorance." If you're experiencing a dualistic world of self and other—and who isn't?—you're under attack.[13] When all dualities heal in the nonduality of darkness, fission is replaced with fusion, and you can finally *feel* what you've never felt before. The very things you took for granted, as axiomatic or given—your sense of self and other—are products of ignorance. As darkness erodes the sense of self and other, it's going after ignorance, and we feel that as fear. The closer you get, the more frightening it can get. Fake news (ego) doesn't handle real news (egolessness) very well.

Agony or Ecstasy?

The following point is subtle but important. It also refines step four from the last chapter. Dark retreat, or deep inner work, only gets frightening when you're not relating to the dissolution process properly. Survival-level instincts (from the biological and developmental dimensions of evolution) barge in as your ego starts to dissolve in the dark, and you misinterpret the experience. If you pay close attention to the first moments of dissolution or opening, they are always blissful. Look underneath any experience to which you would append the label "spiritual" or "mystical," and you will always find some degree of openness. If left alone, opening feels *absolutely* ecstatic. But we rarely leave things alone. Pay even closer attention, and you will see that these lightning strikes of openness are immediately followed by the thunderclap of contraction, which is what generates the *relative* feeling of fear. You open, feel the ecstasy, but immediately slap yourself back into form and back into agony by referring the experience back to an experiencer, generating both in the process. One contraction, two births. Congratulations, ego; it's twins! You've just given birth to duality. It's a superefficient and superfast delivery. But it is not painless because samsāra is born right here.

When things start to fall apart in the dark and you can't handle that much opening or space, you contract not merely in self-defense but in self-generation. You contract to reestablish the very sense of self. This contraction is born of fear, the fear of (ego) death, and it essentially drives the fear into form. It drives the fear into *you*, into the center of your *relative* self, where it festers like an undrained abscess at the core of your (relative) being and effectively serves to keep you away from the center of your centerless (absolute) self.

When the mind falls into itself in the dark and you fall into the Underworld of your unconscious mind, guess what's waiting for you? That nasty f-word.

This fear not only keeps people from exploring the dark (themselves), but it kicks them out of darkness once they relax and fall into these deeper dimensions of their being. "Get me the 'f' out of here!" cries the ego as it trips and falls so deeply into itself.[14] It's a heightened iteration, the very foundational expression of what happens in daily life as we constantly flee from the dark depths of being back to the surface light, just because we're so afraid of the night and who we really are. Life then becomes a sophisticated avoidance strategy, fed by relentless distraction to avoid the harsh noble truth that if we relax our grip on surface structures and fall into the center of ourselves, we fall into the void of infinite space. Which means we don't stop falling.

Paraphrasing Trungpa Rinpoche, "The bad news is you're falling through the air, nothing to hang on to, no parachute. The good news is there's no ground."[15] You (ego, the archetypal "thing") essentially fall into no-thing and disappear. Armed with the wings of right view, the fall converts into flight, and you transform from a terrified subterranean slug in dark retreat into a smiling dakini, or "sky dancer."[16] By dropping in so deeply, you take off and soar fearlessly through the inner space of the mind, even when it's pitch-black, because you finally realize there's nothing to crash into. Emptiness cannot harm emptiness.

One particularly open retreatant shared his experience after three days in the dark: "Releasing fear and just physically feeling my stomach unclenching even though I didn't even know it was clenched. Just the bottom dropping away. Years we accumulate habits of holding ourselves back or acting with resentment. We just don't see it. There was no feeling, 'I've wasted my life,' but more the feeling, 'Well, we have a lot to look forward to.'" The view going forward is so much better when you learn how to fly.

Allow me to restate this critical point: In any form of deep inner work, you open and eventually make contact with reality. But unless you're familiar with your deepest Self as infinite openness (or selflessness; both are synonyms for emptiness), you reflexively contract away from infinity because there's no place for the self in this vast, open space. You'd rather feel bad (contracted) than get real (open) because this level of reality doesn't include you. Openness doesn't include contraction. Ego would rather contract into agony than stay open in egoless ecstasy. It would rather live in hell than die into heaven. Patrick Harpur writes, "It is we who do not take the single step into heaven . . . because to walk through would be to admit of another life outside ourselves, which, having admitted, we would have to lead. We would have to change, and this we cannot do: however miserable my little self, it is mine, all mine, and I won't let go of it."[17]

Deep inner work shows you that life is not about you. Because there isn't one. It never has been, it never will be. The sooner you get over it, the sooner you get over yourself by going deeply within yourself, the sooner you get aligned with truth, the easier life gets in darkness and in light. Bodhicitta returns as the doorway, to show you that heaven is but a single step away.

Ego temporarily drops its guard (habits) in the dark. But due to the power of our contracting habits, when we encounter such openness—such a formless and, therefore, unin*habit*able space—the ego says, "What about me! Where do I fit into this!" Well, it doesn't. Author Carolyn Rose Gimian writes, "The fundamental fear we have to work with is the fear of losing ourselves. When the stronghold of ego is threatened, fear is one of our strongest defense mechanisms. Beginning to dismantle it is one of the greatest gifts we can give ourselves or others."[18]

It is precisely the absence of the contracted ego that makes the experience so ecstatic! The level of spiritual ecstasy is directly proportional to the preceding levels of material agony. If you're really contracted, even a small experience of opening is orgasmic. The contrast makes it so. But if you're already open, the experience is very ordinary. This is why Suzuki Roshi said, "Enlightenment was my biggest disappointment." For someone already so open, the final opening was a letdown. It's the ultimate downer.

Dark Gifts

We're now in a position to refine our understanding of fear. When the Upanishads say, "Where there is other, there is fear," they're also saying, "Where there is *self*, there is fear." The relative self is embodied fear. When you're all alone in the dark, you can finally feel into the core of yourself, the ground of your *relative* being, to find this fear and eventually transform the ignorance. Just above this hot nuclear core, which is way too hot for the ego to handle, you'll discover all the other kleshas that are devoted to cooling you off by keeping you off this thermonuclear truth.

Because of its constancy, you may not know what primordial ignorance feels like because you're ironically always touching it. You're always in touch with it because the very sense of self is embodied ignorance, but you're not aware of it because there's no contrast medium that allows you to feel what's really going on. Darkness provides the contrast. By removing the ability to move, to get away from yourself, you have no choice but to feel deeply into yourself, where some painful but liberating discoveries await. It's painful because when you can no longer cool off, things naturally heat up, and it's liberating because you're finally touching the truth. You also never feel this root ignorance because you're unconsciously trying so hard to get away from its affective expression, or fear. Ego doesn't want you to get in touch with the truth, your empty self, and fear is a powerful deterrent.

Here's the great gift of fear that's unwrapped with deep inner work: We may not know what ignorance feels like, but we all know what fear feels like. Chögyam Trungpa writes, "One of the biggest problems in the world is that people don't feel themselves properly. So we are simple trying to feel ourselves, appreciate ourselves."[19] Darkness physically reduces us into the most nondualistic sense of touch while emotionally reducing us into the deepest root feelings. The deepest *relative* feelings that we're trying to get in touch with are those that rule everything on the surface of our lives. When we get to the depths, we feel fear and the intense contraction that accompanies it, which we can now recognize as the fare that must be paid to get to the underlying feeling of ignorance itself—embodied in the very feeling of your sense of self. Now you're getting down to it, to what *you* (the ego) really feels like. And it doesn't feel so great, which is why we spend our lives trying to distract ourselves from ourselves.

At these depths, dark retreat turns into a laser-guided missile, a bunker-busting weapon of wisdom, designed to penetrate the deepest of all emotions. So we follow our fear—our fear of the dark, of the unknown, of death itself—because we realize that it leads to ignorance and, therefore, the precious opportunity to transform it into wisdom. With the right view, the experience of fear becomes a really good thing. It's a sign that you're getting close to the sizzling truth.

As we've seen, ignorance and the primordial contraction feel like our sense of self. What do wisdom and openness feel like? Selflessness. And that feels like love. While anxiety and fear are the affective expressions of contraction, love and compassion are the affective expressions of openness. That's what makes it all worthwhile. We go into the dark, we do the deep inner work, to transform fear into love. The contraction transforms into expansion, self opens and dissolves into other, and both collapse into the nondual embrace of love.

Meet and Greet 2.0

The journey into darkness is a journey into the Underworld of the unconscious mind. It's not a journey to be undertaken lightly. It takes courage to face the unknown, the unconscious, the dark, yourself. Treat the journey with respect and enter dark retreat as you would a temple: with humility, openness, and veneration. Jungian scholar Robert A. Johnson writes:

> You must understand that when you approach the unconscious you are dealing with one of the most powerful and autonomous forces in human experience. The techniques of inner work are intended to set in motion the great powers of the unconscious, but in a sense this is like taking the cap off a geyser: Things can get out of hand if you are not careful. If you fail to take this process seriously, or try to turn it into mere entertainment, you can hurt yourself . . . it is possible to get in too deep and feel as though [you] are sinking too far into the unconscious.[20]

It's the perfect admonition to keep in mind when you're going into darkness. As with any deep dive into the unconscious, there's always the risk of drowning. Take it seriously. But not too seriously; otherwise, you'll get scared away. When exactly do you gain access to the powers of the Underworld? It varies from person to person and depends on the duration of your retreat. If your dark retreat is a short one, just a few days, you may remain at the upper bandwidths of the unconscious mind and barely begin to unscrew the cap on the geyser. But maybe not. I've seen people drop deep in short retreats. This is why it's important to have some understanding of the levels of the unconscious mind and what might await you in the dark.

Western depth psychology explores the bandwidths of the *relative* unconscious mind; the nondual wisdom traditions explore the deeper dimensions of the *absolute* unconscious mind. You have to drop through the challenging relative levels before you enter the liberating absolute levels. This more complete understanding can inspire you to make the taxing journey through the entry levels because you can now see the light at the end of an otherwise dark tunnel.

If you're feeling anxious or afraid before going into dark retreat, why are you feeling that way? What does darkness represent for you? Are you afraid of the unknown? Are you afraid of death? *Are you afraid of yourself?* These are test questions to reflect upon before going into the dark because darkness forces the exam. It's why the initial stages can be testing. Do this examination now, and you may discover that most of your life is indeed an avoidance strategy to sidestep the center of yourself. Ego does everything in its power to dodge the bullet of truth. But in the confines of your dark room, you can no longer dodge these bullets. You can no longer take any of those sidesteps without bumping into yourself. Darkness puts an end to any evasion tactic and essentially hurls you into the center of your centerless self. Precisely what you have spent your entire life trying to avoid. The harsh but noble truth that you don't exist. You've spent your life trying to hide from (ego) death. No wonder it's so scary to walk into the dark!

You're going into dark retreat to meet yourself. At the deepest levels, you're going to meet your maker (isn't that what happens when you die?). Your unconscious mind. What else is in there? What else could you possibly be afraid of in the dark? This is why it's so important to have a secure space that you can trust, where you feel it's safe to let go and "die."

Tsognyi Rinpoche teaches a "handshake practice," which is about opening your hand, your mind, and your heart to warmly meet and greet every aspect of your conscious and unconscious mind. If you don't open to the negativities, they won't just go away. What you're unwilling to embrace will squirt out in symptomatic ways. First, the negativity gets projected and loaded back onto the darkness, which continues to make it feel oppressive. Second, the negativities remain buried in your unconscious mind and continue to exert their formidable influence on your conscious life from within. Psychologist Bruce Tift writes:

> [B]y organizing our character structure around the avoidance of these unworkably intense feelings [like anxiety and fear], we paradoxically place these worst fears at the center of our [relative] sense of self . . . The very experience we've dedicated our life to not feeling . . . becomes the center of our [relative] sense of self . . . From a Buddhist point of view, our commitment to not feeling disturbing emotions gives rise to a very convincing sense that we have some central, essential nature. Our lives indeed seem to be formed around something, and that something feels deeply problematic to us. By practicing our avoidant strategies over and over, day after day for decades, we become experientially convinced that there must be a central point around which our life revolves. The centerpiece, or our [relative] being, is composed of our core vulnerabilities, which are perceived as problematic. Our life revolves around a problem. And that problem must be our secret [relative] self, because it's always been there and never seems to change.[21]

For the ego, something problematic is better than nothing. It's why the ego delights in drama and even tragedy because at least those Shakespearean plays (ploys, movies, or movements) are entertaining. Tift doesn't make the following important distinction, but his many references to the center of our being refer to our *relative* sense of self, or the intermediate and upper bandwidths of the unconscious mind. The deeper center of our *absolute* Self, at the core of the unconscious, is centerless, selfless, egoless, emptiness.[22] In other words, below the fear is blissful silence, stillness, and spaciousness. It's the experience of unconditional love, a true resting in profound inner peace (RIP). Understanding this can inspire you to follow your fear to get to your bliss, which is what Joseph Campbell could have said. It's precisely our inability to deal with this selfless, egoless, empty core that generates the fear, then the avoidance, all of which gets embodied as egoic structure and expressed as the entirety of our distracted lives.

There is no place for you (ego) in this egoless space, so ego is scared to death of it. It represents the death space. It's why we're so afraid of ourselves and what we might dis-cover if we ever stopped long enough to drop into the center of our being, a stopping and dropping that is the gift of darkness. The prospect of falling into oblivion (emptiness) is dizzying for the ego, what author Milan Kundera referred to as "the vertigo of eternity": "Anyone whose goal is 'something higher' must expect someday to suffer vertigo. What is vertigo? Fear of falling? . . . No, vertigo is something other than the fear of falling. It is the voice of the emptiness below us which tempts and lures us; it is the desire to fall, against which, terrified, we defend ourselves."[23] Our two-faced relationship to evolution comes back into play: Part of us wants to fall, but part of us is terrified of the defeat and the plunge into truth. Knowing this can help us relate to the unconscious conflict of interest.

Ego can't stand (on) this space, so it finds another place to stand, and another, and another (just witness your monkey mind), knowing that if it ever completely stopped moving, it would drop into the truth (of egolessness) and disappear. This is why we're so constantly distracted and always on the move. This is what creates a "human doing." Distraction not only yanks us out of this groundless space, the movement also creates the illusion of ground itself, a place for the ego to take a stand. Dzogchen Ponlop Rinpoche said, "[O]ne of our strongest habitual tendencies as sentient beings is that of moving, or being unstill . . . This is said to be the root of all confused habitual tendencies."[24]

Ego is the very embodiment of distraction, born of fear, and unconsciously whispers into your ear, "Do something, *anything*, to avoid inner truth. Keep moving, keep it *up*." Dark retreat puts an end to all doing and leads to the great fall, the undoing of the ego. Tift continues:

> Oddly enough, this belief [in a central secret self] serves us, because it means we don't have to consider the possibility that

> there is no center to our lives and no independently existing self... when we actually recover what has been disowned and bring it into our immediate experience—and see that it's not going to kill us—we begin to dissolve our sense of having an essential self. We discover that, absent a central struggle, we have no center to our life at all. We just show up each moment and deal with our life as it happens.[25]

Recovering feelings (like anxiety and fear) that have been disowned and owning up to them in our immediate experience is the opportunity afforded with deep inner work. Dark retreat takes the cap off the geyser and allows these unconscious feelings to bubble up, or erupt, into consciousness. Tift suggests the core instruction of dark retreat in his last sentence: Attend to the present moment, no matter how frightful, and everything else takes care of itself. *Hold* your fear properly, and the fear will take care of itself as it gradually transforms into fearlessness.

CONCLUSION

It's this good. Who would have known that life could bear such gifts? From a sober mind. This is crazy. It's like I searched my whole life for this.
—Anonymous retreatant

Darkness is the one remaining revolutionary act. Changing the political order does not matter. Economies are all more or less alike. Governments and cultures rise and fall. The person who chooses to turn off the lights and lie awake in darkness embraces the truth of a life before and beyond all of these. The only way back to the path we once traveled on as a species is through the darkness of deep time.
—Clark Strand

We started our journey into darkness with the youthful face of Janus looking forward. We can now engage the weathered face of Janus and reflect back. Recall that Janus is the god of beginnings and endings and the doorkeeper of the heavens. His two faces allow him to see inside and outside simultaneously, and forward and backward without turning around. He's sometimes called the god of duality, but that's a limited understanding of his unique capacity. It's better to interpret his two faces as contrasting facets of a single entity. Janus approaches his world with a unique and inclusive perspective. His is not a world of black or white, yes or no, dead or alive, asleep or awake, self or other, darkness or light. It's not the exclusive *either/or* view of reality but the complementary and more respectful view of *and*. There is no bias, prejudice, or favoritism with this all-encompassing perspective. He can *hold* two contrasting views at the same time, honoring both darkness and light, inside and outside, until you arrive at the nondual point where you take no sides.[1] Mahāyanā Buddhism calls this common ground "The Great Equanimity." Vajrayāna Buddhism refers to it in terms of "One Taste." Jewish scholar Zvi Ish-Shalom says that at this nondual point, "Everything tastes like God."

Janus upholds the godlike "double vision" of William Blake, the ability to see another level of reality and meaning below the outward appearance of things while simultaneously keeping an eye on external things. This eye-to-eye view allows us to see both relative and absolute truth simultaneously. Rephrasing William Blake, you believe a lie when you see with and not through the eye.

Double vision aligns inside (microcosm) and outside (macrocosm), seeing them as two faces of the same world. There's a hill outside Rome named after Janus, called Janiculum Hill, which offers a multi*face*ted view of the city. Evolution is marked by increased perspective, the ability to face your world in multiple ways, and the capacity to hold opposing views at the same time, all of which result in a more panoramic view of reality. It's a view, a tale of two cities, that's ironically nurtured in total darkness.

Looking back over our journey, we have emphasized darkness and the interior because our infatuation with light and the exterior has led us astray. Dzogchen Ponlop Rinpoche talks about "the extreme path to the middle," which suggests several points. First, whether we know it or not, we're all extremists. Our extreme obsession with light and the great outdoors has thrown us out of ourselves and out of alignment, distracting us into the display of mere appearance. We've turned into light junkies, addicted to all kinds of shiny objects. Darkness invites us into the great indoors and helps us back into alignment by retracting from the display to recapture the essence.

Looking out, seized by sight, creates distance and a lack of sensual intimacy. Looking within, captured by touch, encourages intimacy and leads to love. Lusseyran writes, "[T]his means an end of living in front of things and a beginning of living with them. Never mind if the word sounds shocking, for this is love."[2]

Secondly, to find our way back to the (nondual) middle, an initial overcompensation helps. It's like trying to flatten a scroll that's been rolled up for centuries. One pass of your hands along the surface won't do it. To get the paper to lie flat, sometimes you need to roll it up in the opposite direction. Repeatedly. It's an extreme counterbalancing move that eventually results in equanimity. Dark retreat can seem extreme at first, but that's only because of our lust for light. The path back to the middle mandates a preliminary overemphasis on the power of darkness to balance our extreme diurnal and wake-centric ways. Equanimity arises when light is finally balanced with dark, outer is brought into alignment with inner, the conscious mind is in harmony with the unconscious, surface is squared with depth, and diurnal and nocturnal are seen as but two faces of the One.

Dark retreat is not about bringing light into darkness. It's about bringing darkness to light. It's about giving darkness equal footing in our lives and restoring alignment. It's about solving the equation of consciousness and honoring darkness and all that it represents as much as we do light. Tibetan sage Milarepa said, "Not seeing [night] and day as differing, this is as meditation as it can be."[3] Facing opposites invites them into their underlying unity. Barbara Brown Taylor writes, "Darkness is not dark to God; the night is as bright as the day."[4] It's just not the same kind of brightness. It's the brightness that Lusseyran discovered, which shines when you come to relate to darkness on *its* terms, not yours, and discover an underlying brightness that is emptied of both darkness and light.

In dark retreat, as Patrick Harpur writes, "We are emptied of everything until we are an aching void that, like a vacuum, draws in the mighty rush of Love itself." He continues, "This can result in a vision of God [because God is love]. It takes place, as one anonymous medieval mystic put it, in a 'cloud of unknowing,' where you must 'reconcile yourself to wait in this darkness as long as is necessary, but still go on longing after him whom you love . . . You must enter a state of nothingness . . . a state of 'nowhereness,' where you are not outside or above yourself, nor behind or beside yourself either."[5]

To get to this divine point, you must let go of everything, including this book. Patrick Harpur concludes:

> Even the idea of God Himself has to be given up. The soul enters a profound darkness from which only the grace of God can deliver it. There, in the darkness that is not even darkness but beyond darkness and light, the spirit merges ecstatically with the Uncreated Light, yet its identity is not submerged; for all things in the "Super-essence" are "fused yet distinct." Sometimes the darkness is not darkness at all but the illusion of darkness created by the light of God, which blinds the soul with its brilliance.[6]

Dark Transit

Janus symbolizes transitions, from one condition to another, from one vision to another, from one way of understanding reality to another. We've engaged his spirit to transition from our partial exteroceptive and dualistic stance (a sight-centric, light-centric, wake-centric view of reality, all manifestations of the ego-centric stance) to a more inclusive interoceptive and nondualistic stance (a touch-centric, feeling-centric, egoless nonstance). From surface to depth, from myopic to panoptic, that's the gift of Janus. *Panoptic* means "showing or seeing the whole at one view." Synonyms include *all-embracing, all-encompassing, all-inclusive, overarching, sweeping, including everything*. This transition nurtures the double vision that amounts to a type of X-ray vision, allowing us to see through mere appearances and into underlying realities, cutting through the multitudinous display and into our shared essence. It's the transition from mere seeing to seeing through.

Applied equanimity, discovering our shared essence, comes to fruition as the parity of me and you. I have finally come into alignment with you. Jacques Lusseyran, whose blindsight has accompanied us on this journey, offers his final words of insight: "Blindness has shown me a space other than the physical one, which only serves to separate me from them and them from me. This is the space where the stirrings of the soul and the spirit come into being."[7] When the sage Ramana Maharshi was asked how to help others, his aligned reply was, "What others?" After decades of doing this practice, I have discovered that the secret sauce, that which inspires me to go into darkness and that which keeps me there when "rock meets bone," is doing this inner work for others. It's a transition that changes everything. Dark retreat is not easy. There are times when it still takes me to the edge. But I go there and take the leap because of you.

If I could adapt the traditional image of Janus for this book, I would have his two faces looking in toward each other for the duration of our journey as we come face-to-face with who we truly are in the dark. And I would conclude with the traditional image, with his two faces looking out toward others in the light. We first step inside to learn who we are, to recapture our essence. Then we step back outside, having learned that, despite the distracting display, we're essentially the same.

Janus, as a multifaceted principle, then assumes the role of psychospiritual janitor (derived from the word *Janus*), an earthly manifestation of this heavenly god. A janitor takes care of a building, in this case our recovered temple of darkness, to keep the space clean and in order—free of light pollution. This custodian, caretaker, and guardian removes the dust of diversity to reveal the underlying unity of the human condition, reminding us that we are each children of the night, siblings who simply forgot.

Hide and Seek

The wisdom traditions assert that modern advocates of these ancient schools offer nothing new. It's just a matter of repackaging. Of updating outdated operating systems. Of hitting the refresh button. You can look outside to acquire new knowledge, but that's disempowering. It projects onto others the wisdom within. Or you can make the effort to look inside and remember, which is empowering because you discover the light behind the projector. It's a peaceful transfer of knowledge and power that darkness always invites.

Plato wrote about anamnesis, or learning as recollection. All this effort to learn, when all you have to do is remember. For Plato, evolution was a matter of learning less and less. Taoist master Lao Tzu agrees, "To attain knowledge, add things every day. To attain wisdom, remove things every day."[8] Shift your focus away from shallow relative solutions received outside and turn toward the deeper absolute answers found within.

You already have everything you need within you. You just need to be shown. Dark retreat shows you what's hidden inside by removing the outside. No matter where you set your gaze in the dark, you're always looking within. One retreatant shared the fruits of this vision: "All the burden to try to be something, to try to get something, to try to figure things out. There is nowhere to go; there is nothing to figure out. It's all here and now, available to all of us. And that's it!" Another retreatant echoed this view: "I thought there was always something more. A greater substance, a greater thing, a greater aspect of life. That something greater is already inside. There is no seeking that needs to be done." Seeking denotes the absence of that which you seek. In one final head-spinning contrariety that would make Janus smile: You cannot find it by seeking, but only seekers will find it. And dark seekers seem to find it faster.

We use expressions like "at the end of the day" to convey a sense of the bottom line when everything has been taken into consideration, when you want to deliver the most important point. The phrase communicates a quality of the irreducible, what really matters in the end, what's of ultimate importance, the decisive conclusion, the finale. At the end of the day, it gets dark. It all comes down to darkness.

As gods are prone to do, Janus gives birth to a host of offspring. Janus words (antagonyms or contranyms) are multifaceted words that have developed contradictory meanings.[9] *Darkness* is a Janus word that we've explored using higher- and lower-phase darkness. One hell of a word with heavenly iterations. It's such a slippery sleight of mind, known to every dark trekker, how wisdom hides in the Underworld. Hades, the god of the Underworld, is the "Unseen One." He was also known as Pluton, the "Giver of Wealth," who distributed riches from below. But don't take my word for it. Seek it out for yourself. Step into the dark and trip into yourself. Disclose the treasures within. Then step out of your cave and share those dark gems with an outer world that remains lost in the light.

ACKNOWLEDGMENTS

A deep bow of gratitude to Tess Callahan, Dustin DiPerna, Lihi Eliza, Sean Esbjörn-Hargens, Eric Holsapple, Christof Koch, Adam Leonard, and Stephan Rechtschaffen for their valuable comments on the manuscript. Warmest gratitude to my agent, William Clark, for his skillful guidance in bringing this book to life. My editor, Lyric Dodson, showed her gifts yet again, and Jamie Schwalb at Sounds True sustained the entire journey. Tami Simon has my deepest thanks for her unwavering support. Oleg Gorelik, whose golden heart benefits all who know him, has been steadfast in encouraging my efforts in this book. The visionary Elizabeth Koch, whose kindness, courage, and generosity changed my life, has my infinite gratitude. Finally, my wife Cindy Wilson has been with me every step of the way, championing my countless retreats, enduring the endless writing, and bringing her professional talents to help birth this book.

NOTES

Introduction

1 My psychedelic journeys were never recreational, but always in the spirit of inner work. Almost all of them were guided by therapists, psychedelic researchers, or trained shamans, and the medicines I used include LSD, MDMA, ayahuasca, psilocybin, IM ketamine, and 5 MeO-DMT.

2 John O'Donohue, *Beauty: The Invisible Embrace* (Harper Perennial, 2004), 23–24.

3 When I discovered the work of historian and philosopher Peter Kingsley, I was startled at the resonance with my own experience in dark retreat. In his book *In the Dark Places of Wisdom* (The Golden Sufi Center, 1999), he writes about the ancient Greeks and "people who justified their teachings on the basis of journeys they made into another world, who saw it as their job to bring back what they found and describe what they learned" (p. 104).

4 It's a subtle point, but proclaiming that darkness is the color of nonduality is ironically a dualistic assertion. It could imply that the only way to experience nonduality is in the dark. I will argue that darkness is uniquely qualified to deliver us to the nondual state by withdrawing us from the dualistic display, but the point is to then take that nondual realization back with us when we return to the world of light. In the pages ahead, we'll explore why darkness delivers us so effectively into the space of "not two."

5 Experience (*nyam* in Tibetan) always has a beginning and an end, like morning mist. Realization (*tokpa* in Tibetan) is stable, like a mountain. In techno-speak, integration and maturation are the journey of converting fleeting states into enduring traits. Sharing experiences inappropriately is one sure way of preventing this conversion. See chapter 10 on how to integrate.

6 The one notable exception is *Wonders of the Natural Mind* (Snow Lion, 2000), a marvelous book by Tenzin Wangyal Rinpoche. While this book is for the general reader, it focuses on the more esoteric practice of tantric-level dark retreat.

7 I have received the permission blessing of many Rinpoches to write this book. The admonition for not writing about dark retreat applies to tantra level dark retreat, which I am honoring. This book deals primarily with sutra-level dark practice, which anybody can do.

8 See the many studies of Peter Suedfeld around REST (Restricted Environmental Stimulation Therapy), a relaxation technique using mostly flotation tanks that reduces sensory input and brings about deep states of relaxation. Numerous studies have been published around darkness therapy, also known as "blackout" or "dark room therapy." I'm working with several teams of neuroscientists to study formal dark retreat, but as of this writing, nothing has been published.

9 But unlike psychedelics, you can end the trip with the flip of a light switch. We'll explore parallels between psychedelics and dark retreat throughout this book.

10 "50 Essential Meditation Statistics for 2024, Benefits, Technology & Practice Data," FinancesOnline, accessed January 8, 2025, financesonline.com/meditation-statistics/.

11 "How Many People Meditate," Mindworks, accessed January 7, 2025, mindworks.org/blog/how-many-people-meditate/#:~:text=In%20recent%20years%2C%20surveys%20have,the%20breath%20is%20very%20widespread.

12 Stephanie Hsu, "Meditation Trends Around the World," *Muse*, May 17, 2023, choosemuse.com/blogs/news/meditation-trends-around-the-world?srsltid=AfmBOorthYEvVS3FuLn4WXin0MeibTk0d8Ycae9b6CYkDxzTLwO1TJiL.

13 *Kali* is loosely translated as "dark," so *Kali Yuga* is often translated as "Dark Age." Unless we constantly separate lower-phase darkness from higher-phase darkness, as we'll do in chapter 1, the term *Dark Age* could be confusing. For this reason, we're going to stick with the term *Kali Yuga*, or *Degenerate Age*.

14 Chögyam Trungpa, *The Sādhana of Mahāmudrā* (Nālandā Translation Committee, 1990), 5.

15 Integral Theory is one of the most comprehensive approaches to addressing the complexity of our current age. The five paths of waking up, growing up, cleaning up, showing up, and opening up explore this complexity in detail. I am acutely aware of what integral theorist Ken Wilber calls the "pre-trans fallacy" and of the difference between aduality (which expresses pre-personal fusion) and nonduality (which expresses transpersonal union). I leave it up to the integrally informed reader to decide for themselves if my argument slips into a pre-trans conflation. For more on the five paths, see Ken Wilber's *Finding Radical Wholeness: The Integral Path to Unity, Growth, and Delight* (Shambhala, 2024). For more on the pre-trans fallacy, see Ken Wilber's *Eye to Eye: The Quest for the New Paradigm* (Shambhala, 1990), p. 215–261. Also see the upcoming section "Glorious Deconstruction" in chapter 6.

16 Christopher C. M. Kyba, et al., "Artificially Lit Surface of Earth at Night Increasing in Radiance and Extent," *Science Advances* 3, no. 11 (November 2017), science.org/doi/10.1126/sciadv.1701528; see Dark Sky International for more on light pollution outreach, advocacy, and conservation: darksky.org.

17 Amina Khan, "Artificial Lights Are Eating Away at Dark Nights—And That's Not a Good Thing," *Los Angeles Times*, November 22, 2017, latimes.com/science/sciencenow/la-sci-sn-earth-artificial-light-night-darkness-20171122-story.html.

18 Khan, "Artificial Lights Are Eating Away at Dark Nights—And That's Not a Good Thing."

19 Barbara Brown Taylor, *Learning to Walk in the Dark* (Canterbury Press, 2015), 5.

20 Listen to scientist John Wren Lewis talk about his near-death experience and how he found God in deep and dazzling darkness: "The Dazzling Dark, an Interview with John Wren Lewis by Caroline Jones," youtube.com/watch?v=TDHsi-HOiQU.

21 Christopher Dewdney, *Acquainted with the Night: Excursions Through the World After Dark* (Bloomsbury, 2004), 138.

22 Tarek Asaad, "Sleep in Ancient Egypt," in *Sleep Medicine*, eds. Sudhansu Chokroverty and Michel Billiard (Springer, 2015), doi.org/10.1007/978-1-4939-2089-1_2.

23 Peter Kingsley, *In the Dark Places of Wisdom*.

24 For one rich source, see Gregory Shaw, *Hellenic Tantra: The Theurgic Platonism of Iamblichus* (Angelico Press, 2024).

25 Mantak Chia, *Darkness Technology: Darkness Techniques for Enlightenment*, Universal Healing Tao ebook, accessed January 21, 2024, school.mantakchia.com/product/darkness-technology-darkness-techniques-for-enlightenment/.

26 Ross Heaven and Simon Buxton, *Darkness Visible: Awakening Spiritual Light Through Darkness Meditation* (Destiny Books, 2005), 6.

27 This is my own classification; you will not find this articulation in traditional texts. Virtually every traditional text is about tantra-level dark retreat. I consider sūtra-level dark retreats to be anywhere from one to five days and tantra level to be anywhere from five days to a month or more.

28 To get a sense of the challenges in understanding a tantric text, try reading *The Tibetan Book of the Dead*. This book is a user-friendly adaptation of aspects of the Guhyagarbha Tantra but remains incomprehensible to most readers.

29 Sūtra versus tantra dark retreat (called *yangti nagpo*, or "black quintessence," in Tibetan Buddhism) is akin to the difference between spelunking and speleology. Spelunking is the amateur exploration of caves or going underground as a part-time hobby. I've gone spelunking in some truly spectacular caves and derived great benefit. Speleology is the scientific study of caves, exploring their physical properties, structure, history, composition, ecology, and the processes by which they form and change. I can imagine spiritual thrill-seekers and impatient explorers wanting to rush into the deeper tantric end of the cave, but without the proper motivation, preparation, and supervision, you can get in over your head. Or in this case, under it.

Chapter 1: The Two Faces of Darkness

1 The term *ego* is used in this book in the developmental sense, synonymous with the sense of self. It is not used in the colloquial sense, as when we say, "He has a big ego," even though the two usages are not entirely separate. Unless stated otherwise, all the testimonials in this book are (1) courtesy of dark retreat guide Scott Berman or (2) comments from the many retreatants I have talked to over the years. The majority of these testimonials come after three days of dark retreat. I've taken the liberty to do minor edits to make the statements more readable.

2 This is also when you meet the gods who live in the deepest recesses of the dark: Thanatos, the Greek god of death, and Yama, the Tibetan Lord of Death. When Yama is accessed in the dark, he can be transformed into Prajñāpāramitā, and the Lord of Death transforms into the Mother of All the Buddhas. When Thanatos is accessed and transformed, he flips into the

enlightened form of Eros, the Greek god of passion and fertility. In the dark, death transforms into birth. Dark retreat has shown me how immortal gods, qualities, and principles become literally personified and reified into mere mortals.

3 Carl Jung, *Psyche and Symbol*, ed. Violet S deLaszlo (Anchor, 1958), 8.

4 Depth psychology emphasizes the unconscious mind. While its origins can be traced to Sigmund Freud and his mentor Joseph Breuer, depth psychology reached its apex in the work of Swiss psychologist Carl Jung and Austrian psychotherapist Alfred Adler.

5 Quoted in Ross Heaven and Simon Buxton, *Darkness Visible: Awakening Spiritual Light through Darkness Meditation* (Destiny Books, 2005), ix.

6 Peter Kingsley, *In the Dark Places of Wisdom* (The Golden Sufi Center, 1999), 64–65.

7 "To hide," from the Old High German *tarchanjan*; the "place where dirt collects," from the Middle Low German *dork*. See John Ayto, *Dictionary of Word Origins: The Histories of More Than 8000 English-Language Words* (Arcade Publishing, 1991), 157.

8 Kingsley, *In the Dark Places of Wisdom*, 68.

9 Quoted in Barbara Brown Taylor, "Barbara Brown Taylor: In Praise of Darkness," *Time*, April 17, 2014, time.com/65543/barbara-brown-taylor-in-praise-of-darkness/.

10 Quoted in G. A. Gaskell, *Dictionary of All Scriptures and Myths* (Dorset Press, 1988), 250.

11 Quoted in Reginald A. Ray, *Touching Enlightenment: Finding Realization in the Body* (Sounds True, 2008), 63.

12 This quote has also been attributed to Josh Billings, Artemus Ward, Kim Hubbard, and Will Rogers.

13 Someone might proclaim they have no racial prejudice, for example, but when presented with a reaction-time test where pleasant and unpleasant words are paired with the words *white* or *black*, the words with pleasant connotations are more rapidly paired with the word *white*, while words with unpleasant overtones are quickly paired with the word *black*. See A. G. Greenwald and M. R. Banaji, "Implicit Social Cognition: Attitudes, Self-Esteem, and Stereotypes," *Psychological Review* 102, no. 1 (1995): 4–27, doi:10.1037/0033-295x.102.1.4. During unconscious mental processing, activity in the dorsolateral prefrontal cortex (DLPFC) decreases. "As you become more aware of being aware, the DLPFC becomes more active . . . Meditation can both enhance the function of the DLPFC and lessen unconscious bias"; see Daniel Goleman and Richard J. Davidson, *Altered Traits: Science Reveals How Meditation Changes Your Mind, Brain, and Body* (Avery, 2017), 142. In other words, meditation—diurnal or nocturnal—can bring unconscious processes into the light of consciousness, blind spots into sight, and hidden biases into full view.

14 Barbara Brown Taylor, *Learning to Walk in the Dark* (Canterbury Press, 2015), 108.

15 Jacques Lusseyran, *Against the Pollution of the I: On the Gifts of Blindness, the Power of Poetry, and the Urgency of Awareness* (New World Library, 2016), p. 43 and 48.

16 Andrew Holecek, *Dream Yoga: Illuminating Your Life Through Lucid Dreaming and the Tibetan Yogas of Sleep* (Sounds True, 2016), xi.

Chapter 2: Installing the GPS

1. Patrick Harpur, *The Secret Tradition of the Soul* (North Atlantic Books, 2011), 127.
2. Thomas Moore, *Care of the Soul: A Guide for Cultivating Depth and Sacredness in Everyday Life* (HarperCollins, 1994), 5.
3. Paul Tillich, "You Are Accepted," accessed April 23, 2025, wedgeblade.net /files/archives_assets/20810.pdf.
4. Gregory Shaw, *Hellenic Tantra: The Theurgic Platonism of Iamblichus* (Angelico Press, 2024), 88–89.
5. Chögyam Trungpa, *The Myth of Freedom and the Way of Meditation* (Shambhala, 1988), 96.
6. Greater and greater degrees of alignment are one way to look at the stages of the path altogether. When there's less and less of you, the ego, blocking the natural flow, then there's more and more grace, blessing, and Providence that pours through you.
7. Thomas Moore, *Care of the Soul*, 26.
8. Henry David Thoreau, *Walden and Civil Disobedience* (Signet Classics, 2012), 74.
9. *Retreat* and *retraction* are essentially the same word, both derivative of the Latin *retrahere*, which means to "draw back" or otherwise withdraw.

Chapter 3: Dark Retreat as an Observatory

1. Also translated as "Great Completion," or "Great Connection." I now view it as the Great Alignment tradition. These teachings will show you that every moment, if left alone, is already complete and perfect. They also reveal how we're inextricably connected to every other living being on this planet as well as the planet itself.
2. Troubles arise in the dark, or in life, when we solidify or reify things. With nothing to distract you in the dark, everything gets concentrated. A near enemy of concentration is reification, or mis-taking the contents of your experience to be so real. Madness is a consequence of reification, an "endarkened" view; enlightenment is a consequence of dereification, an enlightened view.
3. Shunryu Suzuki, *Zen Mind, Beginner's Mind: Informal Talks on Zen Meditation and Practice* (Weatherhill, 1985), 21.
4. Mahāmudrā, or the "Great Seal," is practiced as a series of investigations into the nature of the mind. Questions are posed that "lead the witness" into exploring the nature of the mind in stillness, in movement, in the body, and in appearances. Mahāmudrā leads to a state of awareness where appearance and emptiness are unified, which is virtually synonymous with enlightenment itself.
5. Philosopher Ken Wilber writes, "At *any* point on the developmental cycle those deep structures which have not yet emerged from the ground-unconscious are referred to as the emergent-unconscious." See Ken Wilber, *Eye to Eye: The Quest for the New Paradigm* (Shambhala, 1990), 114.
6. Jeffrey J. Kripal, *How to Think Impossibly: About Souls, UFOs, Time, Belief, and Everything Else* (University of Chicago Press, 2024), 32.
7. Taking an audio version of this book into the dark may not be a bad idea. But don't listen to it as a form of distraction or entertainment. Check your motivation, and only listen to it in brief chunks. As a general rule, leave everything behind. But if you feel in your heart that select instructions about dark retreat would help, trust that intuition.

8 I recently saw a cartoon of a crusty old man standing pensively with a wooden staff along a mountain trail, with the thought-bubble, "The older I get, the more I regret all the people I've lost over the years. Maybe being a trail guide wasn't such a great idea after all." The gallows humor haunts me a bit with the writing of this guidebook.

9 Yongey Mingyur Rinpoche with Helen Tworkov, *In Love with the World: A Monk's Journey Through the Bardos of Living and Dying* (Random House, 2019), 10.

10 George Mason University, "Letter from John Keats to George and Thomas Keats, 21 December, 1817," accessed August 31, 2024, mason.gmu.edu/~rnanian/Keats-NegativeCapability.html.

11 Yongey Mingyur Rinpoche with Helen Tworkov, *In Love with the World*, 20.

12 John Welwood, *Journey of the Heart: The Path of Conscious Love* (Harper Perennial, 1990), 18.

13 Self-liberation, or sahajayāna, is arguably the highest form of liberation. It's like writing in water. Phenomena self-liberate the instant they appear. In *The Sādhana of Mahāmudrā* (Shambhala, 2025), Trungpa Rinpoche wrote, "Good and bad, happy and sad, all thoughts vanish into emptiness like the imprint of a bird in the sky." Birds don't leave imprints in the sky. No imprint, no karma.

14 The universe seems to have a network topology analogous to the human brain. A network topology is the physical and logical arrangement of nodes and connections in a network. I've had experiences in dark retreat that are remarkably similar to what I experience when I look up into the nighttime sky. As a duality decimator, dark retreat breaks down the duality of inside and outside. Astronauts and psychonauts share much in common.

15 *Dark matter* and *dark energy* are terms thrown onto the mystery of the unknown. *Dark* means "we don't know." The terms explain nothing, but they make people feel better because at least we can throw a label onto these mysteries, creating the illusion that this level of "articulation" actually describes something.

16 To further explore the dance between appearance and reality, see the film *Mask*, where a blind girl is attracted to a severely deformed boy and connects to the reality of who he is behind the mask of mere appearance: *Mask* directed by Peter Bogdanovich (1985, Universal Pictures).

17 Quoted in Jeanette Winterson, "Shafts of Sunlight," *The Guardian*, November 14, 2008, theguardian.com/books/2008/nov/15/ts-eliot-festival-donmar-jeanette-winterson.

18 Nothing—or more accurately, no-thing—is a synonym for emptiness. At deeper levels of dark retreat, emptiness is happening in the dark because darkness is homologous to emptiness. This is why dark retreat is such an emergent phenomenon, because everything arises from nothingness, and nothingness is heightened in the dark.

Chapter 4: Why Do Dark Retreat?

1 The five nocturnal meditations are liminal dreaming, lucid dreaming, dream yoga, sleep yoga, and bardo yoga.

2 Jeff Warren, *The Head Trip: Adventures on the Wheel of Consciousness* (Random House, 2007), 11.

3 Quoted in Adam Zeman, "The Big Idea: How Do Our Brains Know What's Real?" *The Guardian*, February 10, 2025, theguardian.com/books/2025/feb/10/the-big-idea-how-do-our-brains-know-whats-real.

4 Michael Pollan, *How to Change Your Mind: What the New Science of Psychedelics Teaches Us About Consciousness, Dying, Addiction, Depression and Transcendence* (Penguin Press, 2018), 290.

5 Patrick Harpur, *Daimonic Reality: A Field Guide to the Otherworld* (Pine Winds Press, 2024), 20.

6 Isaac Lidsky, *Eyes Wide Open: Overcoming Obstacles and Recognizing Opportunities in a World That Can't See Clearly* (Tarcher, 2017), 20–22.

7 Arthur Koestler, *The Act of Creation: A Study of the Conscious and Unconscious in Science and Art* (Dell Publishing, 1964), 314.

8 Goodreads, "Werner Heisenberg Quotes," accessed August 15, 2025, goodreads.com/quotes/64760-what-we-observe-is-not-nature-itself-but-nature-exposed.

9 Bernardo Kastrup, *More Than Allegory: On Religious Myth, Truth and Belief* (Iff Books, 2016), 76.

10 Clarissa Pinkola Estés, *Women Who Run with the Wolves: Myths and Stories of the Wild Woman Archetype* (Ballantine Books, 1995), 48.

11 Or a radical change in the direction of thought, as in the work of psychologist and pedagogue Edward de Bono and his "lateral thinking" (see his book *The Use of Lateral Thinking*, Pelican/Penguin Books, 1972); or the craze over fuzzy logic and fuzzy thinking (see Bart Kosko's *Fuzzy Thinking: The New Science of Fuzzy Logic*, Hyperion, 1994; and Paul Freilberger and Daniel McNeill's *Fuzzy Logic: The Revolutionary Computer Technology That Is Changing Our World*, Touchstone, 1994).

12 Brian D. Josephson, "'We Think That We Think Clearly, but That's Only Because We Don't Think Clearly': Mathematics, Mind, and the Human World," Cornell University arXiv, September 8, 2019, arxiv.org/abs/1307.6707.

13 Goodreads, "Albert Einstein Quotes," accessed July 24, 2025, goodreads.com/quotes/320600-we-can-not-solve-our-problems-with-the-same-level.

14 Clark Strand, *Waking Up to the Dark: Ancient Wisdom for a Sleepless Age* (Random House, 2015), 54.

15 The question is FedEx'd directly into some cosmic routing center, and the answer is beamed back to me with startling speed. How fast? According to the science of scotobiology, which is the study of biology as directly affected by darkness, darkness travels at the speed of light. That's 186,282 miles per *second*. By other accounts, darkness is even faster than the speed of light, based on the notion that shadows "move" faster than light. A thought experiment reveals this mind-bending truth: "Imagine you have a light that's powerful enough to reach the planet Jupiter. Imagine also that it casts that beam in a cone that's broad enough to cover the entire diameter of the planet. When you pass your finger over the lens, the shadow will cross the entire diameter of the planet—a distance of 86,881 miles (139,821 kilometers). The speed of light is 186,000 miles per second (299,338 kilometers per second). So if it takes you less than half a second to move your hand that distance, then that shadow will have 'broken' the speed of light." See Reuben Westmaas, "Darkness Is Faster than the Speed of Light," *Discovery*, August 1, 2019, discovery.com/science/darkness-is-faster-than-the-speed-of-light.

16 This is precisely the opportunity that's also afforded in dream yoga, a hybrid state of consciousness where the conscious mind can face the unconscious mind directly. To the question of whether karma can come to maturation in the dream state, scholar B. Alan Wallace writes, "Definitely yes . . . rather than having it come to full maturation in some waking state. Better to get rid of it in the dream state"; see B. Alan Wallace, *Dreaming*

Yourself Awake: Lucid Dreaming and Tibetan Dream Yoga for Insight and Transformation (Shambhala, 2012), 133.

17 BrainyQuote.com, "William James Quotes," accessed March 24, 2025, brainyquote.com/quotes/william_james_157162.

18 This classic liturgy is called "The Four Dharmas of Gampopa."

19 Jacques Lusseyran, *Against the Pollution of the I: On the Gifts of Blindness, the Power of Poetry, and the Urgency of Awareness* (New World Library, 2016), 53.

20 Barbara Brown Taylor, *Learning to Walk in the Dark* (Canterbury Press, 2015), 105.

21 Jacques Lusseyran, *Against the Pollution of the I*, 52–53.

22 It is noteworthy that the Buddha attained his awakening not during the day but after going through the four watches of the night. His final steps to enlightenment were in the dead of darkness. Sthāvarā is yet another goddess waiting for you in the dark. In the context of yogic philosophy, touch (samsparśa) is a form of transmission and a type of knowledge. Abhinavagupta, the medieval philosopher-sage of Kashmir, outlined ten stages of unfolding spiritual power (kundalinī) as a somatic language of consciousness "translating" itself through the body. This unfurling revelation culminates in the state of avācya, the inexpressible or indescribable, an experience that transcends ordinary language and can only be understood through the wisdom of the body: contemplation, inner yoga, or deep meditation. According to Abhinavagupta, the degree of one's experience of this ineffable state is directly proportional to how deeply one touches the infinite. In other words, when you go so deep into your (nonverbal) body, you finally get in touch with reality itself. Dark retreat then becomes a real contact sport, hitting you with the unspeakable truth of the absolute.

23 Ross Heaven and Simon Buxton, *Darkness Visible: Awakening Spiritual Light through Darkness Meditation* (Destiny Books, 2005), 6.

24 In his book *In the Dark Places of Wisdom*, Peter Kingsley counters this external trajectory in a narrative we'll explore in the tantric companion to this book: "Perhaps you've noticed it—that our awareness is completely motionless, never changes. When we walk down the road we're really not going anywhere. We can travel around the world and we're not going anywhere at all. We never go anywhere; if we think we do we're just caught in the web of appearances, caught in the web of our senses." Remove the web of your externally oriented senses and you're no longer caught in mere appearance.

25 Stephen Fry, *Mythos: The Greek Myths Reimagined* (Chronicle Books, 2017), 20.

26 Matthew Walker, *Why We Sleep; Unlocking the Power of Sleep and Dreams* (Scribner, 2017), 57.

27 Cloud Dragon Dharma Works, "Joan Sutherland, Roshi: The Radiance of the Dark," YouTube, February 10, 2022, youtube.com/watch?v=zlwSOyrgScI.

28 David R. Loy, *Lack & Transcendence: The Problem of Death and Life in Psychotherapy, Existentialism, and Buddhism* (Wisdom Publications, 2018), 35.

29 What eventually happens after the projections wear off is that we fall out of love and into reality. We fall out of conditional and romantic love and into the reality of the person below our projections. In dark retreat, we can take all this a step further: We fall out of reality and into love. As we will see in chapter 6, as the mind falls into itself in darkness, we fall through relative and conditioned reality into absolute and unconditional love, which is the

irreducible matrix of reality, what Buddhism refers to as emptiness. As we'll see, emptiness is just a funny way to talk about unconditional love.

30 Peter Kingsley, *In the Dark Places of Wisdom*, 185–187.

31 Gregory Shaw, *Hellenic Tantra: The Theurgic Platonism of Iamblichus* (Angelico Press, 2024), 193.

32 Alistair Appleton, "The Magic of No Escape," Mindsprings, February 4, 2023, mind-springs.org/post/the-magic-of-no-escape.

Chapter 5: Why Is Dark Retreat So Transformative?

1 "Joseph Campbell: The Privilege of a Lifetime Is Becoming (Being) Who You Truly Are," Mystery of Existence, accessed October 1, 2025, absentofi.org/2025/04/carl-gustav-jung-the-privilege-of-a-lifetime-is-to-become-who-we-truly-are/.

2 Bruce Lipton, *The Biology of Belief: Unleashing the Power of Consciousness, Matter & Miracles* (Hay House, 2005), 122. Astrophysicists estimate that ninety-five percent of the universe is made up of dark matter and dark energy. Ninety-five percent of every moment is mysterious to us.

3 C. G. Jung, *Psychology and Alchemy*, vol. 12 in *The Collected Works of C. G. Jung* (Princeton University Press, 1968); C. G. Jung, *Alchemical Studies*, vol. 13 in *The Collected Works of C. G. Jung* (Princeton University Press, 1968).

4 Goodreads, "Gospel of Thomas Quotes," accessed April 15, 2025, goodreads.com/quotes/126072-if-you-bring-forth-what-is-within-you-what-you.

5 Robert A. Johnson, *Inner Work: Using Dreams and Active Imagination for Personal Growth* (Harper & Row, 1989), 9–10.

6 Ken Wilber, *Eye to Eye: The Quest for the New Paradigm* (Shambhala, 1990), 101–123.

7 IFS refers to Internal Family Systems, and EMDR refers to Eye Movement Desensitization and Reprocessing. These are just two of countless methods that are helpful in the ongoing journey of transformation.

8 Chögyam Trungpa, *The Myth of Freedom and the Way of Meditation* (Shambhala, 1988), 69.

9 Barbara Brown Taylor, *Learning to Walk in the Dark* (Canterbury Press, 2015), 93.

10 This would be a most interesting thing to study scientifically if participants would be willing to be so shocked. How long would one have to be in the dark for this level of sensory assault trauma to occur? What exactly happens to the body neurologically, hormonally, physiologically, and biochemically when one is assaulted by light? What would be the phenomenological impact, and how long would it take to recover?

11 As we'll explore in the tantric companion volume, darkness is feminine. In tantra, the female penetrates the male. Light is masculine in Buddhist tantra, and runaway luminosity manifests as all the pathologies of patriarchy dominating our wake-centric, light-centric, and sight-centric world. If we're careful, dark retreat can be viewed as a form of radical spiritual feminism designed to put the world back into alignment, into harmony, by penetrating and melting the runaway male energy that manifests in what we label as form itself. Form is nothing but frozen light, and darkness melts that light as all forms disappear back into the primordial womb from which they arose.

12 Jacques Lusseyran, *Against the Pollution of the I: On the Gifts of Blindness, the Power of Poetry, and the Urgency of Awareness* (New World Library, 2016), 45–46.

13 Tess Callahan, "The Love Affair Between Creativity and Constraint," TEDx Talks, YouTube, October 2016, youtube.com/watch?v=VZbv9c0ruPU&t=1s.

14 This maxim takes on mind-bending status at tantric levels of dark retreat when all appearances, including matter, are discovered to be frozen light.

15 For those familiar with the twelve nidānas and the bardo teachings, this principle is represented at the most cosmic levels in the transition from the twelfth nidāna, death, to the first nidāna, ignorance. Death conditions ignorance and initiates the process of involuntary rebirth. Ignorance, represented by a blind grandmother, is blinded by the light of the luminous bardo of dharmatā, the thermonuclear nature of the awakened mind that is revealed at the moment of death. The unprepared mind contracts so intensely from this light that it blinds the mind back into the shade of form, a body, and one's next life.

16 For a rich romp into this world, see Zoë Schlanger, *The Light Eaters: How the Unseen World of Plant Intelligence Offers a New Understanding of Life on Earth* (Harper, 2024).

17 Jacques Lusseyran, *Against the Pollution of the I*, 59.

18 Marsilio Ficino, *Meditations on the Soul: Selected Letters of Marsilio Ficino*, ed. Clement Salaman (Inner Traditions, 1997), 167.

19 Cristiana Caria, "The Concept of Light in the Ancient Times," accessed March 13, 2024, blog.cristianacaria.com/2014/06/22/the-concept-of-light-in-the-ancient-times/.

20 This movement that steals the mind takes on weight when thought is defined as "movement of mind." This is when we see the crime in action most intimately and most ceaselessly, as one thought after the other steals our awareness.

21 Jacques Lusseyran, *And There Was Light: The Extraordinary Memoir of a Blind Hero of the French Resistance in World War II* (Morning Light Press, 1998), 19.

22 Clark Strand, *Waking Up to the Dark: Ancient Wisdom for a Sleepless Age* (Random House, 2015), 46.

23 Strand, *Waking Up to the Dark*, 48–49.

24 Jenny Gargarello, "Am I a Mystic or a Psychotic," Medium, accessed May 16, 2025, medium.com/mental-asylum/am-i-a-mystic-or-a-psychotic-d32c86dd1192.

Chapter 6: Where Does the Healing Come From?

1 Ross Heaven and Simon Buxton, *Darkness Visible: Awakening Spiritual Light Through Darkness Meditation* (Destiny Books, 2005), x–xi.

2 Yale Medicine, "How Inflammation Affects Your Health," April 8, 2022, yalemedicine.org/news/how-inflammation-affects-your-health.

3 This quote is commonly attributed to Mark Twain, but the source is unknown.

4 David R. Loy, *Nonduality: In Buddhism and Beyond* (Wisdom Publications, 2019), xx.

5 Iamblichus, *On the Mysteries*, trans. Emma Clarke, John Dillon, and Jackson Hershbell (Society of Biblical Literature, 2003), 255.

6 Jeffrey J. Kripal, *How to Think Impossibly: About Souls, UFOs, Time, Belief, and Everything Else* (University of Chicago Press, 2024), 9.

7 This quote is often attributed to Meister Eckhart, but the source is unknown.

8 BrainyQuote, "Erwin Schrodinger Quotes," accessed September 13, 2024, brainyquote.com/quotes/erwin_schrodinger_304799.

9 History of Information, "John Archibald Wheeler Postulates 'It from Bit,'" accessed January 17, 2024, historyofinformation.com/detail.php?id=5041.

10 In tantric iconography, this nondual union is represented by the yab-yum (father-mother) deities in intercourse. All kinds of mischief take place in the dark. This sensory withdrawal is termed pratyāhāra, the fifth "limb" of the eightfold path, or ashta-anga-yoga (aka Ashtānga), of Patanjali; or the first of the Six Yogas in the completion stage practice of the Kālachakra Tantra in Tibetan Buddhism.

11 A classic teaching called the four yogic contemplations summarize the point: (1) Outer objects are observed to be nothing but mind. (2) Thus, outer objects are not observed as such. (3) With outer objects being unobservable, a mind cognizing them is not observed either. (4) Not observing both, non-duality is observed.

12 Christof Koch, *Then I Am Myself the World: What Consciousness Is and How to Expand it* (Basic Books, 2024), 205.

13 Ken Wilber, *Finding Radical Wholeness: The Integral Path to Unity, Growth, and Delight* (Shambhala, 2024), 352.

14 If you're literally blind, replace "darkness" with "nondistraction" to arrive at the same nondual point.

15 Iamblichus, *On the Mysteries*, 63.

16 David Bentley Hart, *All Things Are Full of Gods: The Mysteries of Mind and Life* (Yale University Press, 2024), 48.

17 Thomas Merton, *Conjectures of a Guilty Bystander* (Image Books, 2009), 140.

18 Jung's complexes are psychic fragments, like subpersonalities, each with a voice of its own. We do not have complexes; they have us. They possess us as fixations, obsessions, compulsions, and all manner of uncontrollable impulses. The multitudinous nature of our being has resonance with Buddhist psychology and its teaching on dharmas, or atoms of experience. See also Richard C. Schwartz, *No Bad Parts: Healing Trauma and Restoring Wholeness with the Internal Family Systems Model* (Sounds True, 2021).

19 Michael Gazzaniga, *The Social Brain: Discovering the Networks of the Mind* (Basic Books, 1985), 90.

20 Jacques Lusseyran, *Against the Pollution of the I: On the Gifts of Blindness, the Power of Poetry, and the Urgency of Awareness* (New World Library, 2016), 17–18.

21 Edge of Mind Podcast, "Exploring the Nature of Mind and Reality with Neuroscientist Ruben Laukkonen," August 11, 2021, everand.com/podcast/591090668/Exploring-The-Nature-Of-Mind-And-Reality-With-Neuroscientist-Ruben-Laukkonen-Join-the-neuroscientist-contemplative-and-poet-Ruben-Laukkonen-on-a-br.

22 If you're paying really close attention, the first break actually occurs when you label the sound as "plane." The sound itself is nothing but neutral sound waves to which we append the label "plane." Several orders of fracturing have already occurred before you even comment, "I wonder where that plane is going."

23 Ludwig Wittgenstein, *Tractatus Logico-Philosophicus* (Routledge & Kegan Paul, 1922).

24 Peter Kingsley, *In the Dark Places of Wisdom* (The Golden Sufi Center, 1999), 80.

25 Kingsley, *In the Dark Places of Wisdom*, 92.

26 Kingsley, 80, 144.
27 Kingsley, 143.

Chapter 7: Keys for Successful Dark Retreat

1 Laurie Clark, "'The Man Watching'—A Poem on the Spiritual Power of Being Defeated," The Seminary of the Christian Community, accessed July 16, 2024, christiancommunityseminary.ca/blog/the-man-watching-a-poem-on-the-spiritual-power-of-beingnbspdefeated.
2 Pema Chödrön, *Start Where You Are: A Guide to Compassionate Living* (Shambhala, 2001), 8.
3 Quoted in Dzogchen Ponlop Rinpoche, "Erring and Erring, We Walk the Unerring Path," *Lion's Roar*, September 1, 2009, lionsroar.com/erring-and-erring-we-walk-the-unerring-path/.
4 Johns Hopkins Nursing, "How to Be Like Water," Johns Hopkins University, October 23, 2011, nursing.jhu.edu/magazine/articles/2011/10/how-to-be-like-water/.
5 It's similar to the REBUS approach to psychedelics, or "relaxed beliefs under psychedelics," that gives playful meaning to agents like LSD and the dissolving capacity of acid.
6 *Openness* is a synonym for *emptiness*, and emptiness is the heart of Buddhism and the heart of dark retreat.

Chapter 8: Getting Started

1 For darkness therapy, see the work of Saskia John. For yoga nidrā, see the work of Richard Miller, Kelly Boys, or Uma Dinsmore-Tuli. For liminal dreaming, see the work of Jennifer Dumpert or my book *I'm Mindful, Now What?: Moving Beyond Mindfulness to Meet the Modern World* (Sounds True, 2024). For lucid dreaming, see the many works of Stephen LaBerge, Robert Waggoner, Charlie Morley, Claire Johnson, or my book *The Lucid Dreaming Workbook* (Reveal Press, 2020). For dream yoga, see the work of Tenzin Wangyal or my book *Dream Yoga* (Sounds True, 2016). For sleep yoga, see the work of Tenzin Wangyal, Namkhai Norbu, or my book *Dreams of Light* (Sounds True, 2020). For bardo yoga, see the work of Dzogchen Ponlop, Thrangu Rinpoche, or my book *Preparing to Die* (Snow Lion, 2013).
2 One millimeter is about 0.039 inches. A sharp pencil point or a sewing needle is about 1mm thick.
3 Patrick Harpur, *The Secret Tradition of the Soul* (North Atlantic Books, 2011), 65.
4 Harpur, *The Secret Tradition of the Soul*, p 65.
5 Bessel van der Kolk, *The Body Keeps the Score: Brain, Mind, and Body in the Healing of Trauma* (Penguin Books, 2015), 249.

Chapter 9: How to Prepare for Dark Retreat

1 Sounds True Podcast, "Rupert Spira: The Quiet Joy of Being," May 7, 2024, resources.soundstrue.com/podcast/rupert-spira-the-quiet-joy-of-being/.
2 Peter Kingsley, *Reality* (Catafalque Press, 2020), 154.
3 Analogous ways of thinking would include anekāntavāda ("non one-sidedness") from the Jain tradition, coincidentia oppositorum ("coincidence of opposites") from Carl Jung, catuṣkoṭi or tetralemma from Buddhism, along with Western notions of doublethink, paraconsistent logic, and

compossibility. Whatever the term, darkness leads you to the coincidence of opposites.

4 The moniker for dream yoga is "the measure of the path." Dark retreat abides by the same revelatory principle.

5 This maxim doesn't apply for tantra-level dark retreat. Because once you've freed yourself from the heaviness of the upper bandwidths of the unconscious mind, which is the fruition of sūtra-level practice, the deepest luminous aspects of the deeper bandwidths can now shine through. This is when the archetypes appear in the form of deities or gods. One way to know when you've accomplished tantra-level dark retreat is when all the contents of the unconscious mind have been brought into conscious awareness. At this level, there is no longer an unconscious mind. You know this when sleeping, dreaming, and even dying come to an end. You know this when you attain enlightenment. It may not always be the case, but if you feel a strong desire to keep going into the dark, it could be that you're actually getting attached to the darkness and using it as an escape.

6 Jack Kornfield, "Bringing Home the Dharma: Awakening Right Where You Are," Spirituality & Practice, accessed January 4, 2025, spiritualityandpractice.com/book-reviews/excerpts/view/21950.

7 "I'm not doing this for myself" because there isn't one. The ego, or sense of self, is empty of self-nature. This is why the upcoming teachings on emptiness are so important. Bodhicitta is applied emptiness. Deep meditation in general and dark retreat in particular (because darkness is homologous to emptiness) deliver you to this liberating truth.

8 I have written extensively about the many forms of meditation. For a comprehensive survey of daytime practices, see *Meditation in the iGeneration* (Maitri Publications, 2014), *I'm Mindful, Now What?* (Sounds True, 2024), *Reverse Meditation* (Sounds True, 2023), and *The Power and the Pain* (Snow Lion, 2001). For nocturnal meditations, see *Dream Yoga* (Sounds True, 2016), *The Lucid Dreaming Workbook* (Reveal Press, 2020), and *Dreams of Light* (Sounds True, 2020). For meditations that prepare for death, and have surprising applicability to dark retreat, see *Preparing to Die* (Snow Lion, 2013).

9 See my book *Meditation in the iGeneration* or Pema Chödrön's *How to Meditate: A Practical Guide for Making Friends with Your Mind* (Sounds True, 2021).

10 This liturgy is also known as the Four Divine Abodes, or the Four Faces of Love, and cultivates loving-kindness, compassion, sympathetic joy, and equanimity, respectively. In the words of meditation teacher Ayya Kema, "The only emotions worth having."

11 Ilana Beigel, "Compassion and the Path of Self-Study," Kripalu Center for Yoga & Health, accessed May 11, 2025, kripalu.org/resources/compassion-and-path-self-study.

12 I have written three books on the topic: *The Lucid Dreaming Workbook: A Step-by-Step Guide to Mastering Your Dream Life*, *Dream Yoga: Illuminating Your Life Through Lucid Dreaming and the Tibetan Yogas of Sleep*, and *Dreams of Light: The Profound Daytime Practice of Lucid Dreaming*. An overview of all five is presented in my book *I'm Mindful, Now What?: Moving Beyond Mindfulness to Meet the Modern World*.

13 These practices of tonglen, reverse meditation, guru yoga, photagogia, deity yoga, theurgy, mantra, and formal bardo yoga will be explored in a future volume. In a personal correspondence, dark retreat guide Lihi Eliza shared this helpful tip: "Even though dark retreat necessitates a total surrender

and an attitude of no expectation, traditional dark retreats do provide some form of practice structure beyond just turning the light off. Even opening the day, or session, by setting and grounding in intention can help provide some structure and direction for experience to unfold. In a way, we have to build up to doing nothing by providing something to fall back on—in effect creating a 'safe zone' in which we can relax into the non-doing."

Chapter 10: How to Integrate Dark Retreat

1 On his website, Jeff Holoubek, a veteran psychedelic guide, shared his tips for how to integrate psychedelic experience with life. The parallels are uncanny. "Once you have experienced the medicine, you may notice a number of changes in your life. You may feel an increased sensitivity and openness. You may notice a sense of lightness, clarity, and connection. You may feel free from prior identities, limitations, and beliefs. Your experience will likely leave an indelible impression on your mind and heart regarding the nature of existence and your place in it. All of this is normal. You can support and sustain these experiences by mirroring your preparation process the best you can post-session. While integration is a lifelong process, the days immediately following your session are a potent window for creating new patterns and pathways internally and externally. We encourage you to continue or begin the practices of meditation, journaling, and breathwork. You can also support yourself with solo time in nature. Be mindful of the environments you enter and the media you engage with. Connect with community! Find groups and circles where you can share freely and without judgment. Read and write about these topics and ideas. Deepen your self-exploration through music, art, dance, or any contemplative, creative practices that speak to you."

2 Patrick Harpur, *Daimonic Reality: A Field Guide to the Otherworld* (Pine Winds Press, 2024), 21.

3 Richard Feynman, "The First Principle Is That You Must Not Fool Yourself," Caltech, June 14, 1974, Speakola, speakola.com/grad/richard-feynman-caltech-1974.

4 Philosophically, this is one feature of Spinoza's dual-aspect monism. The *Pauli-Jung Conjecture* is a more recent rendering, as is the work of theoretical physicist Harald Atmanspacher (see "Dual-Aspect Monism à la Pauli and Jung," informationphilosopher.com/presentations/Milan/papers/Dual-aspect-Atmanspacher.pdf). In Buddhism, this principle is represented in the core doctrine of the trikāya, or "three bodies": Gross outer body is nirmanakāya, subtle inner body is sambhogakāya, and very subtle innermost body is dharmakāya. The common denominator is kāya, or body. Neuroscientist Christopher Koch coined the clever phrase "No body, never mind." Mind is always embodied, but the mind and correlative body range from gross to subtle to very subtle.

5 An allusion to Bessel van der Kolk's bestselling book *The Body Keeps the Score: Brain, Mind, and Body in the Healing of Trauma*.

6 John Ayto, *Dictionary of Word Origins: The Histories of More Than 8000 English-Language Words* (Arcade Publishing, 1991), 203.

7 For more on lujong, see Rose Taylor Goldfield's *Training the Wisdom Body: Buddhist Yogic Exercise* (Shambhala, 2013); for more on trul khor, see Alejandro Chaoul's *Tibetan Yoga for Health & Well-Being: The Science and Practice of Healing Your Body, Energy, and Mind* (Hay House, 2018), and

Tibetan Yoga: Magical Movements of Body, Breath, and Mind (Wisdom Publications, 2021).

8 David Gordon White, *Sinister Yogis* (University of Chicago Press, 2010), 167.

9 It's beyond our scope in this book, but "wind" in the tantric traditions is analogous to "light" in the Dzogchen tradition. The problem with too much light can, therefore, be discussed in terms of too much wind. In the Kālachakra Tantra, the "King of Tantras," wind is considered the most powerful of all the elements. When we get physically sick, we're often forced into bed and forced to unwind—un-wind. Wind disorders are at the root of so much dis-ease. When we're dis-tracted, the inner winds are what blow us away from the present moment.

10 Visit Night Club online: nightclubcommunity.com. This platform has multiple gatherings every week, with hundreds of hours of archived webinars and guest interviews, as well as a book study group, dream sharing group, induction support group, meditation group, yoga nidrā group, and sleep medicine group. Night Club also offers a community page where practitioners share posts and ask questions.

11 Kay Larson, *Where the Heart Beats: John Cage, Zen Buddhism, and the Inner Life of Artists* (Penguin Books, 2013), 20.

12 Quoted in Patrick Harpur, *The Secret Tradition of the Soul* (North Atlantic Books, 2011), 19.

Chapter 11: Contraindications for Dark Retreat

1 Personal correspondence from a senior student of Namkai Norbu Rinpoche.

2 *Metanoia* literally means "change your mind" or "change direction." The allusion to Michael Pollan's popular book on psychedelics, *How to Change Your Mind*, immediately comes to mind. In religious frameworks, metanoia refers to a transformative change of heart or spiritual conversion, a reorientation or fundamental transformation of how one sees the world and oneself.

3 Charnel grounds are the most unwanted places possible, classically depicted as open burial sites with vultures, hyenas, and other scavengers. Imagine the most repulsive place possible. Tantric practitioners, in their efforts to transform poison into medicine, seek these locations as grist for the meditative mill. This is called "heroic meditation" in tantra. But please, don't try to be a hero. Be yourself, which is perhaps the most heroic thing you can do.

4 There are studies around darkness therapy, the REST method, and flotation tank sensory deprivation, especially the work of Peter Suedfield. But I am not aware of a single study on dark retreat as it's being explored in this book.

5 This is another instance where sūtra-level dark retreat merges with tantra level. In the bardos, the after-death spaces described in Tibetan Buddhism, it is said that everything is exaggerated seven to nine times. Why? Because just like in a dream, or in dark retreat, mind becomes reality. You can no longer get away from yourself.

6 *Spiritual bypassing* is a term coined in the 1980s by Buddhist teacher and psychologist John Welwood (based on the teachings of spiritual materialism from Trungpa Rinpoche). As Welwood writes, it's a tendency to "use spiritual ideas and practices to avoid dealing with their emotional unfinished business." See John Welwood's *Toward a Psychology of Awakening: Buddhism, Psychotherapy, and the Path of Personal and Spiritual*

Transformation (Shambhala, 2022). See also Robert Augustus Masters's *Spiritual Bypassing: When Spirituality Disconnects Us from What Really Matters* (North Atlantic Books, 2010).

7 According to the bardo teachings, this jet propulsion to escape from ourselves drives us from the luminous bardo of dharmatā into the karmic bardo of becoming, and then into the bardo of your next life. The same process is repeated every single time we're distracted. It's a bidirectional process: We distract in the bardos because we distract in life; we distract in life because we distract in the bardos.

8 The Orphic myth of the dismemberment of Dionysus at the hands of the Titans offers historical footing for this necessary breakdown.

9 Alex Tzelnic, "What Athletes Are Learning by Sitting in the Dark," Yoga Journal, April 27, 2025, yogajournal.com/meditation/darkness-retreat/.

10 Thanks to darkness therapist Saskia John; psychologist Bruce Tift; Mitchell Gershten, MD; sleep doctor Ed O'Malley, PhD; and neuropsychologist Paul Richards, PhD, for their contributions to the following sections.

11 Mayo Clinic Staff, "Dissociative Disorders," Mayo Clinic, August 31, 2023, mayoclinic.org/diseases-conditions/dissociative-disorders/symptoms-causes/syc-20355215.

Chapter 12: Why Is Dark Retreat Challenging?

1 The Gray Matters Collective, "Don't Fear Yourself," accessed March 20, 2024, thegraymatterscollective.com/blog/dont-fear-yourself.

2 Kelsi Klembara, "Forever Elsewhere," 1517 (Christ for You), May 8, 2024, 1517.org/articles/forever-elsewhere.

3 "Let us take time . . . to be bored, to strip away from ourselves the screens we have created to hide the real truths of life and death from our eyes." See Carl R. Trueman, *The Wages of Spin: Critical Writings on Historical and Contemporary Evangelicalism* (Mentor, 2011), 179–180.

4 John Ayto, *Dictionary of Word Origins: The Histories of More Than 8000 English-Language Words* (Arcade Publishing, 1991), 174.

5 Jacques Lusseyran, *Against the Pollution of the I: On the Gifts of Blindness, the Power of Poetry, and the Urgency of Awareness* (New World Library, 2016), 55–56.

6 For an extensive exploration of the power of this level of addiction and how to work with it, see my book *The Power and the Pain: Transforming Spiritual Hardship into Joy* (Snow Lion, 2010). I wrote this upon coming out of my three-year retreat, which amounted to three years of intense detox.

7 Gregory Shaw, *Hellenic Tantra: The Theurgic Platonism of Iamblichus* (Angelico Press, 2024), 224.

8 Gary D. Astrachan, PhD, "Dionysos. Mainomenos. Lysios: Performing Madness and Ecstasy in the Practices of Art, Analysis and Culture," *Journal of Jungian Scholarly Studies* 4, no. 4 (2009), jungianjournal.ca/index.php/jjss/article/view/70/63.

9 Darkness therapy is an exception to this rule, but most people are not yet working with darkness therapists. This situation will change as the transformative power of dark practice is better known.

10 See my book *Dreams of Light* (Sounds True, 2020) for a thorough exploration of the clear-light mind.

Chapter 13: Where Does the Resistance Come From?

1 "Generally speaking" because you can position yourself, situate yourself in the world, without automatically generating the ego. Evolved beings can operate beautifully in this world from an egoless perspective while still echolocating to find their way through the world. But this is a lofty spiritual realization and another instance of "transcend but include." You include the necessity of echolocating but transcend the habit of generating an ego out of that process.

2 I mean this poetically and in the psychological sense. Ego, as an arrested form of development, is finally transcended but included. Once again, you still have recourse to this level of development when relating to others who remain fully identified with it, but you have grown beyond this "loss."

3 Jill Bolte-Taylor, PhD, *My Stroke of Insight: A Brain Scientist's Personal Journey* (Penguin Books, 2009), p. 41 and p. 50. We plan to study this hemispheric shift in darkness, conjecturing that nondual experiences in the dark correlate with this level of right-brain activity and left-brain inactivity.

4 Spending time totally naked in the dark is a worthwhile experiment. What does it feel like to be so open and exposed, where nobody, including yourself, can see you? In the spirit of The Myth of Gyges, from Book Two of Plato's *Republic*, what is it like to be invisible?

5 In classic Freudian suppression, the more you deny the existence of something (your fear), the more you assert its existence.

6 The Dzogchen practice of kadak trekchö, or "cutting through to primordial purity," is all about this tearing and cutting, which is cutting through mere appearance (ego) to get in touch with reality (egolessness).

7 It's beyond our scope, but questioning the traditional egoic (adversarial) relationship to disease comes into play. We go into battle with our disease with an antibiotic, anti-inflammatory, antihistamine, anticoagulant, antibacterial, antiseptic, anti-emetic, antidepressant, antioxidant, antipsychotic, or any other antidote. I'm not saying that's contraindicated, but perhaps a more open relationship to disease could balance this combat. Maybe your body (which according to neuroscientist Candace Pert *is* your unconscious mind) is trying to tell you something. Patrick Harpur offers this alternative view: "As an expression of soul, though, the body is a rich mine of images. Its ailments are metaphorical as well as physical; its symptoms are questions. What burden am I carrying, asks Backache; what do I not want to hear, asks Ear Infect; what am I loathe to swallow, asks Eating Disorder; what is wrong with my emotional life, asks Heart Disease; what is constricting me, asks Lung Problem . . . even crass physical ailments such as a broken leg may be soul's way of compelling the headstrong ego to stop dead and reflect on her. Every pain is a potential portal to the Underworld." See Patrick Harpur's *The Secret Tradition of the Soul* (North Atlantic Books, 2011), 173.

8 When unrecognized, this contraction, and our desire to release the sucky feeling, is the conventional search for happiness. When recognized, it transforms into the unconventional search for enlightenment. Conscious or unconscious, the release of the self-contraction drives everything we do.

9 Discovering your selfless nature means discovering your otherless nature, and from this, compassion is born. You're not wrestling with this material for nothing. You're wrestling with it so you can experience it, then act from that space to help others.

10 This is a subtle form of phowa, or "transference of consciousness," as your identity transfers from ego to egolessness.

11 This quote is variously attributed to Meister Eckhart and/or Nicholas of Cusa. "The metaphor of the infinite sphere makes its first appearance in the pseudo-Hermetic *Liber XXIV philosophorum*, a small book in the literary form of an 'opus propositionum,' which, in twenty-four propositions, describes the ineffable essence of God in the mystical language of Neoplatonic theology. It is in the second proposition of this book that we find for the first time the formulation, 'God is an infinite sphere, whose center is everywhere, whose circumference is nowhere.'" See Elizabeth Brient, "Transitions to a Modern Cosmology: Meister Eckhart and Nicholas of Cusa on the Intensive Infinite," *Journal of the History of Philosophy* 37, no. 4 (1999): 575–600, muse.jhu.edu/article/228744.

12 In stronger bardo language, "die before you die." Let go before you're forced to. Titrate the release on your negotiable terms before releasing becomes nonnegotiable.

13 Key Hero Typing Test, "From a Letter Written While Recuperating from a Heart Attack—Abraham Maslow," accessed October 21, 2024, keyhero.com/test-schrybe/online-tippen-test/3724/.

14 Remember that after the more dualistic senses are removed, dark retreat returns us to the least dualistic sense of touch. But the sense of touch, or feeling, is still subtly dualistic. When ego starts to lose its grip on even that, the very last lifeline into duality, it can really start to "lose it." Staying in touch with something, anything, becomes survival level, a matter of life and death, because the ego knows if things truly stop moving, it will disappear. As a matter of survival, the ego keeps stirring things up to keep itself up. If the stirring stops, so does the ego. And it drops dead in the dark.

15 Alain Joly, "I Don't Mind What Happens," *The Dawn Within*, August 5, 2020, thedawnwithin.com/2020/08/05/i-dont-mind-what-happens/.

16 Patrick Harpur, *The Secret Tradition of the Soul*, 167–69, 170, 172.

17 Quoted in Timothy Leary, Ralph Metzner, and Richard Alpert, *The Psychedelic Experience: A Manual Based on the Tibetan Book of the Dead* (University Books, 1966), 29.

18 Harpur, *The Secret Tradition of the Soul*, 174.

Chapter 14: What to Do If It Gets Challenging?

1 To supplement or train yourself for this approach, reverse meditations really help. See my book *Reverse Meditation: How to Use Your Pain and Most Difficult Emotions as the Doorway to Inner Freedom* (Sounds True, 2023).

2 Jill Bolte Taylor, PhD, *My Stroke of Insight: A Brain Scientist's Personal Journey* (Penguin Books, 2009), 164–165.

3 Chögyam Trungpa, *The Sādhana of Mahāmudrā* (Nālandā Translation Committee, 1990), 19.

4 Bolte Taylor, *My Stroke of Insight*.

5 Avatar Adi Da Samraj, "The Fire Must Have Its Way," spoken by Avatar Adi Da Samraj, The Dawn Horse Press, 1978, CD.

6 Shunryu Suzuki, *Zen Mind, Beginner's Mind: Informal Talks on Zen Meditation and Practice* (Weatherhill, 1985), 63.

7 Scottsdale Institute for Health and Medicine: Center for Mindfulness, "'Mr. Duffy Lived a Short Distance from His Body'—Using Mindfulness to Help Mr. Duffy," accessed September 29, 2024, stressbeaters.com/mr-duffy-lived-a-short-distance-from-his-body-using-mindfulness-to-help-mr-duffy/.

8 See this remarkable video of neurosurgery, with the patient playing his guitar as surgeons are cutting into his brain to remove a tumor: MD Anderson Cancer Center, "Brain Tumor Patient Plays Guitar During Awake Craniotomy Surgery," YouTube, May 2018, youtube.com/watch?v=a3kXCC3hldw.
9 Taken from the Outward Bound website, outwardbound.org: "Outward Bound expeditions are transformative life experiences. With a supportive crew, and the outdoors as their teacher, students learn to dig deep to find greater compassion for each other, and to push the limits of what they thought they could do." Sounds familiar.
10 Hippolyte Taine, *De l'intelligence* (Librairie Hachette, 1870), 13.
11 Anil Seth, "Your Brain Hallucinates Your Conscious Reality," TED, July 2017, youtube.com/watch?v=lyu7v7nWzfo.

Chapter 15: Four Steps for Working with Challenges

1 These four steps are also explored in great detail in my book *Reverse Meditation: How to Use Your Pain and Most Difficult Emotions as the Doorway to Inner Freedom* (Sounds True, 2023).
2 GuidedMind, "7 Life Lessons from Pema Chödrön," accessed November 20, 2024, guidedmind.com/blog/7-life-lessons-from-pema-chodron.
3 This seminal teaching is one of the most frequently repeated statements in *The Tibetan Book of the Dead*, which is equally the book of life.
4 Reginald A. Ray, *The Awakening Body: Somatic Meditation for Discovering Our Deepest Life* (Shambhala, 2016), 41.
5 David R. Loy, *Lack & Transcendence: The Problem of Death and Life in Psychotherapy, Existentialism, and Buddhism* (Wisdom Publications, 2018), 93.
6 Chögyam Trungpa, *Shambhala: The Sacred Path of the Warrior* (Shambhala Publications, 2015), 155.
7 Khenpo Tsültrim Gyamtso Rinpoche, *Mahamudra Shamatha and Vipashyana*, trans. Jim Scott (Vajravairochana Translation Committee, 1991).
8 There are many names for that which cannot be named: clear-light mind, buddha-nature, buddhadhātu, dharmatā, rigpa, sugatagarbha, tathāgatagarbha, isness, suchness, absolute bodhicitta dharmadhātu, vajradhātu, tathatā, basic goodness, pristine consciousness, pure awareness, ālaya jñāna, yeshe, primordial basis, for starters.
9 Chögyam Trungpa, *Smile at Fear: Awakening the True Heart of Bravery*, ed. Carolyn Rose Gimian (Shambhala Publications, 2010), 12.
10 Thomas Merton, *Conjectures of a Guilty Bystander* (Image Books, 2009), 142.
11 David R. Loy, *Lack & Transcendence*, 102.

Chapter 16: How to Work with Fear

1 Author and columnist David Brooks suggests that for conventional growth and success, we should follow our strengths. But for psycho-spiritual growth and success, we should follow our weaknesses.
2 Nikol Chen, "Nothing Is to Be Feared, Only to Be Understood," Laidlaw Scholars, April 20, 2020, laidlawscholars.network/posts/nothing-is-to-be-feared-only-to-be-understood.
3 Chögyam Trungpa, *Smile at Fear: Awakening the True Heart of Bravery*, ed. Carolyn Rose Gimian (Shambhala Publications, 2010), 107.

4 Chögyam Trungpa , *The Sādhana of Mahāmudrā* (Nalanda Translation Committee, 1990), 8.

5 Peter Kingsley, *In the Dark Places of Wisdom* (The Golden Sufi Center, 1999), 71.

6 This is precisely why the first of the three death bardos is called "the painful bardo of dying." It's called "painful" because it hurts to let go. Dark retreat, at tantric levels, works mostly with this bardo and the second bardo, "the luminous bardo of dharmata."

7 Peter Kingsley, *In the Dark Places of Wisdom*, 69.

8 From an immunological perspective, our bodies need to separate self (antibody) from other (antigen) to keep us alive. When this healthy dualistic mechanism fails, you get things like AIDS or SCID (Severe Combined Immunodeficiency Disorder, or "bubble boy disease").

9 Pema Chödrön has made a virtual career about this. See her books *The Places That Scare You* (Shambhala, 2018), *The Wisdom of No Escape* (Shambhala, 2018), *When Things Fall Apart* (Shambhala, 2016), and *Comfortable with Uncertainty* (Shambhala, 2018).

10 Robert E. Buswell Jr. and Donald S. Lopez Jr., *The Princeton Dictionary of Buddhism* (Princeton University Press, 2014), 438.

11 In Western accounts, the number of distinguishable emotions range from thirty-four thousand, according to psychologist Robert Plutchik, down to the four foundational emotions of fear/surprise, anger/disgust, happiness, and sadness.

12 A bigger traditional list of kleshas includes heedlessness, lassitude, lack of faith, sloth, restlessness, anger, hypocrisy, selfishness, envy, agitation, competition, harmfulness, enmity, guile, arrogance, pride, skeptical doubt, and the twenty derivative upakleshas, or "secondary afflictions."

13 Do you want to know what else this root ignorance feels like? Consciousness. Consciousness is that which *separates* reality into self and other, inside and outside, generating duality. When consciousness is transformed into wisdom, it transforms into nondual awareness . (In Sanskrit, vijñāna transforms into jñāna. The prefix *vi-* means "divided, fractured, bifurcated." Consciousness is divided, fractured, bifurcated awareness.)

14 For those who engage the nocturnal meditations, this very gesture of falling is one way to transition from dream yoga into sleep yoga. The next time you have a lucid dream, try falling backward in the dream. The mind, in the form of your subtle dream body, will fall deeper into itself, and eventually through itself, as it "lands" in the formless awareness of deep dreamless (and, therefore, formless) sleep yoga.

15 Chögyam Trungpa, *The Collected Works of Chögyam Trungpa, Volume Two* (Shambhala, 2003), 389.

16 Dakinis are feminine protectors who guard and bestow teachings. They are also enlightened goddesses. For a thorough rendering, see Judith Simmer-Brown's *Dakini's Warm Breath: The Feminine Principle in Tibetan Buddhism* (Shambhala, 2002).

17 Patrick Harpur, *The Secret Tradition of the Soul* (North Atlantic Books, 2011), 209. A "life outside ourselves" is the very definition of ecstasy, from *ek*, meaning "out," and *histanai*, meaning "place," the underlying notion being "displace, drive out of one's (conventional) mind."

18 Chögyam Trungpa, *Smile at Fear: Awakening the True Heart of Bravery*, x.

19 *Smile at Fear*, 95.

20 Robert A. Johnson, *Inner Work: Using Dreams and Active Imagination for Personal Growth* (Harper & Row, 1989), 17.

21 Bruce Tift, *Already Free: Buddhism Meets Psychotherapy on the Path of Liberation* (Sounds True, 2015), p. 136, 137, 139.

22 "Self" with a small "s" refers to ego; "Self" with a big "S" refers to egolessness and is equivalent to the Buddhist notion of emptiness. Big "S" Self is Hindu language for the same (non) thing.

23 Milan Kundera, *The Unbearable Lightness of Being* (Harper & Row, 1984).

24 Dzogchen Ponlop, *Mind Beyond Death* (Snow Lion, 2006), 203–204.

25 Bruce Tift, *Already Free*, 139.

Conclusion

1 A view of reality resonant with quantum mechanical superposition of two mutually exclusive states. Thanks to Christof Koch for this insight.

2 Jacques Lusseyran, *And There Was Light: The Extraordinary Memoir of a Blind Hero of the French Resistance in World War II* (Morning Light Press, 1998), 21.

3 *Songs of Realization: As Taught & Sung by Khenchen Tsultrim Gyamtso Rinpoche* (Nalandabodhi, 2013), 27.

4 Barbara Brown Taylor, *Learning to Walk in the Dark* (Canterbury Press, 2015), 16.

5 Patrick Harpur, *The Secret Tradition of the Soul* (North Atlantic Books, 2011), 122.

6 Harpur, *The Secret Tradition of the Soul*, 123–124.

7 Jacques Lusseyran, *Against the Pollution of the I: On the Gifts of Blindness, the Power of Poetry, and the Urgency of Awareness* (New World Library, 2016), 33.

8 Sabrina Wu, "To attain knowledge, add things every day. To attain wisdom, remove things every day," *Rock and Talk*, December 25, 2016, therockandtalk.wordpress.com/2016/12/25/to-attain-knowledge-add-things-everyday-to-attain-wisdom-remove-things-every-day/.

9 Examples include *citation*, which can denote violation or achievement; *oversight*, which can mean monitoring something or a mistake; and *cleave*, meaning to separate or to unite. Other Janus words are *bolt* (to fasten, or to flee), *bound* (to tie something down, or to go to a place), *clip* (to cut or to attach), *fast* (moving fast, or firmly fixed), *left* (remaining, or to have gone away from), *refrain* (a repetition or to stop/abstain), and *strike* (to miss/fail or to hit/succeed).

INDEX

ABOUT THE AUTHOR

Andrew Holecek is an interdisciplinary scholar-practitioner specializing in Tibetan Buddhism and consciousness studies, known for his ability to make complex spiritual and scientific concepts accessible to students worldwide. He serves as resident contemplative scholar at the Institute for Advanced Consciousness Studies and a research consultant for Northwestern University's Cognitive Neuroscience Program. He has completed the traditional Tibetan Buddhist three-year retreat and is a member of the American Academy of Sleep Medicine.

Andrew has authored nine books on meditation, dream yoga, and end-of-life practices, weaving ancient wisdom and modern science with clarity and warmth. His work has appeared in *Psychology Today*, *Parabola*, *Lion's Roar*, and many other publications, and he is often featured in scientific studies on meditation and lucid dreaming.

He is the founder of Night Club, an international community supporting nocturnal meditations, and the Preparing to Die Program, which helps individuals navigate end-of-life experiences through contemplative practices. Andrew hosts the *Edge of Mind* podcast and teaches internationally on lucid dreaming, dark retreat, and death preparation. He lives in Boulder, Colorado. Learn more at andrewholecek.com.

ABOUT SOUNDS TRUE BOOKS

Sounds True was founded in 1985 by Tami Simon with a clear mandate: to disseminate spiritual wisdom. Since starting out as a project with one woman and her tape recorder, Sounds True has grown into a mission-driven learning and media company, partnering with many of the leading wisdom teachers and visionaries of our time.

Every Sounds True Book is designed to not only provide information to a reader but to also to embody the quality of a wisdom transmission, unlocking our greatest capacities to love, serve, and uplift others.

Sounds True Books are part of St. Martin's Essentials, an imprint of Macmillan Publishers.